THE DIALOGUE BETWEEN THEOLOGY
AND PSYCHOLOGY

ESSAYS IN DIVINITY

JERALD C. BRAUER, GENERAL EDITOR

The Dialogue
Between
Theology and Psychology

BY LEROY ADEN, FRED BERTHOLD, JR., FRANK M. BOCKUS,

DON BROWNING, LELAND ELHARD, JOSEPH HAVENS,

PETER HOMANS, PERRY LEFEVRE, LEIGHTON MCCUTCHEN,

WILLIAM R. ROGERS, CHARLES R. STINNETTE, JR.

Edited by PETER HOMANS

THE UNIVERSITY OF CHICAGO PRESS

CHICAGO AND LONDON

For SEWARD HILTNER

THE UNIVERSITY OF CHICAGO PRESS
CHICAGO 60637
The University of Chicago Press, Ltd., London W.C.1.

Library of Congress Catalog Card Number: 68–16698

Printed in the United States of America

General Editor's Preface

The present volume is the third in a series of eight books being published under the general title "Essays in Divinity." This does not appear, at first glance, as a particularly auspicious moment for such a formidable enterprise. At the very moment the so-called radical theologians announce that "God is dead," an eight-volume series investigating various dimensions of the study of religion or of theology is published. Is this not an ill-timed venture?

In point of fact, however, in America the discipline of theology was never in a healthier state. To be sure, there are no giants such as Tillich or Niebuhr on the scene, but there are many new and exciting factors in the picture. The very presence of the "God is dead" movement is evidence of a new vitality and ferment among the younger theologians. In no sense does such a movement herald the end of systematic theology or the impossibility of using God-language. It is but one of many significant attempts being made now at basic reconstruction and reinterpretation of Christian theology.

One primary fact marks this new age — the pre-eminence of dialogue in all aspects of divinity. Basic conversation between Roman Catholicism, Protestantism, and Judaism is just beginning, and its full effect on theological construction lies ahead. At the time systematic theology entered the preliminary phase of dialogue, Paul Tillich's last lecture pointed to the future of this discipline in relation to the world's religions. Dialogue is not to be understood as the "in" movement in religion today; it is to be viewed as providing a new base that will profoundly affect not only the systematic study of doctrines and beliefs but every dimension of religious studies.

Another mark of the vitality of religious studies today is their dialogic relationship to other disciplines. Studies in divinity have never been carried on in complete isolation from other areas of human knowledge, but in some periods the relationship has been more fully explored than in others. The contemporary scene is marked by the increasing tempo of creative interchange and mutual stimulation between divinity and other disciplines. Several new theological disciplines have emerged recently to demonstrate this fact. The interplay between theology and literature, between theology and the psychological sciences, and between theology and the social sciences promises to reshape the traditional study of religion, as our major theological faculties are beginning rapidly to realize.

The emergence and increasing role of the History of Religions is a case in point. Until recently it has been a stepchild in the theological curriculum. Today it is developing a methodology that probably will prove influential in all areas of theological study. History of Religions also appears to be the way that most state universities will introduce the serious and disciplined study of religion into strictly secular curriculums.

These are but a few of the factors that demonstrate the present vitality of the study of religion today. It makes both possible and necessary a series of books such as this. The particular occasion for the publication of "Essays in Divinity" is supplied by the one hundredth anniversary of the Divinity School of The University of Chicago and by the University's seventy-fifth anniversary.

The editor of this series proposed that this event be celebrated by the Divinity School faculty and alumni by holding seven conferences, each of which was focused on the work of one of the seven academic fields of the School. Out of these conferences have come eight volumes which will, it is hoped, mark the progress in the various disciplines of theological study and point to the ongoing tradition of scholarship in the University's Divinity School.

Though something may have been lost in thus limiting the roster of contributors to these books, this very limitation may have the effect of marking the distinctive genius of one theological center long noted for its production of scholar-teachers in American theology. Also, it will enable an observer to determine the extent to which several generations have been shaped by, and have shaped, a particular institution. It will be possible to note the variations of approach and concern that mark respective generations of that institution. Furthermore, it will help to assess the particular genius, if any, that a given institution possesses. It will demonstrate to what extent its graduates and professors are in the midst of contemporary theological scholarship. It is to be hoped that the series will provide both a bench mark for today's scholarly discussions and research in religion and a record from which future generations can assess the contributions of an institution at the turn of its first century.

None of these volumes pretends to be definitive in its area; it is hoped, however, that each will make a useful contribution to its area of specialization and that the entire series will suggestively illuminate the basic tendencies of religious scholarship at the present moment. The intent has been to devote each volume to a particular issue or area of inquiry that is of special significance for scholarly religious research today, and thus to keep each volume from being simply a disconnected series of essays. It is hoped that these books will be found to have, each in its own terms, a genuine unity and that the reader will note a cumulative effect, as he moves from essay to essay in each volume.

This the third volume in the series, came out of the centennial conference on religion and the personality sciences held at the Divinity School in 1966. Though the theme of the book is important in many respects, it is significant for two basic reasons. First, it deals with problems of primary import both for theology and for psychology and explores a variety of issues that emerge between these disciplines. The various essays seek to analyze some of the consequences and possibilities.

Second, the general subject matter is further evidence of the fresh vitality to be found in theological studies. The "care of souls" or the development of "casuistry" has a long history in Christian tradition. Priests and ministers have always been deeply concerned with the counseling of troubled and disturbed believers. The church succeeded in developing a remarkable literature based on the pragmatic experiences of sensitive and concerned pastors. Out of that, pastoral theology and pastoral counseling developed.

The advent of psychology, psychiatry, and other disciplines concerned with human development introduced an entirely new dimension into the picture. The question now was whether religion was prepared to enter into a genuine dialogic relationship with these disciplines, so that each might learn from the other, or whether religion would simply take certain techniques from the new disciplines in order to educate more sophisticated and competent pastoral counselors. Fortunately, the problem is not one of techniques. The basic question involves the nature of man and the dynamics of personality development. Both theology and the personality disciplines have much to say about these realities.

As early as 1950, the Divinity School of The University of Chicago abandoned the usual pattern of handling these questions under the rubric of practical theology. A new field, religion and the personality sciences, was founded alongside such traditional disciplines as theology, Bible, and the history of Christianity. This new field has a content and a method as do the other fields. Its subject matter is the interrelationship between theology and the psychological theories of man. What was started at Chicago rapidly became a pattern in many other institutions, particularly where serious graduate work was undertaken.

This volume contains the first fruits of that new field as it developed in the Divinity School. It is clear that the work is just beginning and that it is building on a solid foundation.

JERALD C. BRAUER, *General Editor*

CONTENTS

CONTENTS

*Mental Health and Ultimate Reality, and of Chaos
to Mental Illness and Alienation*

Introduction

PETER HOMANS

A convention of recent origin in theological discussion distinguishes "classical" from "dialogical" fields of study — thereby juxtaposing the basic disciplines of Bible, Church History, and Theology to those studies which more directly engage some aspect of the culture that has now in a sense engulfed or simply passed by the Christian tradition. No doubt the vices and virtues of such a separation are many. Some will argue that theology is essentially dialogical, while others will insist that purity of theological response is preserved only by a certain distance between faith and culture. Such discussions can easily become overserious, like arguments about whether particular sacraments are of the "esse" or the "bene esse" of the church, or they can become ideological, with the various fields regarded as territories and properties. It is sufficient here to note that, without such a distinction, studies fostered by the field of Religion and Personality at the Divinity School of the University of Chicago would not have been possible. The essays in this volume well represent such studies. The work of this field has clearly conceived itself as moderating a discussion between two broad areas of study, religion and the personality sciences, but more especially between two much more easily definable, but normally unrelated, disciplines within that general area: theology and psychology.

The distinction between classic and dialogical studies was formally recognized in the curriculum of the Divinity School during the early 1950's, when specific divisions were organized to explore in greater depth than was previously possible materials in psychology, sociology and imaginative literature.

1

The Religion and Personality field was formed, and for many years chaired, by Seward Hiltner. Its studies have sought to identify points of reciprocity between Christian faith and cultural form. In psychology, this concern has often been directed toward the work of the minister, and especially toward the resources of the emerging dynamic psychotherapies for that work. Seward Hiltner's concern for pastoral practice was part of a broad view of the implications of psychological dynamics for faith and for theological thought. His conviction that a proper articulation of theological and psychological materials was possible gave the basic direction to this field — and these essays illustrate that direction. Most of the authors studied with Seward Hiltner, and all have benefited from their association with him. The volume is respectfully dedicated to him, in gratitude for his leadership, his teaching, and his personal warmth and encouragement.

These papers, then, are really "working papers" — careful, thoughtful, and in some cases even ambitious in their effort to be comprehensive. The problems they select, the figures they discuss, and the solutions they propose indicate what is considered important in this field, and are also suggestive of trends which may emerge as work continues. Because of the newness of this field, it is relatively easy to put its work into some kind of general context; but for that very reason future developments are less obvious, and more difficult to predict.

Mircea Eliade has prefaced one of his more recent books by recalling Whitehead's familiar remark that the history of Western philosophy is nothing more than a series of footnotes to Plato, but adding that the wisdom of such "splendid isolation" has become increasingly questionable in the modern epoch. Eliade's concern is, of course, with the bearing of primitive and Eastern religions upon the religious and intellectual formations of the West, but it is important to note that he has again and again counted the discoveries of depth psychology as one of several extremely important "outsiders" that have invaded the once closed field of the Western consciousness. These invasions are the basis of Eliade's plea for a new humanism, which, he believes, the West can acquire only by becoming open to the spiritual preceptorship of other cultural and religious traditions.

The systematic theological work of Paul Tillich bears directly upon this statement, partly because, more than any other theologian, he has permitted his theological work to come under the influence of psychology and especially depth psychology, but also because he has recognized in depth psychology and in existentialism as well, not so much the outsider to which Eliade alludes, but rather an "insider," the bearer of a fundamental spiritual perception which has resided within the Western tradition all along. For, as Tillich often noted, depth psychology represents a "rediscovery" of the spirituality of the West, something that the West has known "all along."

In these two approaches we have, in very simplistic and abbreviated fashion, the context for much of the work of this field of study. Does the emergence of the psychological and psychotherapeutic disciplines signify the appearance of an outsider, or are these disciplines really the insider we have so long neglected, but for which we have nevertheless been responsible all along? Are we in the West at the point of rediscovering our theological heritage through the psychological sciences? Or do we find ourselves, in facing psychology, faced with the very different, the outsider, a stranger?

Whichever way that question is answered it creates a new question: How are we — on the basis of a commitment that embraces the modes of reflection and action characteristic not only of Western religious institutions but also those of the psychological sciences — to understand and interpret the meaning of religious life and thought today? It is this central issue that arises when theological statement is forced into an encounter with the claims and knowledge of the personality sciences.

Existentialism and depth psychology have provided obvious and important materials for study. Less obvious, but nonetheless important, is a second set of materials, the work of the Chicago school in the philosophy of religion and the

close association this work had with the psychology of religion, the religious education movement, and theological
liberalism. Taken together, these constitute the primary
sources and orientations of the field of Religion and Personality. The first group reflects a sense of discontinuity between conscious and unconscious, between self and world,
between man and man, between man and God — and, for
that reason, between theology and psychology. On the other
hand, the Chicago school has given us a series of spiritual
perceptions that celebrated a sense of continuity, a sense of
the primary connectedness of things; and it has, therefore,
for the most part chosen to speak of continuity between psychology and religion rather than between psychology and
theology.

The presence of such materials reveals what is perhaps the
greatest hazard of interdisciplinary work. For one usually
works with materials that are themselves the results of
already well-formed and well-legitimated methodological
procedures — the investigative methods of theology and psychology, for example, in this volume. This is one reason, perhaps, why theologians and psychologists have as a rule worked
independently of each other. So we are given the privileges
of two disciplines, and, unfortunately, a double responsibility
as well. Anyone wishing to avail himself of these materials
will not, however, find legitimation for his efforts in the theological and psychological discussions per se. On the other
hand, all dialogical studies strive toward the boundary lines
between disciplines, convinced that knowledge emerges between such disciplines as well as from within particular
methodological confines. Dialogical fields are therefore area
studies rather than disciplines grounded in well formed methodologies. They may become disciplines only if there are un-
clarified presuppositions in their subject matter, and only if
these suppositions are gradually exposed in an explicative,
rather than an ideological, spirit.

We might, therefore, expect that methodology is an important issue in this field. Methodological concerns have been
one of the distinguishing features of the psychological sci-

ences, and modern theology — at least theology of the dialectical sort, with its penchant for prolegomena — has in its own way shared this concern. Essays by Fred Berthold and Perry LeFevre address this question specifically from the point of view of theology. My own essay attempts a critical-psychological discussion of methodological assumptions in theology, proposing what is in effect a therapeutic for theological method. Psychologists and psychotherapists justify their inquiries into the nature of the person in a particular way, and in so doing, question the modes and methods of inquiry employed by the theologian. The personality sciences in effect dare theology to test its relevance for understanding the nature of personhood. On the other hand, do the psychologcial sciences also provide materials for the reformulation of theological method? Are there analogies, metaphors, and primary symbols in psychology that betray crypto-theological gestures? We are now all familiar with the "Freudian slip"; how willing are we to recognize the "theological slip" of a particular psychological theory or psychotherapeutic strategy?

The problem of method surrounds a second important concern of these papers, that of self-understanding, or, as it is often more formally designated, theological anthropology. The "image of man" provides another point of discussion for the student of dialogue, for the psychological sciences also attempt to designate the nature of the person, the structure and dynamics of the psyche, both in terms of its inwardness as well as in terms of its encounter with and appropriation of wider social, historical and cultural meanings.

The meaning of faith is perhaps the point at which theology most closely approaches the question of anthropology. Charles Stinnette, Don Browning, and Leland Elhard attempt a direct exploration of the phenomenon of Christian faith and of the place of psychological understanding in the clarification and explication of the nature of faith. The most comprehensive psychological consideration in this regard is, of course, the development process, as the personality sciences have sought to establish it. The concept of human development symbolizes well the significance of the personality sciences for religious meaning and theological statement.

In what sense is faith a developmental phenomenon, continuous with those stages, tasks, sequences, and the like, of which psychology so often speaks? Are we to think of faith primarily as a developmental attitude, and in so doing assign the task of understanding it to the psychologist? Or are we to think of faith more in terms of its object, thereby assigning the task of understanding to the systematic theologian? In what sense does faith transcend, as the theologian would have it, all other developmental processes, and in what sense is it more simply a reflection of these? Interestingly enough, the papers discussing this problem have chosen the notion of identity to organize their psychological considerations. They come close to saying that faith *is* identity. Less inclusive developmental processes might just as well have been adduced, however.

There is some discussion in theological circles today of the place of professional role and its effects not only upon the minister's work but upon thought and understanding. This discussion can, of course, be heard wherever considerations of professional workmanship, craft, or technique are relevant. It occurs in therapeutic psychology between the subjective and more intuitive clinicians and their more objective, scientific brethren. In theology it occurs between theologians and pastoral psychologists. To what extent does the minister's professional commitments — what some may still prefer to call his vocation or calling — affect not only his pastoral accomplishments but also the way in which he understands his faith? The pastoral psychology movement has given sustained articulation to this question. It is dealt with fully in LeRoy Aden's paper, and others also assign special importance to the significance of dynamic participation for theological understanding.

When this concern for dynamic participation, so highly characteristic of clinical psychological work generally, is carried forward beyond operational considerations, it can be found to bear upon a variety of theological problems. In such cases, methodological propriety no longer holds the foreground of attention, and gives way to a concern with the problems themselves. The essays by Frank Bockus and Leighton McCutchen directly attempt to enrich kerygmatic and doctrinal understanding through psychological analysis — and others argue in varying degrees for the methodological propriety of such an approach. An important issue is raised by such discussions: for psychological understanding is bringing to bear a wisdom of its own. The theologian's methodological position, therefore, appears in the way he selects psychological materials, and the transformations these materials undergo as they are applied to the theological problems. This procedure is neither a simple application of pre-formed psychological understanding, nor is it an attempt to validate theological ideas through simple correlation and matching with psychological processes. In the former we hear echoes of psychological reductionism, in the latter, echoes of a perhaps more subtle reductionism, that of much theological apologetics. The value of these papers will depend finally upon the extent to which their authors manage to avoid reductionism of any sort — psychological or theological. McCutchen's essay bears upon the problem of myth as this has been formulated in the demythologizing controversy, and Bockus brings psychological resources to bear upon christological formulation. Other problems in doctrine and ethics might just as easily have been submitted to this kind of psychological analysis.

The defining intuition of pastoral psychology and of much clinical work generally — that participation affects reflection and that the activity of reflection always resists simple discrimination into theological or psychological form — can be carried forward still further, to apply to problems which, though not doctrinal in themselves, are nevertheless germane to theological thought. The papers in this volume by William R. Rogers and Joseph Havens take up such problems. The first addresses itself to theological formulation through the question of order and chaos as it appears in psychotherapy; the second analyzes the significance of the small group movement in America, in its ethical, cultural and religious aspects. In these two essays we have still another approach to materials in the Religion and Personality field, one that attempts commentary of a theological order upon two important forms of cultural experience: individual psychotherapy and the dynamics of small groups.

The stylistic bias of these essays, along with their particular contents, merits comment. As in much interdisciplinary discussion, one senses in these essays a dissatisfaction with rigid compartmentalization, over-structuring, dichotomizing, and the like. This may well account for their somewhat critical, overbearing, and occasionally even argumentative and didactic style. They betray a sense of disaffection, a sense that "something is wrong," and they try very hard to come to terms with this. Consequently there is a noticeable preference for what might be called an immanental style of thinking about religious and theological problems. Transcendence and judgment are more likely to be understood in the context of nature and grace; repression and social alienation as distortions of a deeper sense of organic sociality and community attachments; and excessively rationalistic categorizing as a reflection of the absence of immediacy and proximity to phenomena. With such an approach, dynamic psychology can hardly be considered an outsider.

If the status of depth psychology as insider or outsider has provoked the dialogue between theology and psychology, we must note that the archoutsider (or -insider), Freud himself, continues to make himself felt whenever religion and theology take psychology seriously. Theological thought today presents no final concensus with regard to the status of Freud's thought, and the papers in this volume reflect this situation, although most writers are quite clear about where they themselves stand. Some of the authors have employed Freud extensively to implement their constructive work; some use psychoanalysis in a partial and limited way; and some have sought to define their normative position in a rather thorough criticism of Freud. Such a plurality of response testifies that the implications of psychology for religious studies are manifold, and that our dialogue has just begun.

How may that dialogue be carried forward? What new work appears to recommend itself? There are a number of promising suggestions in these papers, suggestions which in different ways attempt to expand the psychological base of our understanding of theology and religion. It is psychology that unites a number of different considerations in theological studies. For example, much recent discussion in psychology is concerned with the ego and the self: not so much with the way in which biological and genetic givens are integrated with social acquisitions in order to complete the developmental process, as with intrinsic energies at once psychological and referring at all points in the developmental process both to sociality and transcendence. This increases the necessity of fresh thinking about the psychological bases of theological anthropology and of ethics as well. It is less possible to speak of personality, society, and culture as separate systems, and less possible to separate a psychologically based theological anthropology from moral and social questions.

Such a renewed interest in anthropology points back into the past, to the religious roots of modernity, and also to the not so religious present. In each case, psychology is helpful. The attention given to the work of Erik Erikson in theological circles may seem to be an interest in the psychological profile of the Protestant Christian; on the other hand it may also be taken in a wider sense as a renewed interest in the psychological biography of the religious man. Again the intuitions of pastoral psychology are in evidence, for by insisting upon the study of cases, pastoral psychology has in effect attempted to explore the autobiographical uniqueness of the person. Perhaps closer work with the church historian is called for. Freud's cases seem to have more in common with the historian (did he not conclude that his patients really suffered from "reminiscences"?) and the novelist than with the protocols of the clinician.

Yet much theology is concerned today with its own fate

at the hands of a secularization process which is no longer hostile but simply indifferent to its resources, its intentions, and its good will. What are the dynamics underlying a transition whereby theological existence gives way to the merely secular? It is banal to note that psychotherapy provides for many today the only basis for a personal ethic. Is psychotherapy the cultural heir to religious experience, and is psychology the only kind of theology the future will allow? What shifts in patterns of self-understanding make theological meaning less accessible than ever to the contemporary self?

Such questions may also be taken as questions regarding the nature of religion itself, or, in this instance, the psychological features of religion. The early psychologies of religion, like the earlier anthropological studies of religion, tended to approach other religions "from the outside" so to speak, objectively, with a minimum of apparent participation. While studies in religion are today often more dynamic, and while psychology as a discipline is also more dynamic, we do not yet have equally forceful psychological studies of different religions, or, perhaps even more important, studies of particular problems in this area, such as the patterns of character formation in other religions, the interrelation of myth and dream, or residual religious forms ("high" or degraded) as these may be present in the processes of secularization. Such studies are surely necessary if theological thinking is to have relevance to the modern world.

If considerations such as these are given more substantial attention in the future, it will mean that studies in Religion and Personality have become as concerned with those problems that emerge at the border between theological and psychological studies, as they were in the past with the formal integrity of that dialogue itself. The quest for methodological integrity yields to the desire to understand. Perhaps psychology is neither insider nor outsider.

1

Theology and Self-understanding: The Christian Model of Man as Sinner

FRED BERTHOLD, JR.

Kant's warning "not to venture with speculative reason beyond the limits of experience"[1] has been highly honored by modern theologians. Some have thought to establish their theological concepts on the basis of a scientific or philosophical analysis of experience. Schleiermacher illustrates this in one way, Wieman in another. Others, following Feuerbach's lead, have tried to show that theology is really a disguised anthropology. Still others, like Karl Barth, have been critical of the attempt to give human experience a significant role in the formation of theology. Yet even Barth witnesses to the influence of the Kantian dictum. He entirely agrees that speculative reason is bound to the limits of experience, and that is why there can be no valid natural theology, why our knowledge of God must be given in revelation. In another way, too, Barth illustrates the concern of modern theology with human experience. He insists that the knowledge given in revelation constitutes genuine human knowledge. Once received, it helps us to understand our human situation more fully and correctly than would be possible without it.[2]

What shall we say: that an analysis of experience yields theological insight? Or that theological insight yields an understanding of experience? Both formulations seem to imply

[1] Immanuel Kant, "The Critique of Pure Reason," quoted from *The Philosophy of Kant*, trans. John Watson (Glasgow: Maclehose and Sons, 1888), p. 5.

[2] Barth, *Church Dogmatics*, vol. 1, pt. 1, trans. G. T. Thompson (Edinburgh: T. and T. Clark, 1936), pp. 226–60.

that a "good" theology, however arrived at, ought to be consistent with our understanding of human experience.

But the notion of experience is notoriously vague. Feuerbach was on the right track, I think, in suggesting that theology is most intimately concerned with our understanding of the nature of the human self. In any case, it is this connection which dominates contemporary Protestant discussion. The work of Rudolf Bultmann is more than a case in point; it has been the focus, as well as the source, of much of the most significant theology in recent years.

Bultmann, too, heeds Kant's warning. He regards it as settled that human reasoning cannot transcend the boundaries of experience, cannot find out God. Nor can we speak of God in rational, conceptual terms, for to do so would imply that He is an "object" within the spatio-temporal boundaries of experience. How, then, is theology possible? It is possible for one who sees that its intent is existential rather than speculative. We have no way of speaking conceptually about the God who encounters us, but we can speak of the impact of the encounter upon our understanding of our self and our situation. The proper object of theology is, then, not God but man.[3]

I have done little more than hint at something which I believe to be a dominant characteristic of modern theology: its involvement in the project of human self-understanding. This is by no means to suggest that all would agree with Bultmann that this is the main object of theology. But most would agree, I think, that it is one theological concern. To the extent that this is so, I should like to propose that one criterion of a good theology is that it helps us to understand the human self.

Models

Even if we assume agreement on this point, its implications for theology are not immediately evident. Resisting the temptation to discuss all the methodological alternatives, I

[3] Bultmann, "The Historicity of Man and Faith," in *Existence and Faith*, trans. S. Ogden (New York: World Publishing Co., 1960), p. 93.

wish to pursue one line of thought which has received considerable attention in recent years. This is the general notion that theology provides a "model" for understanding the world — or, in the instance I discuss, for understanding the human self.[4]

In science, a model (a computer, for example, treated as a model of the human nervous system) suggests a way of understanding a set of phenomena that are too remote, too small, too complex to grasp immediately. Most sophisticated workers in the field are aware of the dangers of treating the model as a *picture* of reality. Indeed, the model is useful precisely because we have no reliable picture, because we are baffled by many aspects of the reality we should like to know. It is impossible to verify a model by comparing it with that to which it refers, since we do not have independent access to its referent. Nevertheless, there are certain rational criteria for distinguishing a good from a bad model. Ramsey discusses these in connection with theological models. The model must, he says, "chime in with the phenomena; it must arise in a moment of insight or disclosure."[5] That is, there must be something in man's experience which fits in with the model. For example, there must be something in man's experience of the universe which makes it appropriate for him to think in terms of a "loving father."

Most important for our purposes is the criterion of adequacy.[6] Clearly, it is impossible to verify or falsify a model in any simple way, for the model suggests certain facts and relations in a region that is largely mysterious and baffling. Nevertheless, we can at least put the matter negatively: such

[4] I am using the term "model" in much the same way that Max Black speaks of an "analogue model" and Ian Ramsey, a "disclosure model." There are also affinities with S. Toulmin's use of "map." Black, *Models and Metaphors* (Ithaca: Cornell University Press, 1962); Ramsey, *Models and Mystery* (Oxford: At the University Press, 1964); Toulmin, *Philosophy of Science* (New York: Harper & Brothers, 1960). See also the article by F. Ferre, "Mapping the Logic of Models in Science and Theology," *The Christian Scholar*, 46, no. 1 (Spring 1963), pp. 9–39.

[5] Ramsey, *Models and Mystery*, p. 15.

[6] See K. Bendall and F. Ferre, *Exploring the Logic of Faith* (New York: Association Press, 1962), p. 74.

facts and relations as may be suggested by the model ought not conflict with what we do know. Admittedly, this is a difficult and tricky criterion, since, in the mysterious regions where models are most at home, one may always ask: but what, after all, do we *know*? Yet in many cases we do know something, at least with considerable confidence, and it may be relevant to a judgment of the model. In this respect, a model functions like a theory. As Carl Hempel has pointed out,[7] most scientific theories include some relatively direct reference to "observables" even though other portions of the theory may be connected with these observables only by indirect inference. At some points, a good model must be directly related to concrete experience. At these points, at least, it must be applicable to, and consistent with, what we do experience. For example — the example I wish to pursue in this paper — in Christian theology the "sin of Adam" constitutes a model which allegedly helps us to understand a vast range of human experience. Many of the things it suggests are no doubt inaccessible to our observation. Yet surely, among other things, this model also suggests something about human behavior that in principle is open to observation. The model would justly be judged inadequate if men were seldom or never aggressive, or if they customarily gave to the needy to the point of jeopardizing their own survival. The model must be applicable to, consistent with, such observations and well-founded theories as we do have.

In his discussion of a "new style natural theology," John Macquarrie says, "It has been important that the theist has exposed his conviction to a confrontation with the observable facts of our world and has shown that it is at least not incompatible with them."[8] To show the model to be compatible would be a minimal requirement. The "disclosure" function of the model suggests the further requirement that the model help us to understand better what we experience. Macquarrie accepts this function of theology, too. Philosophical theology

[7] C. Hempel, "The Concept of Cognitive Significance," *Proceedings of the American Academy of Arts and Sciences*, 80 (1951–54): 61–77.

[8] John Macquarrie, *Principles of Christian Theology* (New York: Charles Scribner's Sons, 1966), p. 49.

provides "a bridge between our everyday thinking and experience and the matters about which the theologian talks."[9] The starting point of theology is man himself, and "faith can be seen as something that is rooted in the very constitution of our human existence."[10] Macquarrie asks whether the descriptions provided by theology point to situations "typical of our human existence in the world."[11] Further, theology is to "make sense" of existence, and his discussion of alternative ways of interpreting the human situation makes clear that, ideally, theology should make better sense than other formulations.[12]

The notion that theology provides a model for the understanding of experience and, particularly, for the understanding of the human self, seems to me a promising one. However, most of the discussion to date has centered on methodological and logical issues. So far as I know, no attempts have been made to apply the general notion to specific theological models — that is, to examine whether a specific model is or is not applicable to the relevant data. In what follows, I wish to inquire whether the Christian theological model of "man as sinner" is adequate to, or in conformity with, the facts of human experience.

One reason why such an inquiry must be seriously pursued is that a number of important writers have suggested that Christian theology provides a model which leads us to *misunderstand* human experience. For example — and this is also relevant to the concrete topic we are to pursue — Sigmund Freud has contended that Christian theology leads to illusions about the self and the human situation. My point is that, if we think of theology as providing a model, we are clearly taking our stand with those who insist that theology has cognitive import — that it is not simply an expression of an attitude, or a set of values, but that it presumes (rightly or wrongly) to tell us something about the nature of reality — in this instance, about the nature of man.

[9] *Ibid.*, p. 51.
[10] *Ibid.*, p. 53.
[11] *Ibid.*, p. 62.
[12] *Ibid.*, pp. 59–64.

Man as Sinner

How are we to understand man, his nature, his achievements, and his failures? Christian theology has much to say on these topics. Normative for its statements are the biblical images or models of man: Adam in the midst of a good creation, Adam the sinner, and Jesus Christ, the new Adam. Of course, the Bible has much to say about man that is not directly connected with the Adam motif, but this motif is certainly central enough to provide a focus for our discussion.

Man is created good and is destined for fellowship with God. God's intention is that man live in love and trust with his fellow men and with God. This intention is not imposed upon man as an alien command, but it represents the genuine good for man himself, since its realization leads to man's peace, joy, and blessedness. We have an image of this goodness in Adam before his fall. For Christian theology, we have the definitive image of Jesus Christ. He is the "first fruits" of the new creation, and in him man is to receive adoption as the son of God; in him man is to be clothed with that glory for which the whole creation groans and travails.

In fact, however, men do not live in this way. They do not love and trust God or their fellows. Instead, they turn away from God's fatherly providence and seek to gain control of their own destiny. In their pride they reject dependence upon God and, indeed, seek to "become like the gods." This condition may be called "unfaith," a basic mistrust of God. And it leads to a similar mistrust between man and man.

The above characterization of the Christian view of man confines itself, I think, to statements which would be acceptable to the vast majority of Christian theologians. If we were to address ourselves to more detailed and specific questions, however, we would find that the unanimity vanishes. Some theologians stress man's reason as the crucial factor in man's goodness; others his freedom; others his conscience. Some think of man's sin primarily in terms of his finitude; others stress his sensuality; others his ignorance; and still others his pride. In short, it is not clear whether we can talk of *a* Christian model of man as sinner, or whether we must deal with a number of overlapping (and to some extent competing) models.

Since my purpose is not to do a history of theology, but to exemplify the need for the testing of models, I shall confine myself henceforth to that understanding of man as sinner which seems to me central and dominant in Protestant theology. For the sake of specificity, I shall focus upon the theology of Karl Barth, whose writings on this topic are both influential and, I think, representative of the central tradition that goes back to Luther, Calvin and indeed to Augustine.

Barth's View in the "Church Dogmatics"

The knowledge that man is a sinner is not, according to Barth, something available to our general human understanding apart from the revelation of God in Christ. Nevertheless, once that revelation is given, it helps us to understand the riddle of human existence.

> It is true, of course, that in and with the knowledge of actual sin we do win through to a very useful insight into the problematical nature of human existence. It is true that, while this is not identical with man's disharmony with God and his neighbour and himself, with the real breach in his existence, it can be an analogy to it which may help to make his guilt and need all the more plain.[13]

One strange thing about Protestant discussions of sin is the refusal to face, or the unconscious omission of, the question of the dynamic root of sin in the human personality. What is it about man that leads him to sin? This omission seems especially glaring when the situation of Adam in paradise is so portrayed that it becomes incomprehensible how or why he should have fallen into sin. As we shall see later, this omission is important for our assessment of the adequacy of the Christian model. Perhaps Kierkegaard came as close as any to dealing with this question of the dynamic root of sin. But

[13] Barth, *Church Dogmatics*, vol. 4, pt. 1, trans. G. W. Bromiley, p. 361.

he, too, is wary of the topic. Psychology may properly show, he says, that human nature is such that sin is a possibility; but it can never deal with "causes" of sin. To treat sin causally is to deny its absurdity and to deny that it becomes something actual only with the leap of the human free decision.[14]

Barth, too, refuses to discuss the question of the root of sin, for "sin has no positive basis in God . . . no positive place in His will and work."[15]

> Turn it how we will, if we regard this [sin] as a possibility of the creaturely nature of man, we shall always find it excusable because it is grounded in man as such. But in the final meaning of the term it is inexcusable. *It has no basis. It has, therefore, no possibility* — we cannot escape this difficult formula — *except that of the absolutely impossible.*[16]

At the descriptive level, Barth deals with sin in terms of "unbelief" and "pride."

> He sins in that he rejects the confidence that God is the source of all goodness and good to man. . . . Sin is therefore unbelief . . . unbelief is *the* sin, the original form and source of all sins.[17]

For some reason that we cannot understand (because it has no foundation in human possibility), man turns away from God. We can, however, say something more concrete about this sin; namely, that it is pride.[18] It is true that God gives freely to man, gives Himself and all that is good. But He gives Himself "in His divine lordship." Man may accept this gift, may live in peace and trust with God, but only with the God whose man acknowledges to be completely sovereign over him. This, man is unwilling to do. Why? Because of his pride, because man "only wants to exalt himself and to be as God."[19]

[14] Soren Kierkegaard, *The Concept of Dread*, trans. W. Lowrie (Princeton: Princeton University Press, 1957), p. 20.
[15] Barth, *Church Dogmatics*, vol. 4, pt. 1, p. 409.
[16] *Ibid.*, pp. 409–10 (italics mine).
[17] *Ibid.*, p. 414.
[18] *Ibid.*, p. 417.
[19] *Ibid.*, p. 419.

"There is no explanation of this human will to be as God. We can only state it as a fact that it is our desire."[20]

This pride reflects itself in every phase of human life. It makes man self-centered, aggressive, suspicious, and therefore the disharmony between God and man spreads to man's relations with his fellows.

Is the Model Applicable?

Does this model of man as sinner help us better to understand the human self? Does it "fit the facts"? Does it fare well in comparison with other possible models? Does it yield self-understanding, or illusion? Does it need modification?

If the model is considered as a description of human behavior, it has much to commend it. Here I would simply point to the impressive work of Reinhold Niebuhr, who has made a strong case for the view that this model is superior to the various forms of rationalism or idealism which tend to obscure man's devious and apparently inexhaustible self-interest. In short, I want to assume, for present purposes, that the Christian model of man as sinner is a fairly good one. Obviously this assumption can and should be challenged, but it is to further issues that I wish to devote my attention at this time. Even if the model is "fairly good," are there points at which it is lacking? Can it be improved?

There are several respects in which the model may be questioned. For one thing, we ought to question the failure to deal adequately with the origins, causes, or root of sin. Further, we may directly question whether pride is really at the root of the problem of sin. And we may also ask how the model fits with certain other portions of the total theological model.

The Question of Dynamics

We have noted the reluctance of Barth to deal with the basic question, Why does man pridefully turn away from God? A reason is given for this failure: namely, to suggest a basis or cause of sin would seem to give it some status in human nature. Barth fears that in the end this would seem to make

[20] *Ibid.*

19

sin something natural and excusable. Barth, on the contrary, regards it as absurd — as an uncaused and irrational irruption of man's free act. Such a position seems to me unjustified for several reasons. First, it is both natural and inevitable that our reason, when confronted by any "fact," should ask about its origins or causes, should seek to understand its connections with other facts. This is not to say that such a quest is always successful, but no theological dictum can keep us from it, and certainly not in the absence of some cogent explanation why the use of reason is here forbidden, or inappropriate. Further, insofar as any explanation is offered, it is invalid. It is just not the case that causation and freedom are incompatible. To trace the causes of human act, to whatever extent we can do so, is not to prejudice one way or the other its status as a free act. The notion of an uncaused act is unintelligible. Further, as many philosophers and theologians (perhaps most eloquently, Jonathan Edwards) have, I think, demonstrated, the notion that human acts are free and responsible, demands that we understand them, not as un-caused, but as caused in significant degree by factors internal to the self. If my reaction of pride is not somehow grounded in my self (my character, my dispositions), it may be viewed as a sheer chance irruption; it would provide no basis for saying that "I" am a sinner — for, lacking any stable internal basis, there would be no reason to suppose that my next reaction (and the one after that, etc.) would not display just the opposite characteristics. A free act, for which my continuing self is somehow responsible, must be thought of not as uncaused but as causally grounded in some aspect or aspects of my self.

Actually, I suspect that there are two other closely interrelated explanations for the relative lack of discussion of what lies behind the sin of pride. I think Barth is quite correct in saying that, for Christians, concern for and understanding of sin arises within the circle of faith in Christ. Our starting point is not the origins of sin — either individually or in terms of the history of the race. We start with an awareness of Christ, and in his light we come to understand the horror of that sin which made necessary so great a sacrifice. In short, not the origins but the overcoming of sin is the focus of concern. And that concern is practical, not theoretical. That is, in the awareness of the horror of sin, the attitude of the Christian is not one of curiosity but of rejection.

Suppose we agree that Christian theology is to understand sin christologically. How does sin appear in that light? The classic answers are: Christ's humility versus our pride; his obedience versus our disobedience; his faith versus our unfaith. "From the particular christological standpoint which is our present norm, the answer is that the sin of man is the pride of man." [21] Later in this essay I shall return to this point, for I want to question quite seriously whether it is true that, viewed christologically, the pride of man can be regarded as the essence or root of sin. For the moment, it is enough to note that traditionally this has been affirmed. The man who humbles himself, even unto death, is contrasted with the man who would exalt himself to the heavens.

This view of sin is also reflected in traditional Christian preaching and biblical exegesis. Most typically, its aim was to produce "conviction of sin." And how is this done? By trying to convince man that *he thinks too highly of himself,* to remind proud man that he is nothing, that he is worthy of condemnation. Think of the powerful opening of Luther's "Lectures on Romans":

> The sum and substance of this letter is: to pull down, to pluck up, and to destroy all wisdom and righteousness of the flesh . . . and to implant, establish, and make large the reality of sin. . . . For even if by his native and spiritual gifts a man is wise, righteous and good in the sight of men, *he is not so regarded by God,* especially if he himself regards himself as such. Therefore, we must keep ourselves humble in all these respects, as if we were still bare.[22]

[21] *Ibid.,* p. 413.
[22] Martin Luther, *Lectures on Romans,* trans. and ed. W. Pauck, The Library of Christian Classics, vol. 15 (Philadelphia: Westminster Press, 1961), p. 3 and p. 5 (italics mine).

My point may be summarized as follows: traditionally, at least within classical Protestantism, sin is traced to pride and no further. When we see the pride of man we have seen to the root of the matter.

The Relevance of Psychoanalytic Theory

If we think of theology as providing a model that helps us to understand man, we must ask whether the model fits the facts. I have already stated that, at the level of the description of much human behavior, the model seems to fit rather well. But we need to push our inquiry further. For one thing, we cannot repress the legitimate question about the dynamic origins of sin. Another point is that not only the Christian model of man as sinner, but other models as well (say, those provided by Nietzsche, or by Freud), might be said to fit equally well with the facts of human selfishness.

Does the model fit "the facts"? What facts? Reference to "the facts" throws the door open so wide that one is bewildered. How can one select the relevant facts without undue arbitrariness? Unfortunately, there is no simple answer to this question. In principle, we should test the model against all kinds of facts, and against all kinds of theories which interpret the relevant facts. When a given fact, or interpretation of it, is questioned, the whole theoretical framework surrounding its presentation as a fact is also brought into question. Obviously, we cannot undertake here such an exhaustive and literally endless inquiry.

I propose to focus upon the facts as seen within psychoanalytic theory. In a sense this is arbitrary. We have no antecedent reason for supposing that psychoanalysts are wiser or more perceptive than anyone else, including theologians. But in another sense this choice is not arbitrary. For I do not contend that we know in advance that psychoanalysis has the right to challenge or correct theology, but only that it presents us with a body of data systematically explored and critically interpreted by a community of serious researchers. Furthermore, psychoanalytic theory has given a great deal of attention to the very phenomenon which looms so large in our theological model; namely, man's pride. For my part, I am convinced that this comparison will be rewarding: for it will suggest (not establish) a correction of the traditional Protestant view of the roots of sin — a correction not only more conformable to the data but more in accord with other central aspects of the total Christian model.

The Dynamics of Narcissism

Pride, inordinate self-love, defensiveness, lack of trust — all these phenomena are well known to psychoanalytic theory. They appear there in connection with the concept of narcissism. Narcissism implies a withdrawal of love from others and a lavishing of love upon the self. The self becomes the focus of everything. To this extent the narcissistic person lacks a realistic relation to the world. This is rooted in a very early failure to develop a proper distinction between the self and others, and this failure goes back to an unsatisfactory relation between the child and the mother. (I will use the term "mother" for convenience, but we must remember that psychoanalysts are well aware that it may not be the biological mother who is important; it is whoever does the early "mothering".)

> As a result of this distorted mother-child relationship, the infant's capacity for differentiation of 'you' and 'I' is severely crippled; he does not create a core of himself, his individuality, and the libido becomes invested in the self; his own body remains the sole object of love (narcissism).[23]

Psychoanalysts have no doubt about the fact of narcissism, nor the fact that it finds expression, in greater or lesser degree, in the later life of all people. The matter of degree is, however, very important, for, in the development of the "normal" person, this narcissism is to some degree outgrown — or, perhaps better, it is modified by a growing capacity of the person for genuine love of others.

[23] Beata Rank and D. Macnaughton, "A Clinical Contribution to Early Ego Development" in *The Psychoanalytic Study of the Child*, ed. Ruth S. Eissler et al., vol. 5 (New York: International Universities Press, 1950), p. 63.

But what is the root of narcissism? Certainly it expresses itself as pride, self-love, self-centeredness. But do we really understand it if we simply content ourselves with such behavioral descriptions? No — for it is necessary to comprehend the dynamic root from which the behavior springs. And when we try to do this, we see that, behind the pride and self-love, there lies a more primary and basic situation, and a more fundamental response to that situation.

Basic to all psychoanalytic theory is the view that the characteristics of adult personality are continuous with, and outgrowths from, those of childhood. According to Erik Erikson, man has an "unconscious determination never to meet his childhood anxiety face to face again."[24] It is out of this childhood anxiety that narcissism develops.

In the very early phases of life, the situation of the infant gives rise to both basic trust and basic mistrust. The first basis of trust is ease of feeding, depth of sleep, and relaxation of bowels. The trust depends upon two things: the gradually developing homeostasis of the child's own body, and the gradually dawning awareness of the mother as an "object" who is dependable, who is present, and who provides for the needs of the child. To be sure, she cannot always be present, and relief from inner tensions or outer threats are seldom instantaneous. In the face of these tensions and threats the child is helpless, dependent to a large extent upon the mother. But in most cases, maternal care and growing bodily control combine to keep these tensions, and the resulting anxiety, within tolerable limits.

> The infant's first social achievement . . . is his willingness to let the mother out of sight without undue anxiety, because she has become an inner certainty as well as an outer predictability.[25]

No matter how kind and gentle the earliest environment, however, the child is soon thrust by its own development into

[24] Erik H. Erikson, *Childhood and Society* (New York: W. W. Norton, 1950), p. 360.
[25] *Ibid.*, p. 219.

24

a situation which, says Erikson, is the source of an "evil dividedness."

> It is, of course, impossible to know what the infant feels as his teeth 'bore from within' — in the very oral cavity which until then was the main seat of pleasure, and a seat mainly of pleasure; and what kind of masochistic dilemma results from the fact that the tension and pain caused by the teeth, these inner saboteurs, can be alleviated only by biting harder. This, in turn, adds a social dilemma to the physical one. [Here Erikson refers to biting the breast and the anger and withdrawal of the mother. Even where breast feeding does not continue into this phase, however, the aggressive feelings of the infant lead to actions on his part which bring a response of withdrawal and disapproval.] . . . Anger against the gnawing teeth, and anger against the withdrawing mother, and anger against one's impotent anger, all lead to a forceful experience of sadistic and masochistic confusion, leaving the general impression that *once upon a time one destroyed one's unity with a maternal matrix. This earliest catastrophe in the individual's relation to himself and to the world is probably the ontogenetic contribution to the biblical saga of paradise, where the first people on earth forfeited forever the right to pluck without effort what had been put at their disposal; they bit into the forbidden apple, and made God angry.*[26]

The aggressiveness which comes with the biting stage causes the child to hurt himself and his mother. The mother withdraws or otherwise expresses disapproval. The anger expressed toward the mother is also turned inward. "I have hurt myself and my mother and she is angry." Erikson calls this "a primary sense of badness."[27] It is both a feeling of inner guilt and a fear of the loss of all that is good. This situation is also referred to as "primal anxiety."

Melanie Klein, though she traces primal anxiety back to an

[26] *Ibid.*, pp. 74–75 (italics mine).
[27] *Ibid.*, p. 220.

even earlier stage in the child's life, is in general agreement with the above descriptions. She is a bit more explicit, however, in relating these phenomena to rejection of the mother and to the desire for independence and mastery, two characteristics which find their parallel in the Christian doctrine of sin. But it is important to note that, according to Klein, behind the child's rejection of the mother, and his desire for mastery, lies a basic anxiety — the child's fear of being rejected and, therefore, also his fear of being dependent. The child is, of course, radically dependent upon the mother. Before the ego-other distinction is achieved, this dependence is, of course, neither perceived nor feared. But it is the very situation of deprivation that gradually awakens the ego-other distinction — for example, the situation in which the infant is hungry and the mother not present. Then "dependence is felt to be dangerous because it involves the possibility of privation."[28] The dynamic sequence is as follows: privation or need, awareness of the absence of the mother, the feeling of being alone-helpless-rejected, anxiety, aggression. The aggression takes the form of wishing to master the situation for oneself, turning away from the mother, and desiring oneself to be able to provide for one's needs.

This desire for mastery also gives rise to feelings of guilt. For the aggression leads to hurting or wishing to hurt the mother. But insofar as the infant also loves and needs the mother, it feels its aggression to be dangerous and evil.

We may note in passing, though we cannot take the space to develop the implications, that Erikson regards primal anxiety and the disruption of the maternal matrix as both inevitable and, in a larger sense, good. This is not to deny that it is also evil, in the sense that the aggression may be turned inward and may lead to an oversevere narcissism. But it is also good, for without the break-up of the symbiotic relationship, there could be no social development, no adaptation of the child to the demands of outer reality, and no growth in his abilities and desires to manipulate and master the environ-

[28] M. Klein and J. Riviere, *Love, Hate and Reparation* (London: Hogarth Press, 1937), p. 7.

ment. "Parents and cultures use just these infantile encounters with inner gremlins for the reinforcement of their outer demands."[29] The development of coordination and skill, and also of conscience, presupposes these inner tensions which, just because they are felt to be evil, must be struggled with and overcome.[30]

I must resist the temptation to treat at length the phenomena of narcissism as they appear in adult life. Suffice it to say that the basic inclinations we have noted in the infant remain and are expanded upon. Turning away from the mother, the feeling of mistrust, the desire for independence and mastery — all these represent the seeds which grow into full-blown pride and self-centeredness. On this topic, however, I should like to make two brief comments. However one-sided or exaggerated the theories of Alfred Adler may seem, his views in general fit well with the theory of narcissism and, I think, with common experience. We do sense in the excessively prideful and self-centered adult an underlying fear, a background sense of his smallness and unworthiness. It is this alone that can explain why his achievements must be made to appear to himself extraordinary and grand, and why he cannot accept the verdict that his achievement and his worth are, like those of ordinary mortals, mixed with failure and fault.

Also, I think that the theory of narcissism sheds light upon the longstanding disagreement between Erich Fromm and Reinhold Niebuhr on the relations between love and self-love. For psychoanalytic theory strongly suggests that inordinate self-love, full-blown narcissism, is dynamically based upon an infantile and continuing sense of one's smallness and unworthiness. He who cannot freely and genuinely love others, who is obsessed with self-concern, need not be told that he is wretched, need not be humbled; for precisely that feeling already holds sway within, and gives rise to his narcissism.

Without an early experience of a sufficient love he has not become a securely independent person — not created

[29] Erikson, *Childhood and Society*, p. 75.
[30] *Ibid.*, p. 361.

a core of himself — and unless he becomes an independent person, he cannot make himself in turn love. . . . We love out of leisure from self-concern, and we are always self-concerned unless we know that someone other than ourself is prepared to maintain the significance of our being.[31]

What I wish to stress here is the psychoanalytic understanding of the roots of narcissism or excessive self-concern. "Primal mistrust" is not, as our theologians would seem to suggest, simply another formulation for "pride." Rather, it is a response that lies behind pride and constitutes its dynamic source. This response, furthermore, cannot in the first instance be attributed to the infant's willful "turning away from the other." Rather, behind this turning away lies the infant's sense (whether well-founded or not) that "the other" has turned away from him. Included in this sense is the feeling of guilt, of unworthiness; and because of the smallness and helplessness of the infant, this sense drives him in desperation and anger to focus his tender feelings and hopes upon himself. Referring to the theological analogue, the suggestion is that, if man is led to contend with the Almighty, it is in desperate reaction to his fear of being unworthy and rejected.

Relations Between the Models

We have now before us a sketch of the theological model of man as sinner, and of the psychoanalytic model of narcissistic man. How are the two to be related?

The psychologist is likely to judge theological ideas by the methods and results of his own inquiry, and vice versa. If we think of theology as a body of truths fallen from heaven, we will have no sympathy for the task of adjudicating between the models. But, if we think of theology (regardless of its ultimate source) as providing a model, one function of which is to help us understand the human self, and, if we admit even provisionally that the psychologist offers a plausible inter-

[31] G. Stuart, *Narcissus* (London: Allen and Unwin, 1956), p. 45.

pretation of a range of relevant data, we should be led to a more flexible view of the relations between theology and psychology. On the basis of the theological model, we may ask if, after all, the psychologist has correctly interpreted his data. And, in view of the data as structured by the psychologist, we may ask if the theological model needs to be expanded, revised or rejected.

I think that the data as understood psychoanalytically should lead us both to expand and to revise the theological model. (The obverse, reviewing the psychoanalytic theory in the light of the theological model, should also be pursued, but I shall not here undertake this important and enormous task.)

The theological model needs to be expanded because we have good reasons for refusing to accept pride or self-concern as brute facts which cannot, or should not, be viewed in terms of their dynamic, psychological origin. This expansion will be of enormous significance for theology. It will demand a deeper and closer look at the whole concept of the goodness of creation, of the basic relation between God and his creature, man. It will help to shed light on that perennially perplexing problem, Whence could temptation come in a good creation?

It is, however, with the possible revision of the theological model, rather than with its expansion, that I propose to conclude this essay. Protestant theology has too long stated or suggested that the root of man's sin lies in a prideful overestimation of the self. This is stated insofar as such theology insists that man's sin *is* unbelief, and that the concrete form of unbelief is pride; and insofar as it refuses to permit any inquiry into what lies behind sin. The same basic conclusion is suggested by the way in which Protestant theology has typically dealt with the problem of man's conversion from sin to faith. In this connection, the strategy has been to try to convince man of his sinfulness, to deepen his sense of unworthiness, to reduce him to nothingness before God.

Psychoanalytic theory suggests, I think, that neither the understanding of the nature of sin nor the strategy for overcoming it are quite correct. With regard to the nature of sin, the theological model may be correct at the descriptive level — that is, insofar as man does in fact separate himself from God and does in fact make himself the center of his concern. But do we not better understand the nature of any phenomenon when we see it, not simply as brute fact, but in relation to other phenomena which serve to explain its quality and, indeed, its very existence? Thus, psychoanalytic theory can perhaps give us an understanding of the roots of sin; and this in turn will reflect upon our understanding of its essential nature. My own conclusion is that we should view sin, not primarily as an inexplicable and willful self-assertion, but as a fearful and desperate response to a radical feeling of one's smallness and unworthiness. This does not mean that sin, in its overt manifestation, cannot take the form of prideful self-assertion.

I have already suggested that this understanding of sin would go along with a strategy for overcoming sin quite different from the traditional one. It will do no good to hammer away at the wretchedness of man's sin if man is, in fact, already overconvicted of sin. It is precisely this woeful and guilt-ridden feeling that is inextricably bound up with the real root of sin. It does not follow that awareness of our sinful condition should have *no* place in Christian preaching. It does follow, I think, that this awareness is not the first or foremost precondition for reconciliation and the new life in faith.

The Heart of the Gospel

These conclusions have resulted from a comparison of the theological and psychological models. But we have focused on only one part of the theological model, namely, the model of man as sinner. I should like to suggest that, if we bring into view another and absolutely central portion of the theological model, we will gain support for the revisions that I have proposed.

Karl Barth has correctly insisted that the Christian understanding of sin must be based upon what God has done in Christ. I want now to urge that traditional Protestant theology has been misled by a false reading of the implications of such a christological norm.

When we view man's sin in the light of Christ, what do we see? The traditional answer has been that we see how hopeless and wretched man must be, if it required such an unjustified sacrifice to rescue him. This leads to the thought that man is the antithesis of God: self-love, instead of love; pride, instead of humility.

In spite of Barth's emphasis upon sin as pride,[32] he insists that the traditional Protestant interpretation, just sketched, is a distortion of the Gospel.[33]

To be sure, neither Barth nor I would wish to deny that the New Testament speaks often and eloquently of man's sin. But if that were its basic message, it would be superfluous. That testimony abounds in the Old Testament. The heart of the Gospel lies elsewhere; namely, in the proclamation of the fact that God loves us and accepts us. This grace of God is poured out upon us not in virtue of what we might become if we try hard enough, not on the condition that we submit to the woeful sentence upon our wretchedness, not in blind unawareness of our self-centeredness, but it is poured out upon us as we are. "While we were yet sinners, Christ died for us."[34] Implicit in the Gospel is the awareness that it does no good simply to condemn man for his sin, for it is precisely that awareness which drives the religious man to seek to justify himself. Further, the Gospel implies that the dynamic change from pride to love results from the conviction that God already loves and accepts us. The two things fit together: the dynamic root of man's sin is his fear that he is unworthy (which leads to his "boasting in the law"), and the medicine for sin is the conviction that he *is* accepted by God.

> He does not despise men, but in an inconceivable manner esteems them highly just as they are, takes them into

[32] Barth, *Church Dogmatics*, vol. 4, pt. 1, pp. 413ff.

[33] *Ibid.*, vol. 4, pt. 1, pp. 3ff, and vol. 3, pt. 1, especially 228ff. See also Barth, *The Humanity of God*, trans. J. N. Thomas (Richmond, Va.: John Knox Press, 1960).

[34] Rom. 5:8.

His heart and sets Himself in their place. . . . Thus He affirms man. . . . It would not do even partially to cast suspicion upon, undervalue, or speak ill of His humanity, the gift of God, which characterizes Him as this being. . . . He does not reject the human! Quite the contrary![35]

Some colleagues, responding to an earlier draft of this essay, complained that I have been unfair to Barth — and, for that matter, to Luther and Calvin. Their basic understanding of sin is put in terms of unfaith, not pride. Also, even more basic than their harsh judgment of man is their stress on his pre-eminent status and value 'in Christ.' I gladly accept these corrections, as perhaps my closing comments on Barth might suggest. However, I should like to add two observations. Especially in Calvinist orthodoxy, and in both Lutheran and Calvinist popular preaching, the emphasis upon man's pride, and the strategy of humiliating man, are certainly prominent. Finally, if I understand Barth correctly, I have no quarrel with the *substance* of his view of sin, and its relation to grace. However, I think that his own basic insight would stand out more clearly if he would avoid equating unfaith with pride. Unfaith is prior to and provides the dynamic wellspring of pride. This formulation is, I believe, consistent with his basic position. And, as I have tried to show, it is more consistent with the understanding of the root of sin that is suggested by the psychoanalytic model.

[35] Barth, *The Humanity of God*, p. 51 and pp. 53–54.

2

The Snare of Truth

PERRY LeFEVRE

One of the haunting issues confronting every theologian is the question of truth. For the theologian this may be the question whether the teachings of the church are true in some objective sense, but his concern may also be focused on the relation of such discursive truth to what some would call religious or existential truth. In Kierkegaard's Journals there is an interesting entry, dated 1854. Kierkegaard wrote: "The truth is a snare: you cannot have it, without being caught. You cannot have the truth in such a way that you catch it, but only in such a way that it catches you."[1]

There are three things about this journal entry that call for special underlining in any consideration of the impact of therapeutic psychology on theology, when the particular emphasis is on knowing and believing. First, Kierkegaard is clearly distinguishing what he means by truth from what most men have meant by truth. Most men have called truth something that "can be had" by a person who himself does not get caught. Much of what men normally call truth can be known in an objective, detached fashion. Furthermore, such truths are discovered, or in some settings perhaps it is better to say, uncovered. In going beyond these two assertions, Kierkegaard is maintaining the positive point that truth can be had only in such a way that it catches you rather than that you catch it.

These Kierkegaardian assertions about truth help to bring into focus the problem of the interrelation between truth

[1] Soren Kierkegaard, *The Last Years*, ed. and trans. Ronald Gregor Smith (New York: Harper and Row, 1965), p. 133.

and psychotherapy. Kierkegaard was concerned to explore the "healing truth" for the sickness unto death, as he calls it. The psychotherapist is interested in the truth that heals the psyche. Perhaps an examinaion of the similarities and differences in the two cases may illuminate the relations between theology and therapeutic psychology. The observations to be made are, of course, made from the standpoint of the theologian. Others must bring to bear the raw data of therapeutic experience to test them. With respect to the "sickness unto death," perhaps all stand on equal grounds and have common experience as a basis for judgment.

Apart from the conditioning therapies, most of the therapies for the psyche appear to emphasize the phenomenon of insight. There are many discussions of the nature and function of insight in psychotherapy, and although there is a wide range of meaning and some ambiguity about the use of the term itself, perhaps it will be sufficient to indicate that the development of insight is the development of the understanding of connections, of seeing patterns of relationship which make one understand why one acts, or feels, or thinks as he does. A classical example of the development of insight might be drawn from one of the first case studies published in Breuer and Freud's *Studies in Hysteria*.[2]

Breuer had been treating a twenty-one old girl who had been very disturbed for a number of months. Among her symptoms were paralysis of the arms, hallucinations, alterations of sight and speech. For no apparent reason, she had difficulty in taking a drink. She would take a glass of water in her hand, but as it touched her lips she would push it away again, unable to drink it. Under hypnosis she disclosed that she had once entered her room to find a disgusting little dog (which belonged to her English governess, whom she also disliked) drinking out of a glass. She said nothing because she wanted to be polite. In the course of this disclosure, Breuer recounts, "she gave energetic expression to her strangulated anger." She then asked for a drink, and without any inhibition

[2] Joseph Breuer and Sigmund Freud, *Studies in Hysteria*, trans. A. A. Brill (1937; reprinted Boston: Beacon Press, 1958).

drank a great deal of water, awaking from the hypnosis with the glass at her lips." With this, the disturbance disappeared.

Breuer continues, describing his further discussions with the patient.

> Every single symptom of this complicated morbid picture was separately taken up and the various occasions during which it appeared were related in reverse order, beginning with the days before the patient became bed-ridden, and backward to the time of its first appearance. When this was related, the symptom was thereby permanently removed.[3]

The capacity of insight to free an individual from a bondage to his past has been demonstrated again and again, although the methods of establishing insight have been developed in very complex ways. The problem arises when we find that this kind of insight does *not always* free the person. This realization has sometimes led to a distinction between intellectual insight and so-called emotional insight. Or we may find insights described as "verbal" or "merely intellectual." It is not enough to see or to acknowledge patterns or connections. It is claimed that there must be an "affective" component. An emotional response must be released or set off by an insight, if it is to be therapeutic. French summarizes Freud's understanding of the goal of therapy:

> Freud (1904) first formulated the goal of therapy as filling in the gaps in the patient's memory, undoing the patient's repression, making what was unconscious conscious. Disappearance of the patient's symptoms was hoped for as an automatic consequence of making what was unconscious conscious.
>
> . . . .
>
> Later, Freud (1918) formulated the changes effected by therapy in terms of the relationship between the "Ego" and repressed drives or wishes. By becoming conscious of repressed wishes and of the conflicts that arise out of

[3] *Ibid.*, p. 23.

them, the "Ego" gains control of the energy (libido) that activates them and can then utilize this energy in the service of its efforts to find satisfaction in the real world.[4]

But how can the "Ego" get control of this energy by becoming conscious of a repressed wish or conflict?

The answer is that conflict can be handled only when it is understood. Insight must guide behavior. But insight — in the sense of merely becoming aware of the root of one's difficulties in some hitherto repressed material — is not enough. Insight must also be inclusive of the underlying conflict between the infantile wishes and reality. There must be a "working through," a disillusionment to the extent that one accepts "reality."

This, I take it, is what Alexander is demanding when he calls for a balance between the curative factors of emotional abreaction and intellectual insight.[5] As Frieda Fromm-Reichmann has put it:

> No cure is accomplished according to present classical and modified psychoanalytic knowledge, by any single, one-time understanding of any single symptom or any single previously disassociated experience. All emotional experiences which are made accessible to the patient's awareness and mature emotional judgment have to be recognized and accepted ("working through") repeatedly in various contexts. . . . Working through should be continued until the time is reached when the intellectual understanding of his problem, of its previously disassociated causes, and of its various interlocking mental and emotional ramifications is gradually transformed into real creative emotional insight.[6]

But let us get back to Kierkegaard, and through him to Socrates. It looks very much as if what psychotherapy is pur-

[4] Thomas French, *The Integration of Behavior* (Chicago: University of Chicago Press, 1958), 3:16.
[5] Franz Alexander, *The Scope of Psychoanalysis* (New York: Basic Books, 1961), pp. 226–27.
[6] *Psychoanalysis and Psychotherapy* (Chicago: University of Chicago Press, 1959), p. 95.

suing through the development of insight parallels what Socrates envisaged in his maieutic method. It further appears that the theory of the healing and freeing truth implicit in such psychotherapy runs parallel to the Socratic theory of recollection. We could, of course, go directly to the Socratic dialogues for confirmation, but since I wish to raise questions in the light of the contrast between the Kierkegaardian dialectic and the Socratic, let us turn to the opening paragraph of the *Philosophical Fragments*. Kierkegaard begins:

> How far does the Truth admit of being learned? With this question let us begin. It was a Socratic question or became such in consequence of the parallel Socratic question with respect to virtue, since virtue was again determined as insight. In so far as the Truth is conceived as something to be learned, its non-existence is evidently presupposed, so that in proposing to learn it one makes it the object of an inquiry. Here we are confronted with the difficulty to which Socrates calls attention in the Meno, and there characterizes as a 'pugnacious proposition'; one cannot seek for what he knows, and it seems equally impossible for him to seek for what he does not know. For what a man knows he cannot seek, since he knows it; and what he does not know he cannot seek, since he does not even know for what to seek. Socrates thinks the difficulty through in the doctrine of Recollection, by which all learning and inquiry is interpreted as a kind of remembering; one who is ignorant needs only a reminder to help him come to himself in the consciousness of what he knows. Thus the truth is not introduced into the individual from without, but was within him.[7]

According to Kierkegaard, for Socrates essential knowledge is self-knowledge through recollection, and the teacher bears merely an accidental relation to its development. This maieutic relationship is the highest one man can bear to another. In analogous terms the therapist is the Socratic midwife. His

[7] Soren Kierkegaard, *Philosophical Fragments* (Princeton: Princeton University Press, 1944), p. 5.

relationship is accidental in the sense that he could be interchanged with another therapist, for the significant work the therapist does is to bring to birth meanings and connections and patterns which are already present but not acknowledged or known in awareness. Even in those forms of therapy where fairly explicit interpretations are offered, they are intended to express what was "there" below awareness all the time. Socrates' dictum "know thyself" could be taken as the therapist's goal for his patient.

Just as Kierkegaard found some puzzles in the Socratic dialectic as a means of moving man toward authentic existence, so we may find some puzzles in the parallel interpretation of the healing truth implicit in the psychotherapeutic understanding of insight. One of the puzzles has to do with the relation of interpretation to self-knowledge. There exist, of course, various frameworks of interpretation, and the different interpretations that result from the different frameworks appear to have comparable potentiality as "healing truth." Whether or not Fiedler's studies [8] of the relative success of various kinds of therapists working from different ideological perspectives (and so offering diverse interpretations) can be duplicated, it does seem that divergent types of insight therapy are effective. Some, indeed, may be in radical conflict with each other, and yet be effective. This problem is not unique to psychotherapy. It is true also of theology. Various theologies may inform one or another expression of the religious life, and yet transformation to new life may occur against the background of all of them.

Whatever may be the function of insight as "healing truth" or in "healing truth," the question is, is it a sufficient clue to successful therapy? A further puzzle leading to the same question is created by seemingly interminable insight therapy. Apart from the defense that the insights may not be "real" or are merely intellectual, insight is again called into question

[8] Fred E. Fiedler, "A Comparative Investigation of Early Therapeutic Relationships Created by Experts and Nonexperts of the Psychoanalytic, Nondirective, and Adlerian Schools" (Unpublished doctoral dissertation, Department of Psychology, University of Chicago, 1949).

as *the* therapeutic factor. Pursuit of insight can become a way of life, not a healing truth for some. Allen Wheelis, himself an analyst, writes of the

> psychoanalyst with the sad yellow face, shoulders stooped as if by an invisible weight . . . stretched on [his] couch . . . four times a week for—how many? years; for a while analysis itself becoming for him the meaning of life, a kind of formal minuet in which the learning of new psychic steps replaced lost illusions; with insight to spare, but no change, coming in time to feel betrayed, but still on the couch for years . . . years . . . saying, I came to this hospital as a resident and still remember how it was. And how I was. Patients would arrive sick and leave well. Something would happen — insight — that made a difference. So I thought. It's the same now; but I'm different, and they muddle along for a while with ups and downs and then come back. And the second time is like the first — some new insights, some new 'realizations,' some new turning points . . . like the wind turns.[9]

Some might say that what has gone awry in cases like this is that there has not been adequate working through, that one should not really talk about the achievement of insight unless such insight has been tested and assimilated through try-out in behavior. It would seem that working through in this sense *is* desirable or necessary for some insights to have healing power, and the question from a Kierkegaardian standpoint might well be whether such a working through may not involve that break with immanence — that something coming from the "outside" which makes the healing truth a truth that ensnares you rather than a truth that you uncover or discover.

Kierkegaard, of course, in the *Philosophical Fragments*, puts alongside the Socratic dialectic of immanence, the dialectic of faith. He does this in a hypothetical way. Suppose, he says, that things were otherwise. Suppose the Moment in time

---

[9] Quoted by Perry London in *The Modes and Morals of Psychotherapy* (New York: Holt, Rinehart, and Winston, 1964), p. 229.

does have a decisive significance. Suppose that the teacher is not interchangeable, that healing truth is not within, recoverable through self-knowledge. If all this were the case, the learner, if he were to acquire Truth, must have the Teacher bring it to him. Not only so, but he must also be given the condition for understanding it. To be sure, Kierkegaard is speaking of the truth that heals the sickness unto death. He is talking about the personal embodiment of that truth in the Paradox — the Christ, and he goes on in the *Unscientific Postscript* to fill in the hypothetical picture. Christianity is not a doctrine; it cannot be communicated directly. Christian faith is a *how*, not a *what*. Kierkegaard's point is that the Socratic doctrine of recollection of a truth that is already there — of insight through the discovery of patterns and connections one had previously been unaware of, is not enough. Something has to happen *to* man, not simply within him, since there is a sickness deeper than repression.

Whatever we may believe about "sin" as a category for understanding the human situation, it may be that there is a clue here for understanding a further dimension of the "healing truth" which goes beyond insight and its appropriation. My own conviction is that this is the case. We need to return once again to the therapeutic process for further reflection. I would hypothesize that in therapy the relationship itself heals, and that the healing truth is the truth-in-relationship shared by the participants. Doubtless it would be commonly acknowledged that the relationship is important because it provides the means whereby insight can emerge and be appropriated. Or if we think of the relationship as a transference phenomenon, then relationship provides some of the "stuff" that can be subjected to analysis or interpretation in order to produce insight. One wonders whether such a view of the function of relationship is sufficient.

Consider, for example, the case materials which are reported for John Rosen's direct therapy,[10] or the reports of Mrs. Sechehaye in the *Diary of a Schizophrenic Girl* and

[10] John N. Rosen, *Direct Analysis* (New York: Grune and Stratton, 1953); *Direct Psychoanalytic Psychiatry* (New York: Grune and Strat-

Symbolic Realization.[11] In all of these, verbal interpretation and intellectualized insights were not enough or were inappropriate. The individuals in question "were lost in a land where no one spoke their language." There were genuine needs and impoverishment in early life which had never been met. Symbolically or in actual fact, the early maternal environment had to be recreated, and the needs of that period had to be met through relationship, through what I would call the concrete language of event. It is the *relation* to the patient as a *mother to a child* which seems to be the embodiment of the "healing truth." There is a factor beyond insight involved, and this leads me to doubt also the adequacy of orthodox theories and uses of transference phenomena. Perhaps Boss is correct. So-called transference love or hate may be a genuine interpersonal relation. There may be no need to doubt the genuineness of the patient's present feelings, as if they were somehow transferred from earlier relationships to the present. Boss writes:

> The analysand begins to love the analyst as soon as he becomes aware that he has found someone — possibly for the first time in his life — who really understands him and who accepts him even though he is stunted by his neurosis. He loves him all the more because the analyst permits him to unfold more fully his real and essential being within a safe, interpersonal relationship. . . .[12]

Boss goes on:

> As we have said before, all genuine love of one person for another is based on the possibility which the loved one offers to the lover for a fuller unfolding of his own being by being-in-the-world with him. On the other hand, the patient will hate his analyst as long as he is

ton, 1962); *Psychoanalysis, Direct and Indirect* (Doylestown, Pa.: Doylestown Foundation, 1964).

[11] Marguerite Sechehaye, *Dairy of a Schizophrenic Girl* (New York: Grune and Stratton, 1951); *Symbolic Realization* (New York: International Universities Press, 1951).

[12] Medard Boss, *Psychoanalysis and Daseinsanalysis*, trans. Ludwig B. Lefebre (New York: Basic Books, 1963), p. 239.

still (because of his childhood experience) open only to a child-father or child-mother relationship which limits his perception of adults to frustrating experiences.[13]

Boss further believes that the analysand's being-himself will mature into ever more differentiated forms of relating if (and only if) the more primitive forms of relating are first permitted to unfold themselves fully. If this is allowed, maturer forms of behaving appear spontaneously. Thus the gradual detachment from the analytic situation happens *because* acting out is permitted. It is not produced by a misinterpretation of acting out as a renewal of childhood memories. The additional point needs to be made that the neurotically inhibited person "can attempt to open himself in his relationship to the analyst only if the latter meets him on a level which is genuinely his."[14] For many this may mean that the language of relationship is more basic than the conceptual, intellectual and verbal level.

The critical issue of the relation between objective knowledge and "relationship" recalls an answer Martin Buber gave to a question several years ago. Speaking of the great and contradictory variety of the schools and the methods of psychology, he said: "Every genuine therapist can heal with any of the methods which have been developed; every psychotherapist can destroy with any of them. What matters and what is inseparable from the being and becoming of the person — is the right relation to the Thou."[15] Perhaps Buber is right about what is the real carrier of the healing truth.

But what then is the connection between such a view and the Kierkegaardian contrast between Socratic dialogue and the dialogue of revelation? If we take seriously the notion that the relation to the Thou is the carrier of the healing truth, then we would conclude that Kierkegaard is right. Recollection, in the sense of remembering, of making conscious that

[13] *Ibid.*, pp. 239–40.
[14] *Ibid.*, p. 242.
[15] Sydney and Beatrice Rome (eds.), *Philosophical Interrogations* (New York: Holt, Rinehart, and Winston, Inc., 1964), p. 49.

which was unconscious, is not enough. Bondage to the past may still remain bondage unless the past itself is transformed. A new beginning must occur. It is not enough to uncover or recover the old: the new must break into the old life. And the new is this healing truth, healing because it allows him to be what he is and at the same time makes possible what Boss calls the unfolding of his real and essential being.

Why does relationship of the kind Buber speaks of carry with it the healing of the new beginning, of the transformation of the past? Various ways of putting the answer to this question might be found from a theologian's perspective. The answer is not so clear from a psychological perspective. One of the most promising of the attempts to answer the question psychologically has been that of Eugene Gendlin. In "A Theory of Personality Change" Gendlin holds that the key to therapeutic personality change is a theory of experiencing.[16] Gendlin calls the concrete psychological events "experiencing." Experiencing is the process of concrete bodily feeling. As inwardly felt datum, it contains preconceptual meanings — felt but not symbolized. There is more implicit meaning in such experiencing than we ever can exhaust through symbolization. Symbolic completion of the implicit meanings, or "carrying forward" as Gendlin calls it, is also a bodily felt process. Explicit meanings emerge in the interaction between symbols and implicit meanings. They are not there, so to say — to be discovered: "Symbols must interact with the feeling before we have a meaning."[17]

In psychotherapy, relationship provides the context for changing the manner of experiencing, and with such a change there comes a change in the quality of all the individual's meanings. Insight and better understanding are the derivatives, not the cause, of this process. The implicit meanings to be symbolized are now different ones. In other words, relationship makes possible the "carrying forward" of the process of experiencing, which is "essentially an *interaction* between

[16] In *Personality Change*, ed. Philip Worshel and Donn Byrne (New York: John Wiley and Sons, 1964).
[17] *Ibid.*, p. 114.

43

feelings and 'symbols' (attention, words, events)." [18] Relationship of a certain kind makes possible the reconstitution of
the experiencing process. As Gendlin states it, "When certain
implicitly functioning aspects of experiencing are *carried forward* by symbols or events, the resulting experiencing always
involves *other* sometimes newly *reconstituted* aspects which
thereby come to be *in process* and *function implicitly* in that
experiencing." [19]

Such reconstitution goes on within the "self-process," which
Gendlin defines as the interaction of the individual's feelings
with his own behavior (symbolic or actual). But the self-
process is not solely within the isolated individual. Like Mead,
Buber, and Sullivan, Gendlin would hold that the self-process
is interpersonal in character. And interpersonal responses are
not just external events. "They are events *in interaction with
the individual's feeling*. The individual then develops a capacity *to respond to* his feeling. The self is not merely a
learned repertoire of responses, but a response process *to*
feeling." [20] Gendlin would hold that this fact underlies therapeutic change. He writes:

> If feeling did not have implicit meaning, then all mean-
> ing would depend totally on the events or responses
> which occur. Again then, the self could never become
> anything but the repetition of the responses of others.
> The individual would always have to interpret himself
> and shape his personal meanings just as others had inter-
> preted him.
>
> But feeling has implicit meanings. Therefore, to the
> extent that a feeling process is ongoing, we can *further*
> respond to it differently than others have. However, to
> the extent to which we respond to our own feeling so as
> to skip or stop the process rather than carry it forward,
> to that extent we need others to help us be ourselves. Not
> only the genesis, but the adult development of the self
> also may require interpersonal responses. Such responses

[18] *Ibid.*, p. 129.
[19] *Ibid.*, p. 131.
[20] *Ibid.*, p. 135.

are required not because of their appraisal or content, but because we need them concretely to reconstitute the feeling process.[21]

The effect occurs through the other's response to our concrete feeling process, which in some respect helps to reconstitute it and carry it forward. Gendlin sums up his view: "Personality change is the difference made by *your* responses in *carrying forward my* concrete experiencing. To be myself I need your responses, to the extent to which my own responses fail to *carry* my feelings *forward.*"[22]

Gendlin's theory of therapeutic personality change makes it possible to understand the success of various nonverbal therapeutic interventions, such as the direct action therapy of Rosen, or some forms of play therapy with children, or even some aspects of Sechehaye's work with the schizophrenic girl. There is a language of events and action as well as the language of words. Indeed, there is a language of silence. Gendlin himself calls attention to this in his account of his own work with psychotics. Even where the patient is unable or unwilling to speak, or when his utterance makes no logical sense, the therapist may try to verbalize what he imagines may be the patient's feelings, or he may respond to the other by expressing his own feelings. A felt interaction process may still take place. Gendlin holds that the therapist's behavior alone may aid the therapeutic process: "One person's behavior can *reconstitute* the interaction and experiencing process of the other person."[23]

Pointing in the same direction without quite the detailed sophistication of Gendlin's theory is a paper by Arthur Kovacs. Trained in orthodox psychoanalysis, Kovacs abandoned traditional conceptions and technique. He writes: ". . . I have come to believe that therapy cannot be a self-conscious cognitive process. Therapy depends upon shared experiencing . . . The therapist must give himself up to the encounter

[21] *Ibid.*
[22] *Ibid.*, p. 136.
[23] *Ibid.*, p. 144.

with his patients and be lived by it." [24] Kovacs holds that psychopathology is really a disturbance of the cyclical "ebb and flow of intimacy and detachment" as the result of previous growth distorting interpersonal relationships.

> In learning to tolerate and cherish increasing doses of intimacy with the therapist in the therapy relationship the patient learns or rediscovers what Benedek calls 'trust' or 'optimism' which in turn can serve as a talisman to hang onto as experiments in intimacy are haltingly conducted in the outside world.[25]

Why such relationships of shared experiencing and intimacy are therapeutic could, of course, be understood in Gendlin's terms.

One could use the language of Marcel and Buber to describe what must happen if healing is to take place. Marcel speaks of "presence." [26] The notion of presence is based on common experience. Someone may be in the same place we are. We can even put out our hands and touch him, and yet we may feel quite strongly that he is not really "present." Physical proximity does not really determine whether another person is "there" *for us.* I may be close to others in space and time, and yet they are really strangers to me. I treat them as "absent." Indeed, I can speak to another, he hears my words and may answer me, and yet he does not really "hear" me or respond *to me.* He hears, but in the same way that a radio picks up signals from a broadcasting station. No genuinely personal response is made. To be "with" another in the existential sense means to be present to him and for him.

What Marcel is speaking of is difficult to conceptualize, and perhaps finally impossible to objectify, since it is transobjective. Yet it is not subjective. It is felt and known in the relationship, in the "in-between," in the reality of a new kind

[24] Arthur Kovacs, "The Intimate Relationship: A Therapeutic Paradox," in *Psychotherapy, Theory Research and Practice,* 2, no. 3 (May, 1965): 100.

[25] *Ibid.*

[26] Gabriel Marcel, *The Philosophy of Existence* (London: Harvill Press, 1948).

of being that emerges when persons are present to and for each other. It is intersubjectivity. To be "with" another is not to be alongside. It presupposes a mutual openness and response, a binding unity of shared experience.

Another way to point to the reality of presence, of being with, is to speak of Marcel's term *disponibilité*, "availability." There are some who seem able to be available when another suffers. They are at our disposal. Others are unavailable. Again, it is not a matter of being physically present or not. It is not a matter of being attentive or distracted. What Marcel is referring to is the capacity of some persons to give one a place within themselves. There is, says Marcel, a way of listening which is a way of refusing — of refusing one's self — and there is a way of listening which is a way of giving — of self-giving. Availability may be communicated in a glance, a smile, an accent, a touch of the hand, as well as in modes of speech.

What is it that makes it impossible for some people to be available? Marcel thinks the answer lies, not in whether the other has good will or not, but in whether the other is encumbered with self or not. Opacity, impermeability, these are related to one's own egocentricity. It is most frequently the result of preoccupation with self. Marcel writes of the one who is transparent and available for others; he "knows that [he] is not his own . . . that the most legitimate use [he] can make of his freedom is precisely to recognize that [he] does not belong to [himself]; this recognition is the starting point of [his] activity and creativeness." [27]

But presence is the source of personal being. It is also the key to restoring and maintaining wholeness, in the face of isolation, loneliness, suffering, and sorrow. And creative fidelity — which is the perpetuating of presence, maintaining presence "in spite of," no matter what — aspires toward that unconditionality that may make it possible for an individual or a group to face life's deepest crises with courage.

These notions of Marcel find their parallel in the thought of Buber. For Buber, much human talk is simply speechifying.

[27] *Ibid.*, p. 28.

People talk past one another; they do not make the other really present, and they are not really present to the other. Everything depends, according to Buber, on whether each thinks of the other "as the one he is, whether each, that is, with all his desire to influence the other, nevertheless unreservedly accepts and confirms him in his being this man and in his being made in this particular way." [28] He must make the other present by "imagining the real." To imagine the real in relation to another means "to cross over to the other side," to try to share in imagination the reality of his wishing, feeling, perceiving, and thinking in this very moment, not as a detached content but in their very reality in this man.

> Relation is fulfilled in a full making present when I think of the other not merely as this very one, but experience in the particular approximation of the given moment, the experience belonging to him as this very one. [29]

When such sharing happens in life together, there are creation and healing of human existence. What Buber says of the role of the mother in relation to the child might be said with equal validity of those who are able to be "with" another in the therapeutic relationship.

> Because this human being exists, meaninglessness, however hard pressed you are by it, cannot be the real truth. Because this human being exists, in the darkness the light lies hidden, in fear salvation, and in the callousness of one's fellowmen the Great Love. [30]

One could surely use other language and categories than those of Marcel and Buber to describe this freeing, renewing, truth-in-relationship, but the happening, the event, is the *crucial* reality.

I use this phrase "crucial reality" not inadvisedly and without forethought, not lightly, but reverently, discreetly, ad-

[28] Martin Buber, *The Knowledge of Man*, trans. Maurice Friedman and Ronald Gregor Smith (New York: Harper and Row, 1965), p. 69.

[29] *Ibid.*, p. 71.

[30] *Between Man and Man*, trans. Ronald Gregor Smith (London: Kegan Paul, 1947), p. 98.

visedly, soberly, and in the fear of God. From my point of view, this happening is a Christic happening, a Christic event. What Buber speaks of as the presence of the eternal Thou — the Thou which cannot be made an it — in every human I-Thou relationship, Christians might otherwise describe as the presence of the Christ. As Norman Pittinger has said, the *historical* event of Jesus Christ defines but does not confine.[31] In every human relationship, Christ is present incognito, as judge and redeemer. Indeed, one might go so far as to say with Teilhard and his New Testament predecessors that the cosmic Christ is present at every event and that cosmic process is the process of Christification. The cross pattern is deeply woven into the very fabric of creation, writes zoologist L. C. Birch,[32] but whether or not we see a cosmic Christ present as the logos of all creation, what we find in the event Jesus Christ is the disclosure of the pattern of redemption which is the archetype of God's working in all history. This is what the writer of the prologue of the Gospel of John was saying. C. H. Dodd translates the prologue into another language when he says that it means: "The ground of all real existence is that divine meaning or principle which is manifest in Jesus Christ. It was this principle separable in thought from God, but not in reality separate from Him that existed before the world was, and is the *pattern* by which and the power through which it was created" (my italics).[33] This pattern is the "shape of the engendering deed," which makes it possible to penetrate the incognito of the Christ in all creation and redemption, whether in psychotherapy or elsewhere.

But what of Kierkegaard and his understanding of the dialectic of faith? Though I myself believe Kierkegaard was wrong in his affirmation of the Chalcedonian Christological formulation, with its Greek ontological background, nothing I have said need be taken as denying it. Though the Incarna-

[31] *The World Incarnate* (New York: Harper and Brothers, 1959), p. 47.
[32] *Journal of Religion*, 37, no. 2 (April, 1957): 85–98.
[33] *The Interpretation of the Fourth Gospel* (Cambridge: At the University Press, 1953), p. 285.

tion may be extended to the whole temporal process, as Teilhard suggests, it is so only for faith. For others, the Christic
pattern may be present only in ambiguity or latency. The
point is, rather, that for the Christian all creation and redemption, all opportunities for new beginnings, all reclamation
and redemption of evil, even the overcoming of error by truth
or by a greater truth — all manifests the Presence of a mysterious good, a greater love which was disclosed to man in Christ.
The patterning of this same creative good can be found in
every experience of new meaning and value beyond our control and intention.

And this patterning of events is a form of language. It is
a lure. It is evocative. It is a kind of indirect communication.
It is a calling, a calling of man out of himself into relationship.
But, as Kierkegaard held, here no man can teach another.
The most one can do for another is to be "with" him, so that
the truth-in-relationship can grasp him, draw him into new
life. This is the snare of truth, which you cannot have without
being caught. Another mode of expressing this view is to say,
also with Kierkegaard, that the healing truth is a *way*, not a
result. Consider the distinction by means of an example:

> A man discovers something, gun-powder. He the dis-
> coverer has perhaps spent many, many years of his life
> pondering and ruminating; perhaps many men before
> him have in vain spent a long time in a similar way — now
> he succeeds, now powder is discovered. At the same in-
> stant the way as good as drops out, to such a degree is
> it shortened. What took him twenty years to do, another
> man, by the help of his advance can do, if he goes about
> it rightly, in the space of half an hour.[34]

But it is different when the truth *is the way*. The foregoers
have no advantage over later men. Later men have no advantage over the foregoers. Such truth can be appropriated only
by following the way, and communication of a truth which is
a way can only be indirect by involvement in the way. No

[34] Kierkegaard, *Training in Christianity* (Princeton: Princeton University Press, 1947), p. 203.

man can do it for another. Are not the truth that heals in psychotherapy and the truth that heals the sickness unto death, analogous in this very respect? Both have to do with existence. Their communication is a kind of existence communication. They both involve the communication of a way, not a result, and they both use a kind of indirection.

Should we press this relationship beyond analogy? How should we make more explicit the relation between the truth that heals in psychotherapy and the truth that heals the sickness unto death? This is an old question. My own answer is implicit in what I have already said. The logos of Creation and Redemption is also the creative and redemptive logos wherever redeeming and creating are going on. This, of course, does not lead to the identification of neurosis with sin, or of the goal of psychotherapy with salvation, or of participation in the process with faith. Whether we make the distinction with respect to the depth and universality of the alienation involved, or with respect to the contrast beween neurotic and ontological anxiety, or with respect to the inclusiveness of the healing that is at stake, we need not, indeed we ought not, equate the pairs. Yet we would be equally mistaken to fail to see the interrelation created by the fact that the same reality is the source of healing and creating, wherever such take place, whatever the depth or scope.

I am inclined to go still further and to agree with the late David Roberts that contemporary theologians might well take the lead from Kierkegaard in fixing attention on this healing power, instead of devising schemes for patching together an objective metaphysical entity called God, or of devoting their time as in our own day to affirming God's death. With something of the same conviction, I would hold that we should try to draw together the insights of Whitehead, who saw religion as the art and theory of the internal life of man so far as it depends on the man himself and on what is permanent in the nature of things, with the concern of the existentialists, who ponder the processes which bring man to authentic existence, to transparency, to an integrity wrought by inner transformation. "The conduct of external life," said Whitehead, "is conditioned by environment, but it receives its final quality, on which its worth depends, from the internal life which is the self-realization of existence." [35] The quality of the internal life appears to be the fruit of the quality of the personal milieu within which a man may live and move and have his being.

[35] Alfred N. Whitehead, *Religion in the Making* (New York: Macmillan Company, 1926), p. 16.

3

Toward a Psychology of Religion:
By Way of Freud and Tillich
PETER HOMANS

Within theological studies today, perhaps no question or problem has so successfully earned the indifference of the theological thinker as the "psychology of religion." Nostalgia for it understandably evokes a desire for at least some theological attention, be it constructive or even apologetic in nature. Yet many theologians who in fact pay no attention to the psychology of religion are likely to see in it an apt and ready-made instance of precisely that from which they wish to dissociate themselves, in defining the truly distinctive features of their professional theological work.

If pressed further, the theologian might reply that, after all, the psychology of religion is psychology and not theology, and that religion, for that matter, is not theology either; such an enterprise, therefore, should best be pursued, if at all, by those within the discipline of psychology itself. And yet it is commonplace to note that psychological thought is, on the whole, equally indifferent to the psychological study of religion. In fact, amidst the many conflicts between theology and psychology, one finds this interesting point of agreement: theologian and psychologist join hands to say that there can be no psychology of religion, at least as far as they are concerned, short of contaminating principles basic to their respective disciplines.

Such a state of affairs might best be left alone. Yet I am reluctant to adopt this sense of certainty in so much theological and psychological thought. First, if only because the two terms in question, "psychology" and "religion," continue to be used in relation to each other. More important, they remain unavoidable terms for any theological thinker wishing to address himself systematically to the personality sciences. Whether he wishes to employ these sciences in some constructive fashion, or methodologically to reject them, he will have to make, implicitly or explicitly, a series of conceptual decisions with regard to the meanings he and others assign to "psychology" and "religion." The methodological question in theology, focused as it is on the sciences of man and, in our case, on psychology, remains formidable, and since the psychologist is likely to think of religion before he thinks of theology (he almost never thinks of theology), the theologian will be drawn into consideration of both.

This essay explores some of the theological hazards that present themselves when the problem of a psychology of religion is investigated. In doing so, it argues for the possibility of a reinterpretation of that approach, one that renders it useful for the theological thinker. It is, in brief, an attempt to develop an understanding of what precisely is theologically real in the life history of the person, and to explore the manner in which an interpretation of the theological can at every moment be responsible to psychological understanding. It is in this context that the word religion can be given a psychological meaning. Freud has taught us — and so has much theology — to know the present through the past. Let us therefore begin with a cursory inspection of available solutions to the problem of relating religion and psychology that can be found in the immediate heritage of theological thought.

Three Models for Psychology and Religion

There is a good deal of talk today about models — models for the study of personality, for educational theory, for scientific investigation, and the like. While catchy and probably too fashionable, "model" is also useful in lending perspective to the problem at hand. I shall use the term here to indicate a particular solution to, or integration of, this problem, such that those who work within any one model feel themselves

methodologically comfortable and at ease, both in their sense
of professional work and in the conceptual stance they take
toward their materials. In doing so, I am assuming three facets
in the use of a particular model, each of which has been integrated by the thinker into a unity of life and work: first, a
conceptual integration, strictly at the level of thought; sec-
ondly, a sense that the *professional* context in which one
works facilitates rather than opposes the goals of conceptual
integration; and thirdly, a sense of continuity between one's
intellectual position, his professional work, and his *personal*
identity as this emerges from his own psychological development.[1]

The first model available is, of course, that group of thinkers
directly associated with the phrase "psychology of religion." [2]
As already noted, this approach has been dead for some time,
and students of theology concerned with psychology duti-
fully but impatiently visit its tomb in footnotes and biblio-
graphic pauses, as they hurry on to more pressing and interesting concerns. Let us generalize briefly on some relevant
features.

Immediately apparent in the work of this group is the close
and mutually determinative relation between the definitions

[1] These three facets are drawn from Erik Erikson's work on identity,
but especially from his analysis of the origins of psychoanalysis in Freud's
person and work. See Erikson, "The First Psychoanalyst," in *Freud and
the 20th Century*, ed. Benjamin Nelson (New York: Meridian Books,
1957).

[2] Of many names that come to mind, I am alluding primarily to James,
Starbuck, Coe, Leuba, and Hall. See William James, *The Varieties of
Religious Experience* (New York: Longmans Green and Co., 1903);
E. D. Starbuck, *Psychology of Religion* (New York: Charles Scribner's
Sons, 1903); G. A. Coe, *The Psychology of Religion* (Chicago: Uni-
versity of Chicago Press, 1916); J. H. Leuba, *A Psychological Study of
Religion* (New York: Macmillan Company, 1912); and G. S. Hall, *Ado-
lescence*, 2 vols. (New York: D. Appleton, 1904). See also *The Journal of
Religious Psychology, Including its Anthropological and Sociological
Aspects*, published from 1904 to 1916. For a collection of readings, see
Readings in the Psychology of Religion, ed. Orlo Strunk (New York:
Abingdon, 1959). For a review of this group, see Seward Hiltner, "The
Psychological Understanding of Religion," in *Readings*, ed. Strunk
(above) and Paul Pruyser, "Some Trends in the Psychology of Religion,"
Journal of Religion, 15, no. 2, (April, 1960), pp. 113–29.

of psychology and of religion. The particular understanding of the nature and methods of psychology as a discipline to a great extent structures the manner in which one understands the nature and meaning of religion. James and Hall were formative in the establishment of a broadly functional and adaptive American psychology, and both brought this psychological perspective to bear in determining precisely how and what one should study if he is to study religion. In this instance, the referent for the word religion consisted in a reality, understood as a power, force, or energy, experienced as phenomenologically other or beyond the person's immediate, perceptual awareness. The meaning assigned to this reality always amounted, in the end, to its dynamic and functional facilitation of inner psychic, and also social, adaptation and adjustment. What is important here is the presupposed epistemological frame of reference, which was a predominantly subject-object one. A particular form or type of experience, properly called "religious," was simply and objectively "given" to the experiencing subject, and was subsequently analyzed psychologically.

This stance toward religion made possible the most notable feature of the model we are discussing, namely the conversion experience as the favored paradigm for the "religious" in human experience. Such experiences usually took place during a time of interpersonal isolation; the individual was alone, often in a natural setting, unaware of any impending psychic crisis. In fact, it often happened that the individual sensed just the opposite: that he was very much in control of things; frequently, he had just begun to pursue some activity that did not require the presence of others — reading a book, writing a letter, taking a walk. The onset of the crisis produced its dominant affective tone, that of guilt, with regard primarily to earlier acts, omitted or committed, or to simply a pervasive and nonspecific sense of worthlessness, remorse, and low self-esteem.

One notes that the force of the entire conversion experience was away from isolation and guilt and in the direction of resolution and adjustment, in relation to other persons, but even more in relation to the psychic demands of the experience itself. The resolution, like the onset, occurred in isolation. It was clearly a psychic event with a beginning, a middle, and an end. It was, therefore, an experience one went through as one goes through a tunnel, and although it remained forever memorable in the mind of the individual, it remained just as clearly an event in his past. For this reason, it would not be entirely unfair to liken the typical conversion experience to a psychic thunderstorm, which appears suddenly, asserts itself violently, and then as quickly disappears. As such, the experience was more a homeostatic stabilizing of psychic pressure than a transformation in either conscious awareness or social relatedness.

The psychology of religion group was able to sustain a professional sense of workmanship in the face of common problems because most of them were psychologists or educators concerned primarily with psychology. For our purposes, this means that they were not concerned professionally with institutional forms of Christianity or with theology. And when they were, both were considered proper objects of psychological analysis, rather than a community with which they might identify both personally and professionally. This was equally true of the religious education movement, which, despite its concern with institutional Protestant Christianity, was never integrated into the theological community at the conceptual or professional level. Nor has the adoption of a different name — Christian education in the place of religious education — made its quest for theological acceptance and status much easier.

The reasons for the rather quick and thoroughly undramatic decline of the psychology of religion are far more interesting than the work of the movement itself. It is often noted that the close of the nineteenth century, as an ideological synthesis, occurred at the time of the First World War. Suffice it to say that the abandonment of the psychology of religion as a synthesis by psychologists and religious educators was due, at least in part, to that series of shifts in cultural modalities of self-understanding which produced psychoanalysis in psychology and existentialism in theology. In this sense, the unity of religion and psychology, symbolized by the composite image of the conversion experience as this was constructed by the psychologists of religion, was split, dissociating psychology and theology from any concern with religion. As a result, both theology and psychology underwent changes which, at the level of content, are quite different, but which retain a certain dynamic similarity.

The functional-adaptive approach in psychology, the adherents of which did not consider religion entirely foreign to their interests, gave way, of course, to Watsonian behaviorism, removing permanently the conversion experience and all that it implied from the proper domain of the methodology of psychology. Watson's work may be understood on this level in the sense in which he himself defined it — as a methodological reformulation of the nature and aims of psychology. But his writings may also be viewed from a more programmatic and ideological perspective. For in addition to the methodological contribution, Watson also provided a rallying point for a new sense of both personal and professional identity for psychologists, defining both in opposition to religious moralism and piety. Watson's parting words at the conclusion of *Behaviorism* are to the point:

> Behaviorism ought to be a science that prepares men and women for understanding the principles of their own behavior. It ought to make men and women eager to rearrange their own lives, and especially eager to prepare themselves to bring up their own children in a healthy way. I wish I could picture for you what a rich and wonderful individual we should make of every healthy child if only we could let it shape itself properly and then provide for it a universe in which it could exercise that organization — a universe unshackled by legendary folk-lore of happenings thousands of years ago; unhampered by disgraceful political history; free of foolish customs and conventions which have no significance in themselves, yet which hem the individual in like

taut steel bands. . . . The universe will change if you bring up your children, not in the freedom of the libertine, but in behavioristic freedom. . . . Will not these children in turn, with their better ways of living and thinking, replace us as society and in turn bring up their children in a still more scientific way, until the world finally becomes a place fit for human habitation?[3]

Such programmatic and ideological — one should really say "eschatological" — rhetoric may be seen as an attempt to break out of the kind of psychic bewilderment and confusion produced by religious piety and moralism. In this sense, Watson's attacks on "religion" are really a flight from that particular kind of religious consciousness which so much needed the experience of conversion and which received legitimation in the work of the psychologists of religion. In commending what in theological language amounts to a "kenotic" evacuation of the psyche in favor of the behavioral field, Watson sought a methodological (rather than a psychological) solution to the psychic problem that religious piety created and sought to solve through the experience of conversion. From this point of view, behaviorism may be seen as a methodological flight from the religious super-ego.

Psychoanalysis, in a very different way to be sure, produced a similar kind of critique. Whereas Watson evacuated the psyche, and with it the possibility of "religious experience," Freud created two levels of psychic reality, assigning religious experience to the repressed unconscious, thereby, like Watson, removing it as a factor in any normative understanding or interpretation of psychic life. In commending a restoration of strength and function to the ego as opposed to the super-ego, Freud attempted to depotentiate the binding power of the harsh (religious) super-ego. In this sense, both behaviorism and psychoanalysis may be seen as revolutions in psychological method, directing their critical power against the psychic organization implied in religious experience. Al-

[3] John B. Watson, *Behaviorism* (Chicago: University of Chicago Press, reprinted 1959), pp. 303–304.

though they are first and foremost methodological reformulations within psychology, they are also, as the sudden discovery of a new method, creating a sense of resolution, similar from a psychodynamic point of view to the conversion experience.

Theological existentialism performed the same function for theology that psychoanalysis and behaviorism performed for psychology. It rejected "religious experience" in favor of "theological existence," motivated in large part by the desire to transcend the problematic piety of mere religion. It is hardly accidental that when theological existentialism speaks of psychology it speaks almost exclusively of behaviorism and psychoanalysis. The theological and the psychological revolutions, respectively, eliminated religion, as this was understood by the psychologists of religion. This splitting of psychology of religion into theology and psychology made possible two additional models, which can now be discussed.

First is the pastoral psychology model.[4] Again, it is a model because its representatives have arrived at a working solution to the problem of the relation between religion and psychology, doing so in the context of a sense of both personal and professional identity and workmanship. Although pastoral psychology is administratively part of most theological curricula, a deeper integration is still awaited, recalling the earlier plight of the religious education movement. Since it is a praxis rather than an academic discipline, its associations with psychology are more in terms of the clinical side of the personality sciences.

Its uses of psychology are relatively clear and unambiguous. It is deeply committed to a broad interpretation of what nevertheless remains fundamentally a dynamic, psychoanalytically-oriented psychology, sufficiently broad to include not only neo-Freudian but even Rogerian perspectives.

[4] This reference is to what is sometimes called the American School of pastoral psychology. See Carol Wise, *Pastoral Counseling: Its Theory and Practice* (New York: Harper and Brothers, 1951); Wayne Oates, *The Christian Pastor* (Philadelphia: Westminster Press, 1951); Seward Hiltner, *Pastoral Counseling* (New York: Abingdon, 1959); and Paul Johnson, *The Psychology of Pastoral Care* (New York: Abingdon, 1953).

Theologically it is committed to neo-Reformation modes of thought, religious existentialism and in some cases neoliberal religious thought.[5] From these sources, it has acquired its concern for the theological implications of the pastoral role and its origins in the life of the church, its direct employment of Christian and biblical symbols and vocabulary, and the bearing of these upon a doctrine of man.

The distinctive project of pastoral psychology might be described in an over-simplified way as the use of psychodynamic principles and insights in the clarification of moralistic and idealistic distortions of Christian faith, understood in its more classical forms of statement. Through such clarification, the power of the gospel can be released for appropriation in the inner life of the person.[6] Indeed, one of the outstanding marks of the pastoral psychologist is his insistence upon clarification of his own motives, in order not to be drawn into the moralistic and idealistic claims of his parishioner's faith.

In such moralistic and idealistic claims we may detect residues of that piety which gave expression to the religious experience of conversion so thoroughly analyzed by the psychologists of religion. In the place of such religious experience, however, pastoral psychology in effect substituted the psychotherapeutic experience; and for the inner demands and autonomy of the religious experience itself, pastoral psychology substituted the therapeutic relationship, the strategies of psychotherapeutic technique, and a dynamic psychological understanding of human development. In this way the earlier notion of religious experience, understood as an event with a beginning, a middle and an end, was submitted to critical psychological analysis and related to the entire developmental life-span of the individual. The pastoral counseling process, claimed as a theological reality by its practitioners,

---

[5] The work of Carol Wise and Paul Johnson is illustrative.

[6] For an especially apt illustration of this general description, see Knox Kreutzer, "Some Observations on Approaches to the Theology of Psychotherapeutic Experience," *Journal of Pastoral Care*, 13 (1959): 197–208.

is the formal heir to the conversion experiences of the psychology of religion.

Pastoral psychology was able to dissolve this understanding of religious experience into the psychological and developmental modalities of the dynamic psychotherapies because of its commitment to the theological presupposition that a dimension of faith transcends all forms of religious experience. This presupposition is drawn from what I wish to call the third model for integrating religion and psychology, the "theology-psychology" model.[7] Pastoral psychology is identical with this third model, except for its emphasis upon the professional identity and orientation of the pastor. His commitment to praxis has insisted that his theology be more completely submitted to psychological analysis.

The third model gives us a general and firm consensus with regard to the proper place of psychology in relation to the work of the theologian, and to the place of psychological process in his normative understanding of the development of the person. That is to say, it has approached psychology with its own two most pressing problems in mind, that of theological method and that of theological anthropology. This model thus provides a careful and sophisticated interpretive integration of the proper place and limits of psychology in the theological enterprise.

Whereas pastoral psychology focuses upon the power of dynamic psychology to purify and clarify distortions of faith in the parishioner's existence, this theological group is concerned with the possibly reductive effects of psychology upon an authentic theological understanding of faith. Like the psychology of religion, pastoral psychology attempts to keep a dynamic psychological perspective upon the experiencing of the person at all times, recognizing that the end point of his development is faith, as theological self-understanding.

[7] This third model comprises what is often covered by the rubric "Protestant theological existentialism." However, the specific figures in question are Barth, Brunner, Tillich, and Reinhold Neibuhr. See John B. Cobb, Jr., *Living Options in Protestant Theology* (Philadelphia: Westminster Press, 1962), and Edward Farley, *The Transcendence of God* (Philadelphia: Westminster Press, 1960).

The theology-psychology model, however, while avowedly sensitive to the implications of psychodynamics for theological understanding, tends to view psychological growth, process, etc., as *part-process*. In its most distinctive moments, at least with regard to psychology, this model defines what is theological as opposed to psychological processes, for psychological knowledge is forever under the control of the subject-object relation.[8]

Such a point of view, although articulated by different theologians in very different and complex vocabularies, remains, at least in this respect, rather simple: theological reality in the person transcends psychological reality, just as the self transcends its environment. Psychology, it is said, can clarify distortions in the dynamics of the self; but in doing so it shows only part of the total meaning of the person and his existence. The favored theological formula here is, of course, "transcendence"; anthropologically, the reality to which Christian theology points transcends the developmental and socialization processes of the person, as these are delineated by the psychological disciplines; methodologically, theological method transcends the methods of inquiry employed by the science of psychology. One encounters God as one moves away from — or perhaps I should say as one moves "beyond" — the effects of development and socialization as exclusively formative of the self. In such fashion theologians protect theological meaning from being reduced to psychological interpretation.

The Theology-Psychology Model Exhibited: Freud and Tillich

This model asserts that psychology can tell us about the dissociations within the self, but not about the self in its fullness, wholeness, and ultimate integrity. Therefore, any attempt to explore the possibility of a psychology of religion must begin at this point. But since our discussion of each of these models has been cursory and superficial, we shall analyze with greater care some of the intricacies of this third model by means of

[8] For specific references, see footnotes 15, 16 and 17 below.

two thinkers clearly representative of it, Freud and Tillich. Freud, in addition to being the most influential figure in psychology today, is the psychologist generally studied by this group of thinkers, and has the still further advantage of having given us a psychology of religion matched only by those of James and Jung. Tillich has the added advantage of having explored depth psychology more thoroughly than any other theologian.

We may review, briefly but also with precision, Freud's psychological understanding of religion by means of the notion of transference which, while it rarely appears in theological discussions of his psychology, nevertheless brings together in a unique way both his psychology of the self and his psychology of religion.[9]

As is well known, Freud for the most part spoke of transference as an interpersonal phenomenon (although he did not, of course, use this "revisionist" nomenclature), and he defined it as the attribution by his patients of their unconscious attitudes and feelings to the physician. What is not so well-known, however, and I should like to deal with it here, are his references to transference as an *intrapsychic* or internal phenomenon as well, references which provide an important clue to the basic structure of his psychological anthropology. It is correct to think of the Freudian psyche as divided or alienated: inner division or alienation occurring, for example, between conscious and unconscious processes, primary and secondary process, super-ego and id, pleasure principle and reality principle — that is, between what we could generically call "depth" and "surface" aspects of the total psychic life of the person. In this sense transference phenomena are simply the manifestations of depth or unconscious factors into surface awareness and consciousness. Unconscious or depth forces and energies are "transferred" or carried over into con-

[9] For a concise and thorough discussion of this interpretation of Freud's notion of transference, see Heinz Kohut and Philip F. D. Seitz, "Psychoanalytic Theory of Personality," in *Concepts of Personality*, ed. Joseph M. Wepman and Ralph Heine (Chicago: Aldine Publishing Co., 1963).

scious or surface life. Transference understood intrapsychically is simply the perforation of the (repression) barrier between the unconscious and conscious systems. Dreams, slips of the tongue, symptoms and the transference relation itself were the four main forms of psychic transference, the four ways in which the two different psychic systems became conflictively related.

Consequently, the therapeutic task consists in restoring a developmental or integrative relation between these two systems, to replace the regressive and repressive one. Such restoration occurs only on the basis of continuity between the intrapsychic and interpersonal, because in the therapy the intrapsychic is transposed or embodied in the interpersonal, so that the transference relation itself becomes the disease. Through the resolution of the distortions and projections which appear in the transference relation, the internal or intrapsychic conflicts are at least in part resolved in the interior life of the person.

But what is more important, and often overlooked, is that transference is an extremely helpful notion for understanding Freud's thought at the cultural level as well. For, although a certain amount of "the transference" can be worked through in individual, one-to-one situations, the possibility of working through at the social and historical level remained in Freud's estimation an impossible task. His gloomy pronouncements on the psychic limits of social life are difficult to match; the transference remains formidable. And it is here that religion takes on its most important psychological meaning. Religion is really *cultural* transference, the binding together and gathering up of all the transference residues unresolved in individual living. In the formation of the image of God and in the subsequent ways of relating to this image, men collectively project and then attempt to resolve their individual psychic conflicts. All the wishes, longings and nostalgias — everything unfulfilled, unlived and unexpressed — appear in the guise of the God image.

Freud put the whole matter quite succinctly in a remark to Oscar Pfister mingling both humor and irony:

I note with satisfaction what a long way we are able to go together in analysis. The rift, not in the analytic, but in scientific thinking which comes on when the subject of God and Christ is touched on I accept as one of the logically untenable but psychologically only too intelligible irrationalities of life. In general I attach no value to the "imitation of Christ." In contrast to utterances as psychologically profound as "Thy sins are forgiven thee; arise and walk" there are a large number of others which are conditioned exclusively by the time, psychologically impossible, useless for our lives. Besides the above statement calls for analysis. If the sick man has asked: "How knowest thou that my sins are forgiven?" the answer could only have been: "I, the Son of God, forgive thee." In other words, a call for unlimited transference. And now, just suppose I said to a patient: "I, Professor Sigmund Freud, forgive thee thy sins." What a fool I should make of myself. To the former case the principle applies that analysis is not satisfied with success produced by suggestion, but investigates the origin of and justification for the transference.[10]

It would seem correct and helpful to allude to and to define Freud's psychology of religion as really a psychology of the "transference-god." It is the transference-god, that sociohistorical fantasy of Western man, which must be worked through, a "group" psychoanalysis to be conducted under the auspices of the corporate activity of science, and especially of psychoanalytically scientific psychology. The notion of "curing" culture was foolish for Freud, but the implication nonetheless remains.

Therefore, at least from the psychoanalytic point of view, the psychological interpretation of religion becomes the most important problem for the psychological transformation of the person, whenever this latter process is an anthropological

[10] *Psychoanalysis and Faith: The Letters of Sigmund Freud and Oskar Pfister,* trans. Eric Mosbacher (New York: Basic Books, 1963) pp. 125–26.

consideration. For the (psychoanalytically) psychological interpretation of religion can produce a liberation of the psyche, freeing it from its deepest and most problematic conflicts. A psychology of the person is always, for Freud at least, a psychology of religion.

At this point, a different question moves into the center of the discussion, namely, the fate of the energies formerly invested in this imago. If liberation is from the transference-god, what does it move toward? And it is at this point that, according to the logic of the theology-psychology model, psychological analysis must yield to theological understanding.

The thought of Paul Tillich illustrates a typical instance of such theological understanding. His thought is almost as difficult to enter as Freud's, in spite of being more systematic. We may, however, find an adequate point of contact in the familiar discussion of "the courage to be" [11] and in the analysis of the subject-object relation that underlies this discussion. Here Tillich gives us what is in effect an analysis of precisely those energies formerly bound by the imago of the transference-god, and he is quite clear that this is a distinctly *theological* problem.

Looking at that part of Tillich's thought that relates to the concrete life of the person, we are told that the courage to be emerges as a moral possibility, that absolute faith emerges as a religious possibility, and that transcendence emerges as the theological possibility, when and in so far as the God of theological theism gives ground, in the experience of doubt, to the "God above God." Tillich's critique of what he calls theological theism is, of course, rooted in his ontological analysis of the self-world correlation and his epistemological analysis of the subject-object relation and the dynamics of their transcendence. In these discussions he characteristically presses this theological analysis of the transformation of the person to a point beyond an understanding of God and ultimate reality, a point at which self-understanding is no

[11] Tillich, *The Courage To Be* (New Haven: Yale University Press, 1952). See especially chapter 6, "Courage and Transcendence."

longer under the control of the subject-object structure of reality. The object of theological statement must not be conceived simply in subject-object modes of thinking. Indeed, it is Tillich, perhaps more than any other theologian today, who urges that the transcendence of the subject-object relation permits the appearance of genuinely *religious* reality in the life of the person.

What we have called Freud's transference-god is presupposed in this (Tillichian) theological understanding: the God of theological theism *is* the transference-god, and therefore this latter notion gives us a dynamic, psychological basis for understanding the former. Tillich is quite clear about this.[12] The courage to be presupposes and makes its appearance as a dynamic possibility in the life of the person in a psychological movement in which the transference-god is called into question as the exclusively appropriate symbol for what is ontologically ultimate. Thus psychology must give way to theology, for the former speaks of man's existential plight, but not of his essential possibilities. These are reserved for theology.

A better illustration of the linkage between psychology and theology so characteristic of this model is found in a comparison of the super-ego (Freud) and the bad, moral conscience(Tillich). Tillich has distinguished between a bad, moral conscience and a good, transmoral conscience, indicating that the former is identical with the Freudian super-ego.[13] He also identifies the former with that crisis of conscience which appeared most intensively and received its most dramatic elaboration in the piety of Luther, and which he believed has served as the occasion and condition of grace, at least in the Protestant tradition.[14] We may note too that

[12] See for example Tillich's rejoinder to my paper discussing this point in *The Journal of Religion*, 46, no. 1, pt. 2 (January, 1966), pp. 194–96.

[13] See Tillich, "The Transmoral Conscience," in *The Protestant Era* (Chicago: University of Chicago Press, 1948).

[14] For an interesting and dissident discussion of this interpretation of conscience in the West, see Krister Stendal, "The Apostle Paul and the Introspective Conscience of the West," *Harvard Theological Review*, 5, no. 3 (July, 1963), pp. 199–215.

the bad, moral conscience, as the occasion of a moral and spiritual crisis in the life of the person, appears in particularly exacerbated form in the experiences studied by the psychologists of religion, as well as in the moralistic and idealistic distortions which have so concerned the pastoral psychology movement. The good, transmoral conscience is the fruit of self-acceptance (justification) and transcends its moralistic counterpart, just as the God above God transcends its theological counterpart, the God of theological theism.

This common focus permits the establishment of a series of linkages: first, the bad, moral conscience and the harsh super-ego; second, the fact that both represent phases of socialization in the life of the individual; and third, that both Tillich and Freud commend a moral courage which lies dynamically "beyond" this phase of socialization. Both commend the necessity of moving developmentally beyond the super-ego to a higher form of integrated polarization of self and society. Both set forth a moral and psychological imperative to transcend the super-ego.

The psychodynamic meaning of such transcendence lies in a reorganization of psychic energies which are released as a result of the breaking-up of the imago of the transference-god, the God of theological theism. Put in another way, both Freud and Tillich are concerned with "what remains" after an act of critical reorganization within the self, although they strongly disagree about the creative possibilities resident in such a movement.

Elaboration and Critique
of the Theology-Psychology Model

Here the logic of the theology-psychology model appears most clearly: the proper task and object of theological understanding lies in the analysis of those personal and existential possibilities which lie "beyond" the bad, moral conscience and theological theism. Here the theologian "takes over," so to speak, from the psychologist; here psychological process gives way to theological meaning and reality; here theologi-

69

cal method is deemed more appropriate to the human situation than the methods of psychology.

Such methodological segregation has anthropological parallels as well. Theological categories like "self-transcendence," "spirit," "the encounter of the self with God," all refer to a dimension of personal existence which lies beyond the merely psychological modes of developmental achievement. Development, socialization, integration of the ego into significantly meaningful reference groups, identity-formation, — these are all psychological processes which document the self's attempt to become part of society. Theological anthropology, however, asserts a realm of reality "beyond" the structures and processes discernible by psychological categories and methods.

So Karl Barth gives us an understanding of revelation as the "abolition of religion," and for his formula we may, correctly I think, substitute "revelation as the abolition of the transference-god." [15] Revelation, that reality of which Christian dogmatic statement speaks, lies beyond the psychological processes occurring within the self. In Brunner's familiar delineation of the divine-human encounter [16] we are told that while psychology can comprehend dislocations within the self, only theology can speak of their unity, for the encounter

[15] See Karl Barth, *Church Dogmatics* (Edinburgh: T & T Clark, 1936–62), vol. 1, pt. 1 (1936), p. 438; vol. 1, pt. 2 (1956), pp. 28–97; vol. 2, pt. 1 (1957), pp. 13–23, 56, 61; vol. 3, pt. 2 (1960), pp. 22–27. See also *Prayer: According to the Catechisms of the Reformation*, trans. Sara Terrien (Philadelphia: Westminster Press, 1952), p. 36. These references point to key passages and are not intended to be exhaustive. For further discussion of the subject-object relation and the place of psychology in the thought of Barth, see James Brown, *Kierkegaard, Heidegger, Buber and Barth: Subject and Object in Modern Theology* (New York: Collier Books, 1962).

[16] For one of the most concise statements of this point of view in protestant theological thought, see Emil Brunner's essay, "Biblical Psychology," in *God and Man: Four Essays On the Nature of Personality*, trans. David Cairns (London: SCM Press, 1936). See also *Truth as Encounter* (Philadelphia: Westminster Press, 1964), especially pp. 78–83, 111–18. For a discussion of this aspect of Brunner's thought, see Fred Berthold, Jr., "Objectivity in Personal Encounter," *Journal of Religion*, 55, no. 1 (January, 1963), pp. 39–47.

with God transcends this interpersonal sphere. Reinhold Niebuhr assigns psychology to "nature" and to the study of individual psychopathology and adjustment, but removes it from the analysis of the "dramas" of the self and of history. Psychological analysis is incapable of penetrating to the uniqueness of spirit as it appears in the dramas of history, in permanent myth, and in the familiar Niebuhrian principle of comprehension beyond comprehension.[17]

In each case the equivalent of what has here been called the transference-god appears as the human side of man's relation to God, the projected resultant of human will and desire, which must somehow be overcome, corrected, abrogated — transcended. The really distinguishing methodological feature in these positions is simply the degree of relative limitation imposed upon psychology and psychological understanding in the interpretation and management of the spiritual dynamics of the self.

Now I would like to suggest that this model provides the fundamental resources for what can properly be called a psychology of religion, provided it is critically expanded, for it contains both the possibility and the denial of the possibility of a psychology of religion. It contains the possibility, if seen as an attempt to formulate what is in effect a phenomenology of self and self-transcendence, a delineation of that dimension of reality which lies beyond, while yet remaining dependent upon, development and socialization. Here we need the theologian to define, or at least to begin to define, what in human life is characteristically religious.

There seems to be no inherent methodological reason, however, why this "object of study" cannot be approached in a fully psychological mode of understanding. Is it not possible

[17] See Reinhold Niebuhr, *The Self and the Dramas of History* (New York: Charles Scribner's Sons, 1955), pp. 127–44; "The Tyranny of Science," *Theology Today*, 10 (January, 1954), 464–73; or "The Truth in Myths," in *The Nature of Religious Experience*, Essays in Honor of D. C. MacIntosh (New York: Harper and Brothers, 1937). For a discussion of Bultmann's thought, indicating that his methodological sympathies also lie in this direction, see Schubert Ogden, "Myth and Truth," *McCormick Quarterly*, 18 (January, 1965): 57–76.

to have a psychology — and, more especially, a dynamic psychology — of the self and of the processes of self-transcendence? That is to say, may we not approach that area of human life which is the proper object of theological study, in terms of psychological inquiry?

Note that such an approach is already implicit in certain representative instances in the psychology of personality and personality theory. Here one finds psychological theoreticians attempting to formulate a psychology of the person that considers processes that lie beyond socialization, and, in doing so, attempting to study psychologically the realm of human reality that our theologians have so assiduously claimed for themselves.

For example, Gordon Allport's notions of functional autonomy and propriate striving seek to comprehend aspects of personal inwardness and uniqueness that emerge through the transcending of earlier, more tribal, social integrations.[18] At this point, Allport's methodological strategy is no different from Tillich's. Both speak for a realm of personal integrity and uniqueness lying developmentally "beyond" the superego, and Allport's critique of the Lockean, nomothetic methodological heritage of American psychology is identical with Tillich's protest against technical reason and controlling knowledge.

Abraham Maslow's work is clearly construed on a similar basis. The peak experience, self-actualization, generic guilt, and the like, all attempt a psychology of deep personal inwardness and uniqueness, of "what remains" when the processes of acculturation and the meeting of lower needs has taken place.[19] Maslow's psychology is really a psychology of what theologians call aseity, of the ontic self as it stands over

[18] Allport, *Pattern and Growth in Personality* (New York: Holt Rinehart and Winston, 1961), chap. 10; and *Becoming* (New Haven: Yale University Press, 1955), pp. 28–57.

[19] Maslow, *Motivation and Personality* (New York: Harper and Row, 1954) and *Toward a Psychology of Being* (Princeton, N.J.: D. Van Nostrand Company, 1962. In the latter see especially chap. 13, "Health as Transcendence of Environment," and the discussion of generic guilt in chap. 14.

against, yet at the same time in relation to, social reality. Thus the notion of generic guilt suggests that the phenomenon of guilt need not always be simply a measure of the tension between internal psychic energy and social controls and expectations. And of course Allport and Maslow are further distinguished within the field of personality theory not only by their overt (that is, professional) interest in religion, but by their assigning religion to precisely this sector of the psyche. Their theories of personality move them in the direction of the sort of psychology of religion which may also be understood as the expansion of our theological-psychological model.

Unlike Freud, Maslow or Allport, Carl Rogers has displayed no formal interest in religion. Yet his psychology has engaged the theologian, at least the pastoral theologian, and as such it follows the pattern we are attempting to clarify here. Such Rogerian notions as the fully-functioning person and organismic experiencing process, for example, take their peculiar shape — as does the entire client-centered psychology, for that matter — in a critical stance toward Freud.[20] If we consider this psychology from the point of view of our distinction between the super-ego and a reality that lies developmentally beyond it, then the Rogerian notion of condition of worth corresponds to the super-ego, and the force of the client-centered psychotherapeutic process lies in feeling through (not, as Freud said, in working through) these imposed and introjected norms or conditions, in order to arrive at a novel and more discreet sense of personal uniqueness in relation to socialization norms. In so doing, Rogers has given us a psychology addressed to that dimension of personal existence claimed by the theologian for his own work and method. The more recent client-centered notion of "adient motivation" is still another case in point,[21] for it is a liberation or

[20] Rogers, *Client-Centered Therapy* (Boston: Houghton Mifflin Co., 1951) and *On Becoming a Person* (Boston: Houghton Mifflin Co., 1961).
[21] See John M. Butler and Laura N. Rice, "Adience, Self-Actualization and Drive Theory," in *Concepts of Personality*, ed. Joseph M. Wepman and Ralph W. Heine (Chicago: Aldine Publishing Co., 1963).

rediscovery of conceptual energies and images come upon by means of the imaginative transformation of conventional patterns of socialization and control.

Erik Erikson's work articulates perhaps most directly of all the drift of this argument. For his formulation of identity is mounted by definition upon a dialectical critique of the classical psychoanalytic understanding of the super-ego, and is at the same time a systematically psychological attempt to explore higher integrative possibilities within the self. Thus identification, libido theory, oedipal organization, morality (as opposed to ethics) are set in the larger context of identity-formation.[22] Erickson's reservations about super-ego morality are clearly those of Tillich's with regard to the bad, moral conscience. The extent to which the Eriksonian psychology of identity formation fully explicates the dynamics of the courage to be is not entirely clear; what is clear, however, is that identity, like the fully-functioning self, self-actualization, and propriate striving, constitutes a psychological effort to delineate the dynamics of that sector of personal existence claimed as the proper territory of theology.[23]

Implications: Some Problems in Moving toward a Psychology of Religion

We have suggested that the notion of a psychology of religion seems less irrelevant and out of place, and becomes perhaps even methodologically possible, when we examine critically the theology-psychology model, expanding it in the direction of the more fully psychological. In so doing, we have accepted the theologian's testimony in behalf of the theologically real in personal existence, while remaining reluctant to pursue his corollary claim that such an aspect of human life ever eludes the power of psychological analysis.

The anthropological side of this discussion has largely cen-

[22] Erikson, *Identity and the Life Cycle*, Psychological Issues (New York: International Universities Press, 1959) and *Insight and Responsibility* (New York: W. W. Norton and Company, 1964).
[23] The work of Helen M. Lynd, Allen Wheelis and Erich Fromm could also be adduced in support of this point, since each attempts in his own way a critique of the super-ego in order to set forth more clearly his own reconstructive psychology of the self.

tered upon the super-ego as an important psychological construct that serves the double function of drawing together our three models for relating and integrating psychological and religious notions, and of demonstrating the alleged points of continuity and discontinuity between psychological and theological meaning that so deeply characterize the theology-psychology model. If the analysis of what lies beyond ("transcends") the super-ego, taken in this highly stereotypical sense, is in principle a theological problem, and if it can be approached psychologically, then we may ask, what are some of the implications of such a conclusion? Or, in the language of the third model itself, if the dissolution of the transference-god or the bad, moral conscience can be taken as a crucial event in the life-history of the person — that is, an event about which it is possible to speak dynamically and developmentally — what problems are implied in the resolution of such a crisis?

Perhaps the outstanding dynamic question concerns the fate (or destiny) of those energies organized by the image of the transference-god and by the bad, moral conscience, the release of which creates such a moral and psychological crisis. What other images bind and give statement to these incipiently emergent and vagrant forces in the person and in his society? And how appropriate are such images to the intrinsic energies of the self? Clearly, the images in many instances will be devoid of much, perhaps all, of the symbols, vocabulary, and rhetoric of classical Christian theology. Yet should this disqualify them as appropriate data for theological analysis? For example, one suggestive hypothesis asserts that energies formerly organized by religious ideation are now being absorbed into the popular mythologies and ideologies of mass culture. Images of this nature necessarily become the object of theological analysis, calling as they do for a kind of hermeneutical scanning of those images and symbols projected by various mass media.[24]

[24] This point is the burden of much of Philip Rieff's sociological discussion of Freud. See Rieff, *The Triumph of the Therapeutic: The Uses of Faith after Freud* (New York: Harper and Row, 1966). The familiar motif of the modern self, isolated by the absence of authentic images

Implied in such a psychic transformation of images are two additional notions, those of regression and fantasy. And here Freud and Tillich, taken again as propaedeutic, agree. The psychic crisis of the transference-god produces regression, and Tillich's criticism and transformation of the God of theological theism will create a disruptive sense of anxiety and self-loss, even though it also produces the possibility of a new beginning. Indeed, the very notion of a new beginning implies a going back, a return to something fundamental. Freud, of course, saw in religion developmental failure, and finally even epistemological and moral failure, since it fixed the developmental energies of the person. His preoccupation with the transference-god, supported as it was by the religious situation of his time, prevented him from formally raising the question of a nonpathological form of regression. In the construction we are suggesting here, however, regression can be the source of re-discovery, of a new beginning.

Image and regression suggest fantasy, and taken together these might well constitute elements in a psychology of religion, understood as a psychology of images of self-transcendence. For if the psychology of religious experience provoked a dissociation between psychology and theology, perhaps the psychology of religious *images* can draw them together: the 'image" is all important. Here the recent psychological study by Father William Lynch is apt.[25] He speaks of the phenomenon of hope as possibly the most basic of all religious impulses, believing that it serves as the starting point for both a psychological and a metaphysical understanding of the religious life. What he means by hope is, quite simply, the projecting of one's inward wishing and desiring in the form of images. The capacity for hope, so understood,

---

of social engagement and consequently thrown back upon its own inwardness, which characterizes much imaginative literature, is not unrelated to this problem. For a theological discussion of this motif, see Nathan A. Scott, "Society and Self in Recent American Literature," in the *Broken Center: Studies in the Theological Horizon of Modern Literature* (New Haven: Yale University Press, 1966).

[25] Lynch, *Images of Hope: Imagination as Healer of the Hopeless* (Baltimore: Helicon Press, 1965).

constitutes the first principle of mental wholeness, and its absence in the psychic life of the person is the most fundamental meaning of mental illness. This capacity for hoping or wishing he identifies with the capacity for fantasy. Thus fantasy is the absolutely necessary and indispensable dynamic source for what can become a more stable and pervasive sense of self-transcendence, for it is a moment of opening up of new ranges of energies and symbols which not only lead to religious reality, but which can also be understood psychologically. In fantasy, then, lies the beginning of religion.

Crucial for this understanding of fantasy in Lynch's study is the clear distinction between fantasy as the beginning of religion, and fantasy as the result of the "absolutizing instinct," the kind of fantasy that floods in upon an object, blocking off any capacity to relate to it or to perceive the truth about it. This conception of the absolutizing instinct and its opposition to the hoping or wishing instinct resembles our distinction between the transference-god and the psychological activity of transcending it. For the absolutizing instinct creates the transference-god. The capacity to hope, that is, the capacity for fantasy, which is blocked by the absolutizing instinct, is itself the imaginative core and psychological prerequisite of a sense of selfhood and self-transcendence.

Such notions as fantasy and regression reopen a problem familiar to all three models, one which has been solved by each in its own peculiar way, that of the "psychopathology" of religion. Here we find Tillich's distinction between neurotic and existential anxiety interlocking — as only the theology-psychology model can do — with an interpretation of Freud's psychology as primarily a psychopathology, rendering his psychology of religion as psychopathology of religion. Again the notion of the super-ego is instructive. Tillich finds it exclusively an "image of destructive power," an "existential distortion" of "the essential structure of man's being." [26] But if

[26] Tillich, "Existentialism and Psychotherapy," in *Psychoanalysis and Existential Philosophy*, ed. Hendrik M. Ruitenbeek (New York: E. P. Dutton and Company, 1962).

the super-ego or bad, moral conscience is set in the context of a courage, faith, or capacity for self-transcendence lying developmentally beyond this limitation, both psychopathology and the anxiety of guilt and condemnation become the occasion and means of transcendence. Consequently, any final distinction between psychopathology and the psychopathology of religion is collapsed, for the theological dimension of a person's existence, rooted as it is in a criticism and transformation of the super-ego, becomes the controlling methodological and anthropological reality. And once regression and fantasy are understood in similar fashion — that is, as psychological processes containing the possibility of opening up the imagination to this dimension of reality — then this theological dimension of the person's existence becomes amenable, although not necessarily exclusively amenable, to psychological analysis.

The Argument Summarized: A Concluding Concrete Image

The drift of the discussion can be summarized in a direct and immediate way by the use of a concrete image taken from Rorschach psychology, for in such projective devices we have an extension of the psychoanalytic psychology into the realm of images. And one type of response in particular provides us with an image of transcendence. Needless to say, this use of the Rorschach psychology is an extrapolation from clinical findings into the realm of cultural and existential factors, rather than a simple application.

One of the well-known psychological findings noted by Rorschach and by Rorschach commentators [27] was the presence of a particular kind of response called perspective or "vista" responses and the close relation that obtains between this kind of percept and the psychological processes of self-evaluation. Beck, for example, cites as typical vista responses "a mountain pass, with a bridge," or "a promenade and a flight of stairs," or "a lake, and reflection on the water." In each

[27] See Samuel J. Beck et al., Rorschach's Test, 10. (New York: Grune and Stratton, 1961), vol. 1, Basic Processes, chap. 10.

instance the person projects himself into a relation to his spatial world characterized by a heightened sense of distance, separateness, and perspective.

What is most interesting here is the intrinsic connection between such a sense of vista or distance, and the psychological processes of self-evaluation and sensing of self-worth and self-esteem.[28] Thus vista responses or associations project the more unpleasant and painful emotions associated with feelings of inferiority, guilt, and loss of the capacity for confident and positive self-appreciation. In Rorschach psychology they are characteristically associated with super-ego effect, in contradistinction to the perception of color, which reflects the lively affects of social pleasure and enthusiasm. The imagery of distance is also, therefore, the imagery of the super-ego.

Now, were we to think more at the level of hunches and of let-us-suppose, and to move from the more focused clinical considerations to a broader cultural and historical context, would not some connection seem likely between such a psychological analysis of self-evaluation and *any* experiencing in which the imagery of height and distance becomes problematic, wherever this might be found, whether in biography, in art, or in religious experience? If we turn to religious experience and reflection, we may note that the Christian's characteristic religious concern has been precisely his proximity to, or distance from, God — at least historically in Protestant Christianity and currently in neo-Reformation modes of thought.

So it is that the far removed, the radically transcendent God, the God rich in aseity — or, as is sometimes said, directly employing the imagery of distance, the high God — can become the source and occasion of religious anxiety, and an encounter with this God produces the characteristic states of guilt, condemnation, and the hope of justification. Opposed to this is the experience of a proximate God, the companion of man in his situations, projects and decisions, a God who is the source and occasion of overcoming distance, and of the

[28] See Alfred Adler, "The Problem of Distance," in *The Practice and Theory of Individual Psychology* (New Haven: Harcourt, 1924).

establishment of self-esteem and self-confidence — the courage to be.[29]

What we have called the transference-god is a formidable source of anxiety in self-evaluation. It is this — rather than the metaphysical question of the existence of God — that Freud was really attacking when he spoke of insight into the workings of the harsh, cultural super-ego, and that Tillich, in the context of the imperative to transcend the bad, moral conscience, also agreed "had to be killed." Freud and Tillich help us to recognize that the source of courage is not "out there" — not, that is, distant or beyond — but is, rather, grounded in the structure of being itself; that the emergence of the courage to be consists, dynamically, in the recognition and organic appreciation that this structure is open and accessible, not just in principle but also in fact, to each particular being or self. It is this sense, incidentally, which underlies Tillich's distinction between man as estranged from God and man related to God as a stranger.[30]

To turn again to the first two models: is it not this imago of the distant God and its consequent super-ego affect that have preoccupied the professional efforts of the pastoral psychologist and counselor in his therapeutic struggles to free his parishioner's faith from moralistic and idealistic distortions? And is it not also this imago, harder, perhaps, to detect, that so often created that peculiar conjunction of self-worth and sinfulness and its subsequent violent resolution in the conversion experiences studied by the psychologists of religion?

The imagery of distance, considered in this light, becomes a thread of continuity between our three models, despite their many differences. It offers further support to the possibility of a psychology of religion, understood as having its

[29] For a discussion of this problem from the point of view of religious existentialism, see Martin Buber, "Distance and Relation," in *Knowledge of Man*, trans. Maurice Friedman and Ronald Gregor Smith (New York: Harper and Row, 1965).

[30] See Tillich, "Two Types of Philosophy of Religion," in *Theology of Culture*, ed. Robert C. Kimball (New York: Oxford University Press, 1959).

roots in an expanding of the theology-psychology model. For as we have demonstrated, what theology takes as its methodological point of departure (the bad, moral conscience, theological theism), it also designates as "religious" and as amenable to psychological analysis, claiming to understand in a unique way those modes of personal transformation and unification which lead the individual beyond this problematic state. Surely such modes of transformation in personal existence — unification of self, courage to be, "faith" and the like — can properly sustain an approach that is no less psychological.

4

Reflection and Transformation: Knowing and Change in Psychotherapy and in Religious Faith

CHARLES R. STINNETTE, JR.

The dialogue between psychology and religious truth requires both a rigorous effort to protect the integrity of each
cognitive mode and an effort to demonstrate how these two
ways of knowing are related. Fortunately, both perspectives
meet in a common concern with understanding and influencing human behavior. Integral to each, is the development
of a disciplined and therapeutic mode of intervening in human behavior, that is, psychotherapy and pastoral care.[1] It
is "examined experience" — the resulting feedback of this
disciplined intervention — that provides a new operational
framework for the discussion of such problems as knowing
and change. What have we learned about the phenomenon
of knowing and its relation to processes of human transformation from our common concern with therapeutic intervention?
A further question concerns the role of our presuppositions —
our a priori assumptions — in the interpretation of knowledge
gained from such experience in psychotherapy and religious
faith.

Such presuppositions are sharply illustrated by Freud's in-
flexible assumption that to be religious is to be sick. Religion,
by definition, is the effort to find a cure where none could
possibly exist — beyond the realm of reasonable explanation.

[1] I do not mean to imply that pastoral care is the *only* intervening
mode rooted in religious concern. As one mode of intervention, however, it does provide interesting parallels to psychotherapy.

Freud emphasized the absurdity of faith precisely because his presuppositions about *reality* made it impossible to accept the phenomenon in terms of its own cognitive integrity. Freud's critical perspective, however, is a reminder that faith may appear an absurdity in any strictly empirical discourse. It is a further reminder that if the dialogue between psychology and religious truth is to progress, both sides must be willing to move beyond restrictive definitions to phenomenological descriptions as a way of opening the debate to its more profound dimensions.

Reflection as a Mode of Transformation

We are concerned with psychology as the study of interpersonal dynamics that have their focus in the psyche. Theology, on the other hand, is the methodological interpretation of the meaning and truth of religious faith. So far, the disciplines remain theoretically pure — immune from the influence of the other. Such immunity is short-lived, however, when either the psychologist or the theologian approaches the individual and invites him to reflect upon his experience, utilizing the disciplines and tools developed by either method of knowing. Theory is translated into an immediate and practical concern. Reflection becomes the systematic effort to clarify the meaning of identity, or faith (as the case may be), within the actual community in which the person is in constant process of transformation. All experience — psychological and theological — becomes grist for the mill of interpretation in such a context. And from a strictly pragmatic perspective, the adequacy of any interpretation may be measured by its ability to open the person to his own depths again and restore his responsible freedom.

Whether the goal of the reflective discipline is to clarify the meaning of *identity* (psychotherapy) or *faith* (theological reflection), a phenomenological perspective focuses attention upon the centering process itself by which the person collects and identifies himself en route. Instead of being blocked by a paralyzing struggle between conflicting presuppositions about reality, the way is left open (provisionally,

84

at least) to regard "faith" concerns as the ultimate context in which immediate and human "identity" concerns are pursued. In addition, the dialogue between psychology and religious truth is set within an existential framework, where reflection and transformation must be understood as mutually interacting facets of the mind at work — in what William James called "a theatre of simultaneous possibilities."

The terms "reflection" and "transformation" are pivotal in this discussion. The former may be defined as the human capacity for taking thought, to stand outside one's own experience and to order that experience by means of reason, recollection, imagination, and anticipation. Logical thought is a form of reflection by which order is imposed upon a problematic situation. But reflection includes more. It includes all those creative processes suggested by the terms faith, insight, intuition, gestalt, and the like. Even more, and this is our basic thesis, reflection is integral to change — and change is proleptically present in reflection. The root idea imbedded in the verb "to transform" is *metamorphosis* or *transfiguration.* Our contention is that creative reflection itself is a form of transfiguration, of change. Psychotherapy and pastoral care, both of which employ a methodological form of reflection, centered on the existential concerns of identity (or faith) and meaning, actually effect change in the reflecting person. As new gestalts of meaning appear on the horizon, one finds himself encouraged to *live into* these healing possibilities. Indeed, reflective consciousness, which is one distinguishing mark of the human animal, is at the heart of psychotherapy.[2] It is ironic that this methodological recovery of a humanizing quality emerged at all, in view of the preference of much psy-

[2] M. C. D'Arcy, in *The Mind and Heart of Love*, (New York: Meridian Books, 1956), p. 265, points to the tendency to attribute human feelings to animals. But despite the similarity of the nervous system, "if there be no reflective consciousness in animals," he writes, "no similar awareness of the past and expectancy of the future, and above all no personal sense of humiliation, no personal memory to reinforce the present with imaginative fears, no counting of the hammer strokes of pain, their degree of happiness cannot be estimated accurately by any human calculus."

chology for mechanical or subhuman models of interpretation. Yet this human capacity for "reflective consciousness" has proved to be the means of rediscovering both man's instinctual life, hidden beneath a massive cloak of rationalizations, and his reclamation of these "lost" dimensions through psychotherapy.

We mean to suggest that the inherent relation between reflection and transformation, which is evident in psychotherapy, calls for a reexamination of prevailing concepts of knowledge. Alienation and loneliness are driving modern man to look beyond his technical knowledge for healing wisdom. At the turn of the century, James and Bergson were already objecting to the prevailing tendency in Western rationalism to limit knowledge to mere cognitive abstraction, capable of *prediction* and *control* but incapable of *understanding*. Now the therapeutic disciplines have demonstrated that reflection is, indeed, transformative when personal knowledge is integrally related to experience. Man *is* changed by what he knows when his knowing remains rooted in existential realities — where the ambiguities of pain and joy, anxiety and hope, are mediated through interpersonal experience, symbol, and dramatic reenactment.

Insight and Revelation: A Case Study

Psychotherapy has provided impressive clinical support for James' insistence that the mind is not a mirror but a special kind of human agency, which operates as "a theatre of simultaneous possibilities." This recovery of the active and experiential character of personal knowledge provides a framework for a discussion of a brilliant attempt by Thomas C. Oden to relate revelation and insight.[3] Mr. Oden's basic contention is that, although psychological insight must be regarded as distinct from revelation, it shares a common (if only implicit) ontological assumption with revelation: that God is for us (*Deus pro nobis*). This well-reasoned statement is so impor-

[3] Oden, "Revelation and Psychotherapy I," *Continuum*, 2, no. 2 (1964).

tant to the dialogue between psychology and religious truth that it seems worthwhile to attempt a brief summary:

(1) Mr. Oden maintains that behind the therapist's acceptance of his counselee, there is a tacit ontological assumption that the client is acceptable as a human being, on the ground of being itself. "This implicit assumption is precisely what is made explicit by God's self-disclosure in Jesus Christ." Human acceptance in therapy, therefore, is undergirded in an ultimate sense by divine acceptance.

(2) Insight must not, however, be equated with revelation. It is "a discernment which is achieved by the subject," whereas revelation is God's own self-disclosure. Insight represents *human achievement*, whereas revelation is a *divine gift*. "In achieving insight one grasps, discerns or sees the meaning of something out of his own initiative; whereas one is grasped by revelation."

(3) It is clear, then, Mr. Oden insists, that the new ground that needs to be broken is an inquiry into the ontological assumptions of the therapist. As pastoral counselors, he asks, how can we reconcile the notion of achievement in insight with the assumption of gift in revelation? The proposed solution for this dilemma is found in the *analogy of faith*, in which faith is understood as man's response to God's self-disclosure in Jesus Christ. In the acceptance of his client, the therapist is implicitly "performing a representative ministry to the individual . . . that he [the client] is acceptable in the midst of his guilt." The analogy of faith makes it possible to view such therapeutic acceptance, wherever it occurs, as an analogue of God's action in Christ. Insight, like grace, is a response to the gift of acceptance within a community of acceptance, although Mr. Oden falls back at the last moment from equating insight with revelation. They belong to different orders, he explains.

Mr. Oden's remarkable ability to put his finger on some of the essential methodological problems in relating psychology and religious truth sounds a note of clarity in that discussion. He is correct in identifying the problem of relating insight and revelation as central to all other concerns. But his proposed solution to the problem, informed, as it is, largely by Barthian and Rogerian perspectives, results in serious distortions and injustice to psychoanalytic views and, in addition, fails to throw light on just how revelation (*Deus pro nobis*) becomes insight, or the healing knowledge of God in man (*Deus in nobis*).

Mr. Oden's exclusive emphasis upon client-centered therapy as normative ignores much of the wide diversity and the developmental history of contemporary psychotherapy. He appears to identify psychoanalysis with Freud (and early Freud at that!) without regard for the scope of the schools explored by Ruth Munroe or Clara Thompson.[4] Ego psychology (ignored by Mr. Oden), which shares many of the "here and now" concerns of Rogerian psychology, is in fact rooted in, and a continuation of, psychoanalysis.

The most serious problem with Mr. Oden's analysis is his tendency to dichotomize judgment and acceptance in therapy. Hence the Rogerian is pictured as accepting and the psychoanalyst as judging — relying more heavily on past history than "upon the present understanding of self." In addition to the fact that this blanket statement fails to take into account developments within psychoanalysis, it also projects a false dichotomy. Every form of psychotherapy uses both acceptance and judgment. Indeed, acceptance itself implies some form of suspended judgment (for example, acceptance in spite of unacceptability), which gradually becomes explicit within the responsible selfhood that the therapeutic relation affords. Mr. Oden's dichotomy reaches the breaking point when he considers the relation between the theologian and the counselor:

> He who seriously takes upon himself the task of proclaiming the Christian gospel . . . must be willing to stand in a judgmental relation to his hearer, since the gospel stands in judgment of all false self-understanding. Yet he who seriously takes upon himself the task of pas-

[4] Munroe, *Schools of Psychoanalytic Thought*, (New York: Dryden Press, 1955); Thompson, *Psychoanalysis: Evolution and Development*, (New York: Hermitage House, 1951).

toral counseling must be willing to deny himself all judgmental attitudes towards the parishioner, since the sole purpose of therapy is seeking a context . . . [for] self clarification.[5]

From the perspective of theology, such a statement seems to ignore the incarnational heart of Christology — the ever renewing reality of the Word made flesh, by which God manifests himself not only *for* man but also *in* man: "For our sake he made him to be sin who knew no sin, so that in him we might become the righteousness of God" (II Cor. 5:21). The mystery of the Gospel is precisely the claim that He who embodies judgment identifies Himself with the sinner — judgment and grace are united in the Incarnation. Augustine put it in classic terms with his proclamation that God gives what He commands and commands what He gives. From the perspective of pastoral counseling informed by client-centered psychotherapy, Oden's radical separation appears to ignore the equally important function in Rogerian therapy of assisting the counselee in achieving *congruence* between intention and act. The gap implicit in the need for congruence calls for a context in which judgment and acceptance are united.

The fact is that both godly counsel and psychotherapy, since their common aim is to be both relevant and saving *in* the human predicament, are necessarily and practically involved in acceptance *and* judgment. To separate these two therapeutic activities is to absolutize each and to remove them from the arena of human experience. If *Deus pro nobis* is to become *Deus in Nobis*, He who is for us must effect His transfiguration *in* us. This means that the task of preaching, teaching, or counseling always involves the necessity of becoming interior to another in such a way that distorted judgment, characteristic of dependency, is challenged and transformed into morally responsible judgment — the mark of freedom. Psychoanalysis understands this task as a reworking of the

[5] Oden, "Revelation and Psychotherapy I," p. 249. For a further discussion of the strain between acceptance and judgment as Mr. Oden experiences it in his roles as teacher and counselor, see his footnote, pp. 247–49.

cognitive implications of identification, introjection, and imitation through therapy. The authority of judgment is relocated in the responsible person — a responsibility which, as Paul conceived it, rests not in the spirit of bondage but in the spirit of freedom, which faith affords.

In his otherwise excellent discussion, then, Mr. Oden fails to explain (theologically or psychologically) how *Deus pro nobis* becomes *Deus in nobis*. Although the analogy of faith (following Barth's radical Christology) provides a conceptual correlation between insight and revelation, it hardly explains *how* God's acceptance (or the therapist's) brings about change in the individual. We are left with an impassable chasm — traversed in principle only, that is, christologically.

The gospel affirms that the chasm between God and man is traversed in the person of Jesus Christ — in whom humanity and self-transcendence are perfectly united. Man's true humanity is revealed by the action of God in the Christ-Event. Here, as Calvin insisted, knowledge of God and man's knowledge of himself are reconciled. Man claims his own humanity by the self-transcending act of identifying himself with Christ in faith. But such an act is always rooted in the exigencies of history. If Christ is the ultimate anchor of man's identity in history, every centering act rooted in reflection and self-transcendence is a link with that anchor. Whether perceived as identification with Christ in faith, or as a recovery of humanity, such moments of clarification become the bearers of "kairotic" history. In this sense, theology, as methodological self-understanding based on the premise of faith or trust, is the ultimate context within which one explores and claims his identity.

Our contention is that wherever and whenever man seriously engages himself and his history in reflective activity, he is beginning to be changed — transfigured — in the light of the significant identifying images at the base of his life.[6]

[6] The reader is invited to examine II Corinthians 3, which reaches its climax in the statement (Moffatt translation): "But we all mirror the glory of the Lord with face unveiled, and so we are being transformed into the same likeness as himself, passing from one glory to another — for this comes of the Lord the Spirit."

Where Mr. Oden prefers the christological principle of acceptance as the uniting vehicle of insight and revelation, we would emphasize that acceptance is an existential act, centered in history — where revelation and insight are ultimately inseparable. As Christians, we view man's quest for identity as prefigured in Christ. Man's implicit identity is made explicit in Christ. To be a man is to be fully engaged with the vicissitudes of history, while at the same time actively engaged in finding meaning in that history through insight and revelation. Here ontology is translated into concrete, historical self-understanding. Here reflection and transformation are united in the indicative mood characteristic of the biblical word: *as He is so are we in this world.*

The Phenomenology of Insight

Mr. Oden's stimulating article raises the question of an appropriate hermeneutical method for relating psychology to religious truth. As a christologically oriented apologist, he moves directly to a conceptual and ontological analysis. The resulting discussion suffers from a high degree of abstraction, in which human experience is fitted to interpretative restrictions from the beginning. What would follow if, on the other hand, we were to approach the experience of knowing, which we call insight, from a phenomenological perspective? Perhaps the celebrated episode in the life of Helen Keller will serve to introduce this mode of exploration. Her teacher, Ann Sullivan, had struggled for some time to convey the relation of letters to words and of words to conceptual wholes. On the morning of April 5, 1887, Helen was washing, when she expressed a desire to know the name for water. Miss Sullivan explains what happened later:

> We went out to the pump house, and I made Helen hold her mug under the spout while I pumped. As the cold water gushed forth, filling the mug, I spelled "water" into Helen's free hand. The word coming so close upon the sensation of cold water rushing over her hand seemed to startle her. She dropped the mug and stood as one transfixed. A new light came over her face. She spelled "water"

several times. Then she dropped on the ground and asked for its name and pointed to the pump and the trellis, and suddenly turning round she asked for my name. I spelled "teacher" . . .[7]

Surely the assiduous efforts of teacher and pupil had prepared the way for this creative breakthrough, but the moment of insight revealing a whole new world of words and meaning conveys the impression most nearly described by the theological phrase *creation ex nihilo*. Miss Keller confirmed this impression of inexplicable gift later, when she wrote:

It was as if I had come back to life after being dead. . . . Delicious sensations rippled through me, and sweet strange things that were locked up in my heart began to sing.

A phenomenological approach begins by laying aside prior interpretative frameworks in the effort to examine the object of inquiry, insofar as possible, on its own merits. In the case of Helen Keller's discovery, the temptation to explain the experience is eschewed (initially, at least) in the interest of letting its full impact be communicated. Such differential categories as "human achievement" or "divine gift" (with their assumptive worlds) are avoided. For the moment, our task is to accept the experience without questioning its ontological status. Miss Keller suddenly knew that her discovery had unguessed significance, and she joyfully resounded with its as yet undisclosed possibility — its intentionality. In like manner, the phenomenological method is first of all an effort to "play fair" with human experience, trusting oneself to the integrity of its own mode of communication, as phenomena, before imposing interpretative categories.

Despite its highly dogmatic tendencies (especially in its early stages), psychoanalytic practice has widely used the phenomenological style. The use of free association, the encouragement to relate conflict to here and now relationships

[7] From *Religion and Personality* by Richard Harrity and Ralph G. Martin, p. 69. © 1962 by Richard Harrity and Ralph G. Martin. Reprinted by permission of Doubleday and Company, Inc.

(especially with the therapist), the growing insistence that interpretation (whether by therapist or patient) should be minimized and made functional, are all illustrations of this pragmatic phenomenalism in psychoanalysis. Despite his strong feelings about religion, Freud was able to appraise its clinical role from a functional and phenomenological perspective, as his letters to Oscar Pfister demonstrate.

We suggest that the middle road which phenomenology affords offers not only a new way of relating psychology and religious truth, but also provides a mode of discourse that respects the integrity of the living experience that is the object of inquiry. Apparently Helen Keller regarded her momentous discovery as a kind of revelatory event, having ultimate significance. Such knowledge of, or insight into, the essential nature of reality is precisely the definition of revelation that Joachim Wach has employed in his study *Types of Religious Experience: Christian and Non-Christian.*[8] Apart from the phenomenological perspective, one is apt to do violence to such experiences as Miss Keller's, not only by ignoring its complexity but also by failing to grasp its continuity as well as its discontinuity in relation to other modes of knowing.

The phenomenology of *insight* may be partially identified in the following summary statements:

(1) In contrast to the logical sequence by which reason builds from premise or observation to consequence, insight appears as an instantaneous ordering of a whole series of processes. It is a gestalt, a moment of truth, in which part and whole are fused into one. It is, as Helen Keller put it, as if one had found "life after being dead." Eliot Hutchinson[9] has provided a detailed description of such innovating insight and its creativity, which reaches beyond reason. Whether its setting is science or religion, Hutchinson insists that the

---

[8] (Chicago: University of Chicago Press, 1951), p. 15. Actually Professor Wach is summarizing here a definition of revelation set forth by Nathan Soderblom in his book *The Nature of Revelation.* Although Professor Wach expresses some reservations about Soderblom's overall view, he identifies himself with an "inclusive concept of revelations."

[9] Hutchinson, "The Phenomena of Insight in Relation to Religion," *Psychiatry*, 5, (1942).

shape of the phenomenon is the same: insight amounts to a reorganization of the conceptual field. Insight is a gestalt or meaning — a pregnant moment. Differences appear only in subsequent focus, that is, in the context of immediate or ultimate significance. The direction in scientific endeavor is more or less one of testing and verifying such knowledge in relation to prior structures, whereas the personal and religious significance of insight involves restructuring and redirecting one's life in the light of this significant moment. In one, verification is rigorously objective; in the other it is existential, historical, *and* transformative.

(2) The vehicle for insight is symbol or symbolic acts. The function of symbol calls to mind a distinction between insight and reason as modes of knowing. To use Susanne Langer's [10] terms, insight requires a representational rather than a discursive mode. The symbolic act in Helen Keller's experience was the act of spelling the word "water" in her hand, coupled with the sensation of wetness and, perhaps, a whole "theatre of simultaneous possibilities." Through this symbolic action, Miss Keller was enabled not only to gain a measure of control over phenomena (for example, everything has a name) but also to participate in the coherence of the whole that water, earth, and teacher represent. The clue that she discovered made her interior to a host of other meanings, bringing in their train an integration of subject and object in knowing and a new unification of internal and external history. Reinhold Niebuhr [11] once complained that "reason mechanizes human relations" — leaving them contrived and rootless. The "organic character" of man's relation to man requires myth, Niebuhr argued. This organic quality of human knowing is demonstrated in the function of symbol as the convener of insight — as well as the effectual means of appropriating its truth! The symbol, as Helen Keller discovered, is a means of entering the wider world of human creativity.

[10] Langer, *Philosophy in a New Key*: A Study in the Symbolism of Reason, Rite and Art, 3d ed. (Cambridge: Harvard University Press, 1957).
[11] *Reflections on the End of an Era*, (New York: Charles Scribner's Sons, 1934), p. 73.

(3) The role of symbol in relation to insight also points to man's capacity for self-transcendence. We have previously described this unique human capacity in terms of the intrinsic relation between reflection and transformation. If we examine insight as a phenomenon that presents itself to our awareness, especially as focused in symbol, it reveals the human capacity for self-consciousness — for reflection en route, so to speak. The symbol, which points to this depth dimension in man, is itself a point of articulation between the historical and the ontological realms of man's existence. Even in sleep, the dream is a spontaneous reflection upon the character of man's being-in-the-world, providing an Archimedean point whereby one begins to mold and change his world. For Helen Keller, the moment of truth that changed her life is, perhaps, symbolized by the pause between an abandoned mug and her transfixed reflection upon what had just happened. In any case, the shock of recognition had its consequences in redoubled curiosity about *her* world and a joyful entry into it.[12]

(4) From a phenomenological perspective, the revelatory feature of insight is its communication of a moral imperative. Its intention is the necessity of change. Essentially, art and prophecy share this imperative: "You must change your life!" Freud, the empirical scientist, became both prophet and artist in his insistence that behavioral symptom and style of life (localized in character) are significantly related. Insight is more than a technical understanding of this relation; it is the beginning of a moral responsibility to effect change. It is the truth we know but resist knowing through elaborate rationalization! This prophetic character of insight (which can be observed clinically in therapy), is, we suggest, the "new key" that is required for the recovery of an adequate theory of knowledge. If we make the effort to free ourselves from the limiting halters of prior ontologies, the act of knowing itself may be rediscovered in its existential and ethical dimension.

[12] See Martin Scheerer's discussion of this creative moment in Helen Keller's life in his chapter "Cognitive Theory," in *Handbook of Social Psychology*, 2 vols., ed. Gardner Lindzey et al. (Reading, Mass.: Addison-Wesley Pub. Co., 1954), 1:127.

Indeed, we may be enabled to rediscover the truth of an earlier epistemology in which *to know is to love* — and to love is to care, as the husbandman cares for the earth, not as an absentee manipulator but as a living presence.

Psychotherapy has provided clinical support for Nietzche's dictum that there is no such thing as "immaculate perception." Knowing is inferential, and thought, as Mannheim insisted, always occurs in an "inherited" context. The effort of phenomenology is to recover this organic character of knowing, without imposing premature ontologies. It reminds us that cognition is an active, dialogic phenomenon rather than a passive one, and that truth as known in a personal sense effects change not only in the objective world but also within the knower himself. Indeed, a phenomenological analysis of Helen Keller's insight appears to justify her own conclusion that the new world which had opened before her brought her to new life — a *creation ex nihilo.*

Revelation, Therapy, and History

How does meaning mean? A phenomenological analysis of insight reveals the organic role of meaning in knowing and change — where the quality of what is known is intrinsic to its effectual work in the knower. Such knowledge is indispensable in the humanizing work of psychotherapy or pastoral care. One of the many ironies of modern man, however, is his vast store of technical knowledge, which, apparently, has neither purged his fears nor rendered him more loving. In his zeal for power, he has ignored change in himself. Perhaps we shall have to go all the way back to Augustine to learn again the significance of his insistence that what is not adequately known is not fully loved.[13]

The phenomenological method points to the need for meaning or coherence in knowing, but as a pragmatic method it cannot assess the value or quality of meaning. The discipline of ethics, in which fitting or appropriate "meanings" are

[13] See Robert E. Cushman, "Faith and Reason," in *A Companion to the Study of St. Augustine,* ed. Roy W. Battenhouse (New York: Oxford University Press, 1955).

analyzed in relation to means and goals, is eventually necessary in any discussion of knowing and change. Victor Frankl has built a whole new system of psychotherapy (Logotherapy) upon the need for meaning in human survival, based upon his experience in a war-time concentration camp.[14] Those who discover some objective meaning, some *Logos* beyond themselves, survived the shocks and torments of the death camp. Dr. Frankl has made this search for meaning the central concern in psychotherapy. Survival is hinged to meaning — especially in stress. There must, however, come a time when the content of meaning, its quality, its moral affects, and its embodiment in interpretations, myths, and paradigmatic acts, should be considered in relation to the human quest for self-understanding and commitment. We are suggesting that phenomenology is an important first step in analyzing knowing and change, but that the quest, eventually, must become "for what purpose and to what end or ends?"

We have maintained that revelation is the ultimate framework within which insight occurs. We must now examine how revelation is related to meaning in therapy and history. Revelation, here, refers to that unique self-disclosure of God as healing love that the Christian community celebrates as the event of Jesus Christ. The revelatory event is both relevant to and anchored in human history. H. Richard Niebuhr writes:

> Whatever else revelation means, it does mean an event in our history which brings rationality and wholeness into the confused joys and sorrows of personal existence and allows us to discern order in the brawl of communal histories. . . . In this sense we may say that the relevatory moment is revelatory because it is rational, because it makes the understanding of order and meaning in personal history possible.[15]

[14] See Frankl, *The Doctor and the Soul* (New York: Alfred Knopf, 1955).
[15] *The Meaning of Revelation* (New York: The Macmillan Co., 1952), pp. 109–10.

The question remains, however, How is the meaning of this relevatory event made effectual in man? The traditional answers to this question revolve around the relation of faith and reason. We shall not review that extensive literature here except to say that no rational theological system has yet succeeded in removing the seeming absurdity of faith. The offense of the Gospel remains, despite the impressive work of men like Aquinas or Kant, or a contemporary Tillich, to establish a rational via media between faith and reason. In terms of the current scene, however, Tillich[16] does provide a clue in his insistence that revelation is the "manifestation of the depth of reason and the ground of being." "It points," he writes, "to the mystery of existence and to our ultimate concern." In this view, reason is not destroyed by revelation, nor is revelation "emptied by reason."

The fact is that, although revelation, like insight, is mediated through historical events, its assertions are not factual and literal but ultimately interpretative. Both phenomenology and depth psychology have provided a larger framework for understanding this more inclusive human dimension. In one, we learn that human experience is richer and more complex than our philosophies have allowed. In the other, we have experienced the healing role of metaphor, myth, and symbol in reshaping our lives — and in establishing communication with hitherto lost areas of human experience. It is true, as Thomas Mann once said, that myth, though early and primitive in the life of the human race, is late and mature in the life of the individual.

The problem of how the event of Christ becomes effectual in the believer is first of all a problem of how we are to apprehend the activity of God. While reason serves to clarify and evaluate that apprehension in relation to prior knowledge, reason is not the primary mode of knowing itself. Neither is such apprehension empirically limited or literal, as if tape recorders or cameras were the final word in human knowing. Kierkegaard was correct in saying that faith has no

[16] Paul Tillich, *Systematic Theology*, (Chicago: University of Chicago Press, 1951), I: 130 ff.

real purpose when the literal replaces the indirect. On the contrary, man is changed by truth which comes interior to his own experience, which provides a dramatic encounter with the antinomies inherent in his own existence, and, at the same time, confronts him with the necessity of responding to the question, "Who am I?"

We are suggesting that the function of myth provides a symbolic via media between revelation and reason. As Reinhold Niebuhr has taught us, the understanding of reality by way of myth is fruitful if taken "seriously but not literally." It is understandable that myth has emerged as an important bearer of meaning in psychotherapy as well as in religion — although not enough attention has been given to the epistemological significance of this fact. *It points to the elemental role of mythical apprehension in reflection and transformation, which is prior to, and the presupposition of, rational analysis.* It is also a reminder of the fact that man is a historical creature, whose self-understanding is inseparable from his reflection in time and space. *Myth is the first ontology in human consciousness, and it is eneluctably historical.* For myth relates man to his sacred history, to reality, to what really happened, to the constituting events in human existence.[17] Reinhold Niebuhr writes:

> This is perhaps the most essential genius of myth, that it points to the timeless in time, to the ideal in the actual, but does not lift the temporal to the category of the eternal (as pantheism does) nor deny the significant glimpses of the eternal and the ideal in the temporal (as dualism does). When the mythical method is applied to the description of human character, its paradoxes disclose precisely the same relationships in human personality which myth reveals, and more consistent philosophies obscure, in the nature of the universe.[18]

[17] See Mircea Eliade, *The Sacred and the Profane* (New York: Harper & Brothers, 1957), pp. 95 ff.
[18] *An Interpretation of Christian Ethics*, (New York: Harper & Brothers, 1935), pp. 82–83.

CHARLES R. STINNETTE, JR.

Theological Reflection and Therapy as Change Agents

We have maintained that myth represents a symbolic via media between revelation and reason. Myth provides the dramatic screen upon which man's existential predicament in history is projected — and invested with significance. From the perspective of reason, myth remains, as it was for Paul, *both deceiver and yet true*.[19] In this light, theological reflection, and therapy as well, appear as ways of understanding man's history while engaged in the effort to change it. Revelation and insight are functions of man's passionate concern to understand himself *in his history*, where myth and reason are practical means for that reflective activity. Epistemologically the Pragmatists were nearer the mode of revelation than they realized, when they maintained that the meaning of events is discovered in the course of remaking them. In this sense, one may claim Reinhold Niebuhr as a theological pragmatist, for he came to the question of the meaning of history not with a speculative, detached attitude but with the passion of a prophet. History is understood, he insisted, in the effort to change it. We conclude, then, that both dynamic theology and therapy may be conceived as ways of understanding history in the course of changing it. Methodologically, the reasons for this conclusion may be recapitulated as follows:

(1) Both theology and therapy are ultimately relevant to the human predicament as integrative activities. Certainly a major motif in modern theology has been its concern with the practical significance of faith in man's self-understanding. This is not to say that theology is merely subjective or practical, but rather to insist with H. Richard Niebuhr[20] that in the task of attending to the God of faith, theology must also attend to *faith in God*, if it would understand God. Faith,

[19] See Reinhold Niebuhr, "As Deceivers and Yet True," in *Beyond Tragedy* (New York: Charles Scribner's Sons, 1937). "The temporal process is like the painter's flat canvas. It is one dimension upon which two dimensions must be recorded. This can be done only by symbols which deceive for the sake of truth." p. 6.

[20] *Radical Monotheism and Western Culture* (New York: Harper and Brothers, 1960), see Introduction.

Niebuhr insists, is as much an unavoidable counterpart of the presence of God as sense experience is of natural powers. Now therapy shares this practical mode of knowing with theology in its attention to actual experience and the formative and syncretic significance of symbol.

(2) Both theology and therapy as integrative modes of knowing utilize man's inherent capacity for reflection and action. History is the common focus of this integrative work. Man is understood as a historical creature, who discovers himself and becomes himself within the dialogues of history. His identity is marked with the branding iron of history. He bears the marks of time in his own body and mind and social existence. Yet he bears these marks, not passively but actively, as one who both makes history and reflects upon it. It is this unique capacity for reflection and history that draws theology and therapy into a common cause.

(3) Although psychotherapy has rejected the notion of "free will" as an autonomous faculty in the human psyche, the very possibility of such a discipline depends upon the implicit assumption that human personality is capable of change. Man's freedom is rooted in his knowledge of conditionality, and in his self-transcending capacity for directed action in the light of such knowledge. Man is both determined and free — a frail reed bent by every wind of circumstance, and yet, as Pascal would say, a thinking reed!

Essentially, then, man's freedom to change does not amount to an escape from the consequences of his own history — nor its abrasive calibrations. Rather, his freedom resides in the possibility of perceiving himself in the light of a new image — a new whole — while engaged in taking account of his own historical determination. History is concomitant with man's freedom to respond to meaning, to find himself in new constellations which both incorporate and transform the old. Change, then, is first of all a function of cognitive renovation, in which the new gestalt is perceived as already transforming the present moment. This cognitive process is the heart of reflection and transformation. Phenomenologically, it represents common ground between theological reflection and psychotherapy.[21] The prophetic note in both is the imperative to change.

History as Memory

History, as Bultmann has put it, begins with the awakening of human self-consciousness — with the break with nature. It is precisely this "break with nature" that makes it possible for man to act in the present moment, while remembering the past and anticipating the future. Yet such a "break" does not annul nature. It transforms and incorporates nature historically. Here again, theology and therapy meet in history, for faith cannot reflect upon its knowledge of God, save by historical experience, and reason cannot bring conceptual order to natural processes, save through the continual feedback of sense experience.

Theology and therapy meet in a common concern with history as memory and reenactment. But again it must be emphasized that both disciplines understand remembering as an active engagement with history — as a form of meeting, in which reflection involves transformation. Alice Balint,[22] writing from a Freudian perspective, regards learning as, in part, an act of remembered love. Every triumph in learning is made possible, she insists, through remembered response to investments of love by those who have nurtured the individual. Psychotherapy has been widely described as a "corrective emotional experience," in which "corrections" are applied to the distortions of one's own memory in a "here and

[21] Bernard Meland, in the *Realities of Faith* (New York: Oxford University Press, 1962), emphasizes the transformative quality of revelation in relation to knowledge. Revelation ". . . is an event which transforms or recreates man's sense of knowing and brings to judgment what man's own reason has wrought. In this context Revelation is the encounter with the depth of God's reality in history, an event which man's reason or experience did not, or even could not apprehend on its own initiative," pp. 171 ff. H. Richard Niebuhr, likewise, emphasizes the transformative role of new gestalts of meaning in reflection, in *The Responsible Self*, (New York: Harper and Row, 1963), pp. 102–103. "Reinterpretation" in the light of such gestalts (e.g., revelation) "recalls, accepts, understands, and reorganizes the past instead of abandoning it." Both psychotherapy and theology share this mode of *re-interpretation*.

[22] *The Early Years* (New York: Basic Books, 1954).

now" relationship. Indeed, one might say that the goal of psychotherapy is to restore the individual's sense of participating in real history by recovering his memory from the arid lands of "repetition compulsion." Here it is clinically demonstrable that one who remains ignorant of his own history is doomed to repeat it.

History and self-understanding meet in the active engagement of the reflective person who seeks to fathom the meaning of his own existence in time. Human freedom provides the fulcrum for memory by which the individual grasps time — finds posts to hang duration on — and thereby to transform his own history. Psychotherapy, we have seen, utilizes this human capacity by corrective reexamination of one's history.[23] The historian Collingwood, reflecting on the question "What is history for?" answers,

> History is for human self-knowledge. It is generally thought to be of importance to man that he should know himself: where knowing himself means knowing not merely his personal characteristics, but his nature as man. . . . The only clue to what man can do is what he has done. The value of history . . . [lies] in what man has done and thus what man is.[24]

Collingwood concludes that, in order to know history, one must reconstruct it as a living event, as interior to its meaning, and as a participant in its significance, while remaining critically objective oneself.

Collingwood's approach to historical reason provides a possible framework for a theological understanding of history

[23] See E. Schachtel's "Memory and Childhood Amnesia," in *A Study of Interpersonal Relations*, ed. Patrick Mullahy (New York: Hermitage Press, 1949). Schachtel opposes Freud's explanation of childhood amnesia as due to sexual trauma. He emphasizes the variety and richness of children's fantasy, which, he contends, cannot be fitted into the conventional adult categories and verbal signs of Western culture. The child "forgets" because his adult world provides no acceptable cognitive forms to convey his thought.

[24] R. G. Collingwood, *The Idea of History* (New York: Oxford University Press, 1956), p. 209.

as anamnesis.[25] The faith community, however, understands history as reinterpreted through saving events appropriately recalled in liturgical and theological action. Revelation thus provides the clue to the meaning and foundation of history. It is recognition rooted in the Kairos of history. This does not necessarily involve the abandonment of the critical stance. Biblical scholars, while fully employed in the work of higher criticism, manage also to participate in the celebration of God's mighty acts as here and now events. If the saving events are not to be taken literally, however, it is necessary for the believer to be clear in his mind about the relation of the objective event and its effectual celebration in the ongoing life of the faith community — as anamnesis.

Richard R. Niebuhr has produced a cogent essay, which addresses itself to the methodological problem with which we are concerned, *Resurrection and Historical Reason*. The focus here is how the relation between revelation and history is to be understood. Richard Niebuhr summarizes and compares some major viewpoints within contemporary theology. Brunner and Barth share a radical christological interpretation of revelation. History is a mask, behind which its true meaning is concealed. The event of Christ is the definitive expression of revelation, which "breaks" into history — providing its meaning and its only proper interpretation. On the other hand, Bultmann rejects this notion of revelation as a hole in history. He views history as the bearer of meaning — a meaning not essentially alien to, or discontinuous with, empirical experience, but revelatory of the depths of human existence itself. The event of Christ understood and interpreted existentially brings to birth this profound self-understanding in man himself.

John Knox shares Bultmann's emphasis upon the revelatory significance of history *as history*, but for Knox, meaning is

---

[25] Although Collingwood's method of critical, systematic, and interior knowing sets historical reason in a general framework congenial to this essay, it must be noted that epistemologically he does *not* draw the same conclusion, particularly with regard to our thesis of the reunion of subject and object in the act of remembering. For Collingwood, memory is sheer contemplation!

conveyed in and through *communal* memory and its theological anamnesis. The event as an historical occurrence, recalled and reenacted through personal and communal celebration, becomes the means whereby the truth of revelation is appropriated. To know Christ is to know his benefits in the community which actively remembers him. Apparently, Richard Niebuhr finds this interpretation most helpful in relating faith and historical reason. He writes:

> The mode of historical cognition is remembering, so that to know the resurrection of Christ involves not our occupying the standpoint of the Christian community but our actively participating in its remembering him. John Knox succinctly defines the church as the community which remembers Jesus.[26]

This understanding of memory as the meeting point between revelation and historical reason calls attention to the constructive role of myth and paradigmatic acts in communicating sacred history. Mircea Eliade, in his study *The Sacred and the Profane*,[27] develops the thesis that every religion evolves paradigmatic acts and gestures, especially in relation to sacred space and sacred time, which are intended to recover divine acts and essential origins. Such mythical activities are not necessarily antihistorical, Eliade explains, but rather represent a passion for ontology, for a recovery of the *illud tempus* (this is, the beginnings) upon which a sound contemporaneity may be established. It is thus possible to dramatize and to remember by reenactment the sacred events of history, which recast present history in its proper perspective. The work of anamnesis becomes, then, truly prophetic — an act of reflection which is at the same time transfiguring. Reinhold Niebuhr's theological work has been centered on the moral implications of faith and history as the ingredients of such reflection. "By the symbol of the resurrection," Niebuhr writes, "the Christian faith hopes for an eternity which

---

[26] *Resurrection and Historical Reason*, (New York: Charles Scribner's Sons, 1957), p. 96.
[27] See footnote 17.

transfigures but does not annul the temporal process."[28] History as anamnesis thus becomes an effectual mode whereby faith affirms ultimate meaning *in* and *beyond* the tragic character of history.

Revelation as the Healing of History

It has been our thesis that the human capacity for reflection is at the same time an expression of man's self-transcending potential for change. Knowledge is power, as Bacon maintained, but, in the human situation, knowledge is transfiguring only insofar as it becomes both interior to, and liberating of, the person. Memory as anamnesis is an illustration of such transforming knowledge. In psychotherapy, where identity concerns are paramount, the person is enabled to live into mature images of himself — beyond the distortions of genetic history. In pastoral care, understood as a theological discipline, wherein faith concerns are central, revelation is the healing of history and, therefore, the ultimate framework for all change. Christian faith is rooted in the conviction that, in Christ, God renovates human history. To use an expression of the poet Charles Williams, Christ is "the manifest measure of God's glory correcting time."

We may summarize briefly three implications of revelation as the healing of history:

(1) As a form of remembering, revelation heals by reinterpreting history in the light of judgment and grace. The prophetic word emphasizes the fact that man and his world are under judgment. If we are to understand revelation, we must know what it means to find ourself at the bar of God's judgment. The proper response to such judgment is repentance (metanonia), that is, a turning around. Prophetic religion insists that there is an organic relation between what men do (their history) and who they are (their ultimate identity, ground, ontology). The via media between existence and essential identity is the image of grace in Christ, "The mani-

[28] *Faith and History*, (New York: Charles Scribner's Sons, 1949), p. 237.

fest measure of God's glory correcting time." Grace is the a priori of faith. It is the love that heals in judgment — for judgment is the refining fire of faith, as Job learned.

(2) The New Testament affirms that God manifests Himself as both interior and transformative within human history *in Christ*. Man is confronted and changed by Christ in concrete form. The God-man encounter is forever anchored in the living, concrete issues of history. As Horace Bushnell used to say, in Christ, God preengages our heart before He breaks it. But he does break our heart! He comes with judgment upon our overweening cherishments. He brings not peace but the sword. He demands that we choose, and that we remember who we are in relation to "this man for others." One may choose not to remember, but he cannot escape the consequences of his choice.

The ultimate challenge to man's memory in Christ is the love of God, which is luminous even in its judgment. Here one is confronted by a love which in historical action reveals both the character of God and the true nature of man. In the light of this revelation, this therapy of history, man's anxiety is seen as rooted in flight from existence itself, in unbelief. For man's health depends upon belief — that is, an affirmative response to the meaning of existence, despite its risks. It is precisely at this juncture that the claim is made that Christ is both the end of history and its new beginning. Reinhold Niebuhr writes:

> The affirmation that Christ is the end of history signifies that in His life, death and resurrection the meaning of man's historic existence is fulfilled . . . that "a new age" has been initiated in the history of mankind, means that the wisdom of faith which apprehends the true meaning of life also contains within it the repentance which is the presupposition of the renewal of life.[29]

(3) Finally, revelation is understood as the healing of history in the merging of "identity concerns" and "faith con-

[29] *Ibid.*, p. 139.

cerns" in Christ. Paul Tillich[30] has reminded us that both concerns are rooted in the human thrust toward maturity, in the centered person. Growth, alteration, and self-transcending concerns comprise the transforming processes which aim toward the centered person, and the unambiguous life. The quest for identity and the methodological effort at self-understanding on the premise of faith are, then, different ways of describing a common phenomenon: the quest for the unambiguous life.

Biblical faith affirms that God's action in Christ provides the clue which answers most effectively man's quest for meaning. That action is historical and revelatory. It is inseparable from the forms or components of human identity — continuity, integrity, and mastery.[31] Christ is fully human, and his humanity is transparent in its depths at every stage. Both his wisdom and his stature are manifest in growth, as attested by the Gospel narrative. But the truth of revelation, although manifest in growth and interaction, is historical and action-centered rather than simply evolutionary. Truth is something that happens. It is not a state of mind. The truth of revelation is reborn on every occasion where knowing and believing are united. In such knowledge, man is most profoundly healed, for he is enabled for freedom, free for freedom.[32] Hence man's transfiguration becomes the sign not of mechanical shaping but of freedom which, although set within the limits of conditionality, makes possible the refashioning of his own character in response to the gift of grace.

[30] *Systematic Theology* (Chicago: University of Chicago Press, 1964), 3:108 ff.
[31] Erik H. Erikson, in *Childhood and Society* (New York: Norton, 1950) and *Identity and the Life Cycle* (New York: International Universities Press, 1959), finds in man an "ordered or organizing core." Hence, for Erikson, the centering process involves continuity, unity, and mastery as rooted in the ego — the central organizing agency. Kierkegaard, too, regards the self as centering itself, but here as faith, and by willing to be itself as centered in God. I am indebted to Leland Elhard for these insights relating faith and identity in his unpublished doctoral dissertation "*Identity and Faith*: Soren Kierkegaard and Erik H. Erikson," (University of Chicago Divinity School, 1965).
[32] See F. Schelling, *Of Human Freedom*, trans. James Gutmann, (New York: Columbia University Press, 1946).

Summary

We have focused our attention on the phenomenon of change in psychotherapy and in pastoral care as theological reflection. Both disciplines are practical modes of knowing and believing, whose sustaining matrix is a community of analysis and of commitment. In both, reflection is a mode of action involving transformation. While identity concerns are central in psychotherapy, and the meaning of faith is paramount in theology, both disciplines are directed toward transfiguring knowledge, which is designated as insight or revelation.

A phenomenological study of insight and revelation brings to light both their likeness and continuity and the necessity of developing a via media between reason and faith. We find the clue to this via media in the interpretative function of symbol and myth in reflection, wherein reason is not annulled but transfigured. Psychotherapy appears to confirm the conviction that the problems of human existence are not ultimately accessible to technical reason but, rather, require transfiguring faith in the context of personal commitment — a community of commitment as well as a community of analysis.[33] Theologically, such transfiguring faith appears as a response to the gestalt of grace in revelation. Bernard Meland describes the surprise of grace as a "new structure of sensitivity." It represents the capacity of the human spirit for continual reopening of itself to its own depths. Theological gestalts represent the larger canvas upon which all transfiguring processes are undertaken.

We find the traditional distinctions between insight and revelation unsatisfactory because they tend to ignore the transfiguring quality of all personal knowing. The radical claim of the New Testament is not only that God is for man (Deus pro nobis) but also that God is in man (Deus in nobis) in Christ. Recent studies in cognition tend to provide phenomenological support for a more transformative understanding of knowing than traditional rationalism has allowed. In the

---

[33] See Philip Rieff, "A Schema of Therapeutic Types," a paper presented to the meeting of the American Psychological Association, 1961 (mimeographed).

light of this support, we prefer to distinguish insight and revelation not as human achievement versus divine gift but as one process of knowing, in which revelation provides the ultimate gestalt for all personal knowledge. Reason and revelation, ontology and history, meet in the effectual symbols of grace, which transfigure human personality.

Finally, revelation is understood as the ultimate therapy or healing of history. Here we see the converging of identity concerns and faith concerns in the human capacity for reflection and transformation. Christ enters man's biographical history as the ultimate answer to man's quest for identity and meaning. That saving event, recalled in action (through reflection and transfiguration as ordered thinking and liturgical and moral action) is the agency for the reconciliation and healing of all history.

5

Faith and the Dynamics of Knowing
DON BROWNING

The purpose of this paper is to summarize some information derived from the psychological and psychotherapeutic sciences about the processes of knowing and believing, and to make a few suggestions about what this data implies for a theological understanding of faith. In general, it suggests that every act of knowing is essentially dynamic — an attempt to meet a human need. These sciences demonstrate that there is no such thing as a completely disembodied, abstract way of knowing. Instead, every act of knowing is an intermediate act, anchored to a prior conflictual situation and a subsequent attempt to resolve the conflict. Every act of knowing is basically an attempt to establish a hypothesis which, when acted upon or in some way relied upon, will guide us to a restored state of relative inner wholeness and outer coherence with our environment. That this is the basic character of every act of knowing is something that John Dewey suggested many years ago. But the varieties and complexities by which these general principles manifest themselves in all our diverse modes of knowing may have eluded his own very perceptive intellect.

Knowing and the Real Self

Let us first attempt to specify some of the need systems operating in the human organism, before discussing how they affect our processes of knowing. In doing this, a distinction should be made between need systems relevant to what some psychologists have called the "real self" and need systems relevant to what is commonly referred to as the "phenom-

111

enal" or "empirical self." Concepts of the real self have been presented, with some variation in detail, by Jung, Goldstein, Fromm, Horney, and Rogers. In each instance, the concept refers to a set or irreducible constitutional givens, which an individual brings to his experience for actualization, elaboration, and fulfillment. Charlotte Buhler, in her recent book *Values in Psychotherapy*,[1] has attempted to specify such constitutional givens. She suggests that the real self consists of four congenital tendencies toward (a) instinct satisfaction, (b) expansiveness, (c) adaptation, and (d) order. Roughly speaking, Buhler is including within her concept of instinctual needs what Freud referred to by his concept of libidinal drives. The concepts of expansiveness, adaptation, and order are her way of specifying the basic elements which make up our ego apparatus. I mention her framework, not to enter into a discussion of the real self but because it offers a convenient gathering of basic concepts relevant to the discussion of our thesis — that knowing, as psychology and psychotherapy have come to understand it, is basically the establishment of a hypothesis for action, orientation, or response in the face of conflict and need.

Knowing and Instinctual Needs

Let us discuss an example of a conflict theory of knowing in a psychological system where it was thought that the instincts provide the dominant needs motivating the personality. Such a system can be found in the work of Freud and his expositor David Rapaport.[2] For Freud, the conflict that creates the knowing process first comes in the form of a deprivation or frustration. The hungry infant needing gratification can provide us with a model. Hunger creates a disequilibrium of tension, which propels the infant toward the object that will satisfy the hunger and release the tension. Thought is created

[1] (New York: The Free Press of Glencoe, 1962), pp. 75, 84–87.
[2] For the psychoanalytic theory of thinking and knowing, see Freud's "Formulations Regarding the Two Principles in Mental Functioning," and Rapaport's "Toward a Theory of Thinking," in Rapaport's *Organization and Pathology of Thought* (New York: Columbia University Press, 1951).

when the gratifying object is absent or delayed in coming, and the drive energy cathects a memory image of past satisfying objects. This memory image becomes associated with the drive, and constitutes a primitive thought (hallucination), which may permit temporarily the discharge of tension. If the need gratification continues to be delayed, this primitive thought (cathected memory trace) becomes a hypothesis to guide action in searching external reality for the gratifying object. In this model, knowing becomes a hypothesis about the need-gratifying qualities of external objects. All such hypotheses about the external world find their origin in the moment of delay and frustration. Although this model of thinking and knowing has been modified somewhat by subsequent psychoanalytic formulations, it remains essentially the same. For instance, David Rapaport's systematization of the Freudian theory, although making some use of Hartmann's concept of "conflict free" ego spheres, does not go too far beyond Freud. Higher processes of knowing are basically hypotheses about intermediate means to reach more remote tension-reducing goals.[3] Hypotheses about these intermediate means often become relatively autonomous from their origins, and constitute our fund of so-called mature ego interests and hypotheses about the nature of the world and life in the

[3] Rapaport, "Toward a Theory of Thinking," pp. 699–705. All ego-interests, for Rapaport, are finally what he calls "drive-derivatives" or "quasi-needs" (Lewin's term). He grants that ego apparatuses are structurally independent from the instincts but that their energy is their "own" only in the sense that drive cathexis can become neutralized and "bound" for the purposes of ego functioning. This neutralized energy can then be used to control unneutralized id impulses. This leaves him essentially faithful to Freud, believing that thought and the processes of knowing are a result of a frustration of id drives. Positive ego interests or hypotheses arise only as means to the satisfaction of more basic drives, and gain a relative autonomy only as one learns how to delay his need for immediate gratification. As far as this goes, Hartmann himself does not get too far beyond Freud. Although he posits autonomous ego structures and suggests that they may have a source of energy independent from the instincts, he makes no systematic use of the concept and finally seems to settle for a theory of neutralized libidinal and aggressive drives as being the source of ego energy. See Hartmann, E. Kris, and R. M. Loewenstein, "Notes on the Theory of Aggression," *The Psychoanalytic Study of the Child*, 3, no. 4 (1949): 9–36.

world. Something similar to the psychoanalytic theory of knowing can also be found in the work of certain behaviorists who built their theory around the law of effect — notably Thorndike and Hull.

Psychoanalytic theory probably was in error in emphasizing the ubiquitous role of instinctual dynamics in motivating and guiding the establishment of hypotheses about reality. Of course, instinctual needs doubtless provide the chief motivating force for some of our knowing. But the orthodox analytic theory failed to understand the existence of other need systems that may become involved in the knowing process. It served the purpose, however, of putting us on the search for the dynamic foundations for knowing, and alerted us to the significance of conflict for the stimulation of hypotheses with which to order and make intelligible our world.

Knowing and the Ego Functions

This leads us to a discussion of the second tendency of the real self, what Buhler calls the tendency toward expansiveness. This tendency of the real self or ego, she claims, can have a positive orientation toward reality, relatively free from (not derivative of) the promptings of instinctual needs.[4] Although there are many thinkers who would tend to agree with this, it has been possible only recently to conceptualize the character of the energy systems which may motivate the expansiveness of the ego functions. There have been several efforts along these lines, but the concept of "stimulus hunger" developed by Laura Rice and John Butler appears to contribute the most satisfying understanding of the motivational dynamics behind the positive knowing functions of the ego processes. The concept of "stimulus hunger" points to a highly stable and persistent need of the human organism for varied intensities and novel complexities of stimulation or experience.[5] The drive for new experience and stimulation orients the organism in a positive way toward both social and physi-

---

[4] Buhler, *Values in Psychotherapy*, pp. 71–73.

[5] John M. Butler and Laura N. Rice, "Adience, Self-Actualization, and Drive Theory," in *Concepts of Personality*, ed. Joseph M. Wepman and Ralph Heine (Chicago: Aldine Publishing Co., 1963), pp. 79–106.

cal reality. When confronted by a new source of stimulation, our basic inclination is to get more of it, unless it becomes too intense, and then we retreat. Every individual organism has a history, during which it becomes acclimatized to a certain stimulation level. This Butler and Rice call the chronic level of stimulation. It is the nature of this drive for new experience to try to keep the level of stimulation occurring at any given moment (the acute level) in "match" with the chronic level. Although Butler and Rice conceive this drive for stimulus in basically hedonic terms, they clearly differentiate it from what they call the physiological instincts, including sex — the major difference being that the latter are much more rhythmic and phasic in character, attaining satiation much more rapidly and subsiding into quiescence more quickly than is the case with the drive for new experience. Their theory depends strongly on sensory deprivation experiments, experiments with animals under conditions of instinct satiation, Fox's neural stimulation experiments, and other less systematic observations of childhood curiosity and exploratory behavior.

The thrust of this theory is to demonstrate clearly how all living organisms (especially man) are open systems, maintaining their stability in the context of a positive interest in the intensities and complexities of events and not simply under the guidance of a narrow selectivity dominated by in-instinctual needs, although these are operative at certain times. Of course, experiencing the raw data of the world is related but not identical to knowing. To discriminate the presence of an object in our perceptual field does not mean that we hold a reliable hypothesis about what it is. How do we move from the reception of this data to what we might call an act of knowing?

Once again the concepts of conflict and hypothesis seem relevant. But here the conflict is not between instinctual drive cathexis and reality; it is a conflict between new perceptual data and the cognitive wholes or gestalts that we bring to this data.[6] As we broaden our spheres of perception and ex-

[6] In developing the thought of this paragraph I am relying on the work in cognitive theory reported in the following: Edward C. Tolman,

perience, we are constantly taking in new data, which may not fit readily into existing organizations. This produces conflict between new experiences and old gestalts. It is the nature of gestalts to maintain their integrity and either to reorganize themselves or to restructure events. In an effort to resolve this conflict between new experience and old cognitive maps, a hypothesis is engendered which attempts to guide our efforts to orient toward and assimilate this new experience. The conflict involved is due to cognitive ambiguity and dissonance between old patterns and new data. The hypothesis is an effort to reestablish consistency by making sense out of the new data. Like all other hypotheses, it is a construct guiding action or response to the new data, whether this response be a gross motor action designed to alter the external world or a more subtle internal orientation which reorganizes the consistency of our inner cognitive wholes to include the new data.[7]

This forces us to discuss Buhler's third and fourth tendencies, toward adaptation and order. In terms of what we have said about the expansive character of stimulus hunger as the drive foundation of our positive ego interests, it becomes clear how this positive desire to assimilate new experience must be balanced by innate tendencies to maintain internal

---

"A Psychological Model," in *Toward a General Theory of Action*, ed. T. Parsons and E. A. Shils (New York: Harper and Row, 1951); Ernest R. Hilgard, "The Role of Learning in Perception," and Jerome S. Bruner, "Personality Dynamics and the Process of Perceiving," in *Perception: An Approach to Personality*, ed. Robert R. Blake and Glenn V. Ramsey (New York: The Ronald Press Co., 1951).

[7] It must not be thought that in my use of the word "conflict" I am suggesting simply that anxiety is the chief motivational factor in all knowing. Certainly, I am saying that anxiety is an important co-determinate in motivating our knowing. But anxiety is always a signal of a threat to something man is "intending," whether it be an instinctual need, stimulus hunger, or, as will be mentioned later in the paper, the validation of certain self-values. The concept of anxiety is only meaningful when it is understood as a threat to other needs and intentions of man. More specifically, let it be clear that I am not reducing man's positive interest in the world, whether it be called stimulus hunger or curiosity (Tolman), to what some might call a "defense against anxiety." Our positive interest in experiencing the world may lead to anxiety, which will then produce within us defensive maneuvers.

order and external adaptation in the midst of this change and expansion. The gestalt character of our cognitive processes creates a need to maintain some inner order between the various parts of our cognitive map of the world. But because of the expansive character of the organism, this ordering of cognitive maps can never be accomplished outside of some attempt toward outer adaptation. The integrity of our system of constructs about the world can be maintained only if they are, in fact, reasonably accurate approximations about the nature of external reality, supported and reaffirmed by successive feedbacks from experience. Adaptation, at this level, goes beyond mere coping with reality for purposes of survival. Adaptation here means establishing workable hypotheses about the organization and nature of the outer world, in an effort to find continuity and mutual support between these outer realities and our inner cognitive maps.[8] We need to maintain adaptive continuity between our cognitive maps and the external world, whether or not we are actively interested in controlling and predicting this world, although this certainly constitutes part of our motivation on occasions. We are also motivated by the simple fact that our cognitive gestalts cannot stand the ambiguity of unassimilated data. Thus, in some instances, a man may develop hypotheses of interpretation which may not lead to very immediate possibilities of prediction and control, as is true of all metaphysical speculation and the research of the so-called pure sciences. Man either attempts to maintain the integrity and gestalt character of his world by establishing sensible hypotheses about his experience, or he retreats from the experience so that his cognitive map will not have to undergo the anxiety of a temporarily unassimilable datum. But because of man's innate need for new experience, man has, on the whole, chosen the path of knowing rather than the path of retreat.

It may be appropriate at this time to discuss the relation of knowing and believing. We have pointed out that the process of knowing is an attempt to establish a hypothesis

[8] Hilgard, "The Role of Learning in Perception" (see footnote 6), p. 109.

about an experience which will resolve conflict and meet need, however variously one might define conflict and need. A belief is a hypothesis upon which we have learned to rely. A belief is a meaningful and reasonably well established part of our fund of hypotheses about the world. Many of our beliefs undergo change and refinement, as the feedback from experience presents us with new conflicts and prompts us to find more workable and stabilizing approximations about reality. In general, the more unsure we feel about the viability of our system of hypotheses, the more dogmatically and blindly we will try to force reality to conform to our belief systems. Rogers refers to this process as "intentional" perception, rather than "extentional," which allows the data of experience to fill, broaden and refine our constructs about events.[9] From a psychological perspective, it seems that our hypotheses must be held firmly enough to permit reasonably stable internal order and external adaptiveness, but not so dogmatically as to preclude subsequent refinement. At best, as Whitehead has suggested, our constructs about the world are perspectival and proximate.

Knowing and the Phenomenal Self

So far, we have been discussing abstractly the nature of knowing in the real self, detached from its relation to what we might call the phenomenal self. Theoretically it may be possible to do this, but it is not possible in actuality. For in reality the needs of the phenomenal self provide the most embracing and consistently influential dynamic context for our processes of knowing, and these needs are crucially important for clarifying our understanding of the meaning of knowing and believing as these processes should be thought of in a theological context.

What is the phenomenal self, and how does it come into being? There are several different ways to distinguish between self and ego. For the purposes of this paper, we will

[9] Carl Rogers, "A Theory of Therapy, Personality, and Interpersonal Relationships," in *Psychology: A Study of a Science*, 6 vols., ed. S. Koch (New York: McGraw Hill, 1959), 3:205.

follow the lead of William James and George Herbert Mead. We will associate the ego with the "I" — the observing, perceiving, and thinking apparatuses which guide a person in his transaction with the world. The self will be associated with the "me" — the "I" as "observed."[10] A rudimentary sense of "I" probably develops out of an awareness of bodily functioning.[11] It develops out of the awareness that some things seem to be more under our control than do other things. The self or "me," on the other hand, is the evaluative elaboration that the ego assigns to its functioning. The perceiving, observing ego can look back reflexively upon this functioning; and what it observes, the values it learns to place on this functioning, and the propositions it learns to use in referring to them, constitute the phenomenal self.[12]

It is important to understand that the observing ego perceives the phenomenal self as one of many objects in its perceptual field, an object different from others because, as Allport points out, of the warmth the observing ego associates with this object.[13] The ego gets to know the self in the same way that it gets to know any other object in its perceptual field. It attempts to elaborate and maintain, against the feedback of subsequent self-experience, certain hypotheses and propositions, which will provide a gestalt-like inner consistency of self-perceptions. But the ego's own direct experience, observation, and evaluation of the self does not provide the totality of the data for its attempt to establish adequate hypotheses about the self. It must also take into account the

[10] James, *Psychology: The Briefer Course* (New York: Harper & Brothers, 1961), p. 43; Mead, *Mind, Self, and Society*, ed. Charles W. Morris (Chicago: University of Chicago Press, 1934), pp. 173–78.

[11] Carl Rogers, *Client-Centered Therapy* (Boston: Houghton Mifflin Co., 1951), p. 498.

[12] In this paper, I will use the concept of "phenomenal self" rather than James's concept of "empirical self" or Horney's idea of the "actual self," all of which are roughly equivalent terms. The term "phenomenal self" is associated generally with the work of Donald Snygg and Arthur W. Combs, *Individual Behavior: A New Frame of Reference for Psychology* (New York: Harper and Brothers, 1949).

[13] Gordon Allport, *Becoming* (New Haven: Yale University Press, 1955), p. 40.

propositions and evaluations placed upon itself by its social context. Part of what it means to get to know the self is to get to know the place the self occupies in the totality of other objects and other selves. To know what places the self occupies with other selves, it is necessary for the observing ego to take into account the propositions and evaluations of other people about itself. As Prescott Lecky has stated (although he did not use the distinction I am using between the observing ego and the observed self to express it), it is a fundamental need of man to have a consistent and ordered perception of the self.[14] But, as was mentioned above, in every act of knowing, the attempt to establish inner order must go hand in hand with the attempt to establish outer adaptation to reality. Hence, the ego's attempt to know the self must be accomplished through a perpetual dialogue between its own self-experiences and its perception of the way other people are experiencing its self.[15] Or, to put it less pedantically, a person gets to know himself through pooling his own self-experiences with what he can infer about how other people experience him.

Identity, Knowing, and the Phenomenal Self

This sense of continuity between self-perception and the perception of the self by a significant social matrix is the stuff out of which personal identity is built. Erikson points to this when he states that a person's sense of self-identity is accomplished when "one's sense of continuity and sameness is matched by the continuity and sameness of the other's expectation and recognition of him." [16] This is his way of saying what we have said within the terms of our general analysis of knowing — that self-identity is established when our hypotheses about our selves seem to be confirmed and supported by the feedback that we get from our community. This continuity between self-perception and social recognition makes

[14] Lecky, *Self-Consistency* (New York: Inland Press, 1945), p. 82.
[15] Mead, *Mind, Self, and Society*, p. 174.
[16] Erik H. Erikson, *Identity and the Life Cycle* (New York: International Universities Press, 1960), p. 89.

it possible to orient toward life in a relatively self-consistent and stable fashion.

As Erickson points out, the emerging outlines of an individual's identity should be consolidated sometime before the end of the adolescent years. But its formation was started at the beginning of life and was wrought out of numerous successive stages of crises, conflict, and resolution. According to his view of development, life is a process of moving into ever enlarging circles of experience, which periodically present an individual with new challenges to old self-perceptions and old continuities between self and community recognition. These crises or conflicts are created in part by the maturation of new constitutional givens (the epigenetic principle) and in part by new patterns of expectation coming from our social milieu. Each stage of crisis or conflict can be resolved only when new self-hypotheses are developed which establish a sense of sameness and continuity on a new basis, a basis that is in some way shared and confirmed by the significant others in an individual's life. Because the self is a gestalt and, like all gestalts, must maintain an inner integrity, every new emergence (challenge) constitutes a temporary threat (conflict) to the self, calling present organizations into question.

In the course of development, an individual will have constructed several hypotheses about himself, all of which may not fit together easily into a consistent whole. To bring coherence into this diversity, a person must develop a set of general hypotheses that will serve to synthesize some, and repudiate other, lower-order hypotheses. And these general hypotheses, which integrate lower-order hypotheses and self-experiences, must fit also with the perception of one's identity that seems to be held by a significant part of our community. The best identity is the most inclusive — the one that integrates the largest number of self-experiences, old identifications, biological needs, and capacities of the real self. To this extent, identity must give centeredness to the total experience of the organism as this experience is symbolized in the self.

The importance of the fact that self-identity is derived from a correspondence between self-perception and community recognition, cannot be emphasized too strongly for the purposes of our discussion. It points to the self-world correlation basic to all self-identity. Propositions and hypotheses about the self are also, indirectly, propositions and hypotheses about the world which, through response, recognition, and challenge, helps to form the self's image of itself. A person's self-beliefs reflect highly consistent and reliable ways in which his social world, or at least a part of it, has tended to recognize, respond to, or reflect upon the individual's feelings and actions. Hence, a person's self-identity is an internalization of certain patterns of consistency resident in his world.

Let me make several additional points about knowing and believing as they apply to self-identity. First, it should be understood that, by using the words "proposition" and "hypothesis," I am not suggesting that these self-descriptions composing our identity are always conscious. Some self-hypotheses are preconscious and, in some cases, even unconscious. Nor am I judging the superior validity of either set of self-hypothesis — the conscious or the unconscious ones. That may vary, depending upon the individual situation. Nor am I suggesting that all self-identity hypotheses should be conscious. There is doubtless a place for preconscious self-propositions.

It is true, though, that there should be continuity between conscious and unconscious, surface and depth, figure and ground, before identity can be said to rest on a truly solid foundation. Much of psychotherapy is a process of unifying figure and ground, surface and depth, with regard to identity. That a person can learn conflicting identities and, through an effort to maintain self-consistency, repress one aspect of the conflict, is a phenomenon with which every therapist is quite familiar. Therapy is simply a process whereby the therapist attempts to give a consistently accepting mode of recognition to the client, so that he can develop a new self-identity which will permit a wider inclusion of older conflicting identities.

Furthermore, it is best to understand the hypotheses and

propositions that make up our self-identity as feelings with varying degrees of richness, containing forms that may achieve varying degrees of definite symbolic representation in consciousness. That self-propositions can become relatively dissociated from feelings (what Rogers called organismic experience, or what Gendlin has called "implicitly meaningful experiencing," or what Whitehead and Emmet would call, respectively, perception at the level of causal efficacy, or "adverbial experiencing," is something well confirmed by the vacuous self-references of some schizophrenics and the wooden and anxiety-loden self-descriptions of some neurotics.[17] Self-identity is probably strongest when built upon a foundation of rich interaction with the world at the level of causal efficacy from which clear self-propositions have been gleaned and then tested through a process of acting on these hypotheses — and observing subsequent feedback and response. This explains the perpetual preoccupation of every therapeutic process with feelings. It is not a capitulation to subjectivism. It is the recognition that all propositions, including self-propositions, are basically feeling propositions — feelings with a form that may not become articulated clearly.[18] This truth was recognized philosophically by Whitehead [19] and has been a practical fact for all psychotherapeutic psychology. Before self-identity can become enlarged or changed, the basic feeling propositions upon which self-identity rests must become explicit and available for revision in the light of new experience.

By suggesting that identity is made out of a mutuality of self-perception and community recognition, I do not mean to specify which "community" but only to indicate that the

[17] Rogers, *Client-Centered Therapy*, p. 483; Eugene Gendlin, *Experiencing and the Creation of Meaning* (New York: The Free Press of Glencoe, 1962), pp. 44–62; Alfred North Whitehead, *Process and Reality* (New York: Harper and Brothers, 1960), pp. 255–79; Dorothy Emmet, *The Nature of Metaphysical Thinking* (London: Macmillan & Co., 1961), p. 42.

[18] Martin Scheerer, "Cognitive Theory" in *Handbook of Social Psychology*, ed. Gardner Lindsey (Reading, Mass.: Addison-Wesley Publishing Co., 1954), p. 123.

[19] Whitehead, *Process and Reality*, p. 291.

community must be "significant" for the individual involved, before identity can be built with reference to it. The particular reference group providing support for one's identity may be parents, friends, the upper class, the elite of the profession to which one belongs, or it may, as it has in some instances, consist of ancestors, the church, Jesus and the apostles, or even God. Whichever the group, one's identity will in large part be made up of the consistencies of recognition which one has come to perceive and expect from these significant social sources.

Lastly, the way that we know ourselves has much to do with the way we know other objects in the world. Our self-identity determines, to a great extent, what we are interested in knowing, what we believe we *can* come to know and *should* come to know. Our self-identity includes the value structure by which we judge ourselves. This value system probably will reflect the value system of the reference community in the light of whose recognition we attempt to establish our identity. If one's identity is defined totally with reference to financial concerns and groups, a person may inattend selectively to literary, philosophical, or other speculative concerns.[20] Even if these things are forced upon him, he may not be able to comprehend them; the present gestalt of his self-identity does not include propositional feelings that give importance to these areas or that describe himself as one who can understand such things.

Scientists constitute a segment of our society that attempts to neutralize the importance of self-values for the knowing process. They do this by committing themselves to certain methodologies designed to control the intrusion of personal biases. The difficulty with this is that their commitment to certain methodologies becomes a part of the value system of their self-identity, often heavily reenforced and perpetuated by a reference group likewise committed to these methodologies. This tends to make it difficult for the scientist to grasp data that does not readily fit within the methodological boundaries that have become a part of his personal identity.

[20] Bruner, "Personality Dynamics" (see footnote 6), p. 132.

In order for us to come to know something that our self-system has defined previously as unimportant, irrelevant, or threatening, our self-system must undergo a crisis and a redefinition, so that this new area of the world can become a part of our concern. Hence, the elements of conflict, hypothesis, and testing become important for knowing at every level. Even if we could imagine pure cognitive processes, unrelated to a phenomenal self with a certain identity, the knowing process, as we have seen, would consist of an effort to maintain consistency of cognitive wholes, reconciling new perceptions with old cognitive maps by a process of engendering new hypotheses to be tested. But since all cognitive processes are embedded in a self-system, they never operate independently from the attempt of the self to maintain an experience of continuity and sameness amidst the world of changing perceptions. It is because our cognitive processes are embedded in a self-system formed substantially by our social and cultural context, that the discipline of sociology of knowledge becomes relevant for an understanding of the knowing process.

Knowing and the Structure of Faith

With the help of the foregoing discussions, let me put forward a possible understanding of the nature of "faith" as this word might be used in a theological context. Faith is a series of feeling propositions (hypotheses) that an individual holds with a high degree of certainty. They perform the following three functions: (1) they indicate how an individual understands himself; (2) they indicate how an individual understands the person or group with reference to whom he defines himself; and (3) they serve to organize or center the totality of all other partial self-definitions.

An exegesis of this formal characterization of faith must include the following points. First, this definition points out that faith is neither a totally subjective nor an objective phenomenon. Faith is neither a category which applies totally to one's own subjective self-understanding, nor a set of attitudes totally directed toward an outer, objective event or person.

A person's self-identity is built up through a process of, on the one hand, coming to know another person or group primarily in terms of how they recognize him, and, on the other hand, coming to know himself primarily in terms of how he is recognized by these others.

Faith, of course, contains this subjective and objective pole in relation to one's significant other, or what sociologists might call one's reference group or individual. The point is that faith, as a matter of self-identity, contains within it feeling propositions about both the reference object and the self. These propositions will contain statements or feelings about what the reference object is, what constitutes the nature of its authority, how the reference object perceives and rcognizes the self, and, therefore, what constitutes the definition of the self implied by this recognition. Bultmann, who defines faith as a matter of self-understanding (something close to what we mean by self-identity), is aware of the fact that self-understanding carries within it knowledge about that with reference to which one defines himself.[21] To define faith as self-identity is not to subjectify it; but it does move beyond scholastic definitions of faith as an act of *assensus* to certain propositional truths. Faith as self-identity integrates subjective self-understanding and objective fact into one existential whole.

Second, this characterization suggests that faith is in the same category as other beliefs, hypotheses, or hunches. It suggests that faith propositions are differentiated from lower-order beliefs and hypotheses by (a) their inclusiveness, (b) the fact that they primarily apply to that object in one's perceptual field symbolized as the self and those relations in terms of which the self is defined, and (c) a degree of certainty that transcends the deferential, calculative, and probabilistic character of hypotheses and beliefs guiding more immediate adaptation.

Third, this point of view suggests that faith as a form of self-identity is always fashioned against a background of doubt.

[21] Rudolph Bultmann, *Theology of the New Testament*, 2 vols. (New York: Charles Scribner's Sons, 1951), 1:318.

Self-identity is developed against a background of some uncertainty and conflict about who one is and how one is perceived by significant others. No matter how certain and stable our identity becomes, we never move beyond the necessity of making partial alterations in our self-definitions in the light of new challenges that changing experience brings. That moment of uncertainty between the dissolution of an old identity, no matter how partial or trivial, and the engendering, testing, and validating of new self-propositions, is always experienced as a flash of doubt. To this extent, faith must be understood as an effort to maintain the consistency of the self (its sense of sameness and continuity) by overcoming the dissolving and fragmenting experience of doubt.

It is possible to formulate the relation of faith and doubt in terms of traditional affirmations about the meaning of Jesus Christ. Faith in Jesus Christ can be thought to mean that one has gained his identity with reference to the person of Jesus Christ. In this event, one's identity would be defined in terms of the presumed attitude of Jesus Christ toward one's self, and this attitude would be granted significance according to the kind of authority upon which this attitude was thought to be grounded. But even if the perceived attitude of Jesus is thought to be one of invariant love, and the person of faith has learned to know himself as consistently loved and, therefore, enduringly lovable, the outer boundaries of the believer's self-definition will still always be undergoing change and revision. The contingent and variable character of the totality of finite sources of recognition constantly precipitate major and minor crises in self-definition, even for the man of faith. Faith in Jesus Christ as an invariant source of affirming and justifying love does not transport the person of faith from crises in self-definition produced by the fluctuation of finite events and social situations. Instead, the perceived invariant and divinely authoritative love of Jesus Christ provides, for those who find their core identity in terms of it, an ultimate and unconditioned source of recognition, which then relativizes (renders nonultimate) all other sources of recognition. It makes it impossible for the Christian to measure the totality of his worth or significance in the light of any finite reality. Faith-identity, as we have defined it, provides for the believer a stable framework, in the context of which the contingencies of life become more manageable. In this respect, faith-identity is the ultimate buffer against the anxiety produced by life's finite and transient character. The function of faith-identity can be stated in terms descriptive of the processes of perception. Hilgard points out that the goal of perception is stability, and that when this stability is threatened, one's perceptual processes will attempt to gain orientation by stabilizing the context (ground) at the expense of specific detail (figure).[22] In the light of this, the Christian faith must be understood to be asserting that the context is stable, that there is a ground of invariant affirmation which enables the faithful (those who accept and orient themselves to this ground) to maintain their identity amidst all finite threats to it.

Fourth, it becomes possible, within this understanding of the relation of faith and self-identity, to comprehend the dynamic meaning of all efforts to define God's nature as immutable or *a se*. Within the tradition of classical Greek and scholastic philosophy, defining God as immutable and *a se* was thought necessary to guarantee his perfection. Imperfection was thought to be equivalent to transcience, and perfection, to intransience or immovability. Soteriologically, it was important to protect God's immutability in order to protect his trustworthiness as a reliable source for the maintenance and salvation of the world. Although this was a worthy concern, it is now possible to state the significance of such a concept by pointing out the importance of an invariant source of affirmation necessary for all stable self-identity. It can be said that God is immutable in the sense that he invariantly affirms men in his humanness and in the sense that nothing outside God can qualify his capacity to do this. Of course, when immutability is seen to have this significance, it no longer becomes necessary to assert God's immutability in *all*

[22] Hilgard, "The Role of Learning in Perception" (see footnote 6), p. 104.

respects. From this perspective of faith-identity, the importance of God's immutability is what it implies about his capacity for invariant love. In the light of these considerations, the constructions of Charles Hartshorne gain added persuasiveness. He suggests that God is conditioned at least in one sense: in his *knowing* of man he is qualified (moved) by man's own mutability. But, according to Hartshorne, although God is moved and qualified when he knows man, he nevertheless knows man completely and perfectly. Hence, from the standpoint of the way we are defining faith-identity, it would be important for God to be *a se* in some respects but not in all respects. For instance, it would be important for God to be immutable and invariant in knowing and loving mankind, but it would not be necessary for God to be beyond qualification in every respect.[23]

Lastly, faith as the idea of self-identity grounded in God's unconditioned love has great implications for the freeing of one's cognitive structures. If knowing is embedded in a self with certain values, knowing cannot be free from the selective distortions that these values impose until they have become relativized. A person's values cannot become relativized until he finds a way to maintain his self-identity without absolute reliance upon finite values. It is only when one's values are held heuristically (although in some instances still quite dearly), that one's knowing can possess the flexibility to adapt to reality in all its variety. It is precisely the message of the Christian faith that God's love is *agape* love, unconditioned by the worth, value, or particular values affirmed by the object of his love. Organizing one's identity around *agape* should tend to liberate the cognitive processes of the believing Christian from the distorting maneuvers of overdetermined or absolutized self-values. Since contingent values do not constitute the core of the Christian's identity, he should be relatively free to develop a broad range of hypotheses about reality and to attend to the feedback of experience, without feeling an overwhelming threat to his identity. This suggests that iden-

[23] Charles Hartshorne, *Man's Vision of God* (Chicago: Willet, Clark and Co., 1941), p. 14.

tity based on *agape* is the ground for the bracketing of pre-suppositions characteristic of the phenomenological stance with the flexibility of hypothesis construction characteristic of all science.

Faith-identity, Barth, and Schleiermacher

We have considered briefly what the concept of faith-identity might mean for several theological issues. But to test the validity of this position, we must determine, at some depth, its potency to address and enlighten significant theological debate. The controversy surrounding the figures of Barth and Schleiermacher on the subject of faith constituted an important, though somewhat prejudicially handled, topic for discussion during the post-liberal theological renaissance of the middle third of our century. In some ways, the debate was unfortunate because one party to the discussion was dead and could not speak for himself. Since the debate was somewhat of a monologue, we should not be surprised to note that its historic deposit has tended to suggest the following over-simplification: that Barth's view of faith is objective and that Schleiermacher's was subjective. Although the discussion that follows in this essay cannot probe very deeply into either of these thinkers, it may be possible to bring their apparently divergent views into closer proximity with one another. So we will ask: what would our concept of faith-identity imply for their alleged differences?

Barth would agree with the position of this paper, that faith is an act of the whole personality. In the terminology and conceptual formulations of what psychologists call "self-theory," it was earlier asserted that the self that defines itself on the basis of Christ's perception of our humanity also unifies, centers, and gathers into one coherent system all other anthropological capacities in terms of this identity. Barth states something like this when he asserts that faith is created by the Word of God and "is definitely a determination of the whole self-determining man." [24] Barth rejects all efforts to

[24] Karl Barth, *Church Dogmatics*, (New York: Charles Scribner's Sons, 1955), vol. 1, pt. 1, p. 233.

associate faith with any particular anthropological realm, be it intellect (Aquinas), moral consciousness (Kant), or feeling (Schleiermacher).[25] Barth would have two criticisms of attempts to associate faith with any particular anthropological capacity, and both, he believed, were applicable to Schleiermacher. The criticisms are as follows: efforts to associate faith with a particular anthropological realm may tend (1) to obscure the fact that faith is fully objective, fully rational, and based on fully real knowledge, and (2) to balance human and divine causality in the creation of faith, obscuring the fact that faith is fully determined by the Word of God.

Let us make a few comments about the first point. Barth rejects the concept of faith as naked intellectual assent (*assensus*). Faith is primarily *fiducia* (trust), but includes within it both intellectual assent (*assensus*) and information (*noticia*).[26] Hence, faith (*pistis*) is trust (*fiducia*) which contains knowledge (gnosis) about that which one trusts. One who has faith knows the object of his faith and can give assent to the knowledge implicit in his trust. Faith is a rational (*ratio*) act, although it is more than just a mater of intellect (*intelligere*). Faith includes intellect, but also involves the totality of man's anthropological capacities. It is Barth's thesis that the totality of man's anthropological capacities should be considered, in the broadest sense, precisely as rational capacities.

The second point is continuous with the first, but has a slightly different focus. Barth insists that no particular anthropological realm contains the ground of faith; the Word of God is the ground of faith as it determines the whole self-determining man. This concept of faith, it can be suggested, assumes a theory of knowledge akin to philosophical realism. According to Barth, one can be said to know another object when one completely conforms one's mind to the structure of that object. By this, Barth means to suggest that one knows the Word of God when one completely conforms to its nature

[25] *Ibid.*
[26] *Ibid.*, p. 269.

as revealed in Scripture. Barth insists that man brings nothing to his encounter with the Word of God by which he can attempt to validate it, judge it, or find some ground upon which certainty — other than that conveyed by the Word itself — can be established. Barth does not believe that one can validate faith by appealing to how it makes one *feel*, how it makes one *act*, or how reasonable it seems. All of these are efforts to establish "I-certainty" and place the believer above the Word, forcing the Word to conform to men's standards rather than forming man to its standards and self-validating claims.

One can readily see how Barth would be critical of Schleiermacher. Schleiermacher defines faith as a feeling of absolute dependence on God. To Barth, this implies that Schleiermacher subjectifies faith, denuding it of knowledge and objectivity. Barth would further charge that Schleiermacher's position implies that one's *feeling* of the Word, rather than the Word itself, becomes the object of theological reflection as well as the grounds for authority. Do these criticisms hold? Or do they spring, to begin with, from an incomplete understanding of the nature of faith?

These criticisms are partially justified, and partially misinformed. But a final solution to the question of the nature of faith and knowing must attempt to combine both Schleiermacher and Barth. This is what we feel our concept of faith-identity accomplishes.

Schleiermacher does define faith within the category of feeling. But this means to Schleiermacher something very similar to what we referred to in the earlier part of the paper as one's self-concept or self-identity. Schleiermacher almost equates the terms "feeling" and "self-consciousness."[27] Feeling, as Schleiermacher uses it, refers to the way one feels or is conscious of oneself. It is with this understanding of the meaning of *feeling* that we should interpret the following definition of faith in God and faith in Jesus Christ. Faith in God is the "certainty concerning the feeling of absolute dependence as such, i.e., as conditioned by a Being placed outside of us,

[27] Friedrich Schleiermacher, *The Christian Faith* (Edinburgh: T. & T. Clark, 1928), p. 6.

and as expressing our relation to that Being."[28] Faith in Christ is the feeling of certainty that "the influence of Christ puts an end to the state of being in need of redemption."[29] To put it simply, one has faith in Christ when one comes to the certainty that, through him, one comes to the condition of having God-consciousness dominant in his life.

The following comments on these quotations need to be made. First, faith as feeling is not as subjective, for Schleiermacher, as it may seem. It is (a) the feeling of being dependent upon some power *outside* oneself, and (b) the feeling of certainty that it is through the historical Jesus that God-consciousness becomes dominant. It is clear, then, that although Schleiermacher explicitly denies that faith is a matter of knowledge, he does believe that feelings implicitly contain objective knowledge. He also believes that this objective knowledge can be made explicit and brought into what he calls "objective consciousness."[30] Furthermore, faith, for Schleiermacher, is an experience of having one's feeling or self-consciousness formed, caused, and determined by something outside oneself.

It is probably true that Schleiermacher did not emphasize enough that faith is built on knowledge. But it is also true that Barth does not emphasize enough that faith implies something about how the believer comes to understand and feel about himself. I believe that faith interpreted with the concept of identity can best integrate these two dimensions.

Let us review some of the points made earlier that are relevant to this discussion. First, it was maintained that identity always implies a *self-world correlation*. It implies something objective about how some external source of recognition perceives one; it also implies something subjective about how one regards himself in the light of this recognition. Second, it was asserted that identity is made up of *feeling propositions*. This implies that rational propositions and feelings are not necessarily different things. All propositions about ourselves and

[28] *Ibid.*, p. 68.
[29] *Ibid.*
[30] *Ibid.*, pp. 9–11.

other objects are also feelings about ourselves and other objects. The reverse is also true. All feelings are to some extent propositions. This should help Barth be less skeptical about the importance of feelings for faith, but it also should serve to correct Schleiermacher's assertion that faith is a matter of feeling rather than knowledge. Third, although we have maintained that identity contains both an objective and a subjective pole, we also asserted a slight priority to the objective. We did this when we wrote that a person's self-identity is an internalization of certain patterns of consistency of recognition resident in his social world. By social world, of course, was meant the significant other or others toward whom one orients his life, be it parent, wife, church, Christ, or God. The point is that identity is fashioned from the outside in. Barth is clearly correct at this point. But we can quickly add that Schleiermacher was also well aware of this truth; one had faith, according to him, when one realized that the "whence" of one's active and passive lives comes from God. Our concept of faith-identity joins with Schleiermacher and Barth in asserting the priority of the objective, external, influencing factor in the creation of identity. But, finally, the concept of faith-identity set forth above would support Schleiermacher over against Barth, in allowing for a greater sense of accrued feeling (subjectivity) about "who we are" as an important dimension of faith not always fully accounted for by the great Swiss theologian.

6

Living Faith:
Some Contributions of the Concept of Ego-identity
to the Understanding of Faith

LELAND ELHARD

"For faith is movement and happening,
it is life, fulfilled life."
GERHARD EBELING[1] *The Nature of Faith*

Introduction

It is the aim of this essay to demonstrate the illuminating,
enriching, and unifying relevance to the understanding of
faith of the concept "ego-identity," which is one of the chief
concepts of the modern study of the ego. Developments in
the study of religious faith indicate that this expression of
the perspective of ego psychology on the integrating and relating dimensions of human existence is compatible with such
understanding.

This essay proceeds on the supposition that man's ongoing
experience is always of vital concern to him. Both a relevant
theology and a responsible psychology recognize that their
perspectives are, at least in part, "existential." They must take
into account that their observations and reflections are man's
attempts to "make sense" of his experiences in the world, to
discover his center, to organize his wholeness, and to establish
satisfying relationships to reality in all dimensions, including
the ultimate. This essay holds that no one finite perspective,
theology included, is able, by itself, to exhaust the configuration of this experience. Just as two eyes are better than one,

[1] *The Nature of Faith*, trans. Ronald Gregor Smith (Philadelphia:
Fortress Press, 1961), p. 21.

135

so also two perspectives side by side, in tune with each other, are better than one for perceiving the depths and intricacies of what is really there. Therefore, this theological essay employs the perspective of ego-psychology to enhance its understanding of the believing human being. It uses the concept of identity and finds it especially helpful in relation to the concept of faith as seen from the perspective of theology.

This essay uses a descriptive method. With the help of a number of thinkers in theology and psychology, it keeps describing what it sees as it views from all angles the experiencing, believing, human configuration. As each new glimpse both alters and confirms previous views, we gain clarity and confidence in "what is there."

This essay limits itself and its use of the identity concept to a discussion of faith as personal, dynamic experience in the present. It is concerned with the "subjective" side of faith, the "faith that believes," although the "faith that is believed" is found to be always involved. This essay operates on the basis of Tillich's definition and elaborates on it: "Faith as ultimate concern is an act of the total personality. It happens in the center of the personal life and includes all its elements." [2] In this context of the experience of faith, we observe with Erik Erikson that the attributes of the ego are akin to the attributes of faith. He says in *Young Man Luther*,[3] "I will

[2] Paul Tillich, *Dynamics of Faith* (New York: Harper Torchbooks, Harper & Brothers, 1958), p. 4. For those who are especially sensitive to "psychodynamics," we might suggest that Tillich's definition of faith is in harmony with the growing awareness of ego-psychology that the driving forces and real depths of the person cannot be reduced to isolated, separate, psychological "drives" or to primitive needs for physiological tension reduction, imperative and continuous as they are. It has been rediscovered that the dynamics of man's behavior have uniquely human characteristics associated with the whole configuration of his present experience. The "dynamics of the configuration," the drive to become a centered self, discussed at length in this essay, is understood as the most profound dynamic in human behavior. See G. W. Allport, *Pattern and Growth in Personality* (New York: Holt, Rinehart and Winston, 1961), pp. 196–256, esp. p. 237, and K. Goldstein, "Organismic Approach to the Problem of Motivation," N. Y. *Academy of Sciences, Transactions*, 9 (1947): 218–50.

[3] (New York: W. W. Norton & Co., 1958), p. 206.

try to indicate that Luther, in laying the foundation for a 'religiosity for the adult man,' displayed the attributes of his own hard-won adulthood; his renaissance of faith portrays a vigorous recovery of his own ego-initiative."

Allen Wheelis' portrayal of the "quest for identity" highlights the religious aspects of the contemporary concern for identity. He does so in existential and ultimate terms in his novel, *The Seeker*: [4]

> Having lost the eternity God once promised me I'm not going to get excited by a millennium.
>
> This, I think, is a conflict for which there is no solution. It has simply to be endured. To be human depends upon the awareness of an incommunicable self; to be civilized depends upon an identification of self with the social process. The meaning of my life lies in my contribution to this process, but it is with the interior life that I feel identified. I can endure its destruction, but cannot be reconciled to it. . . .
>
> Maybe nothing could make it easier to die, nothing except some kind of falsehood. But that remains to be seen. I must not prejudge it. What I need is something that will function as religion in making me feel a part of a larger whole, and yet to be free of myth and magic, a faith that will weld me to others and yet not claim to be an absolute.

A Description of Ego-Identity

Four components, inseparably a part of each other, appear to comprise identity. One, identity is a pervasive inner sense of self, of being a unity, a continuity and a mastery in the midst of the confusion of immediate experience. Two, this sense of identity arises only in relationships with others. Three, a number of polar tensions are present in these relationships. Four, this sense of identity is continually "in process," a process impelled by these tensions. Thus, the words "pervasive sense," "relationship," "tension" and "process"

[4] (New York: Signet Book, New American Library, 1960), pp. 187–89.

summarize what identity is about. These components are reviewed successively and interrelatedly in the following discussion.

Erikson describes ego-identity as a *sense*, meaning an overall attitude (*Grundhaltung*) which is deeper than self-concept. Like a "sense of health," or a sense of "being unwell," identity pervades the surface and depth of the person. It is a way "of *experiencing* accessible to introspection" and "of *behaving* observable by others." It is also one of the *unconscious inner states* determined by test and analysis.[5] When one has achieved a sense of identity, he preconsciously feels "at home in his body." He "knows where he's going and has an inner assuredness of anticipated recognition from those who count."[6] In times of not having an adequate measure of these senses and feelings, one stops taking them for granted and becomes self-conscious of the identity problem. He may then more openly assert *his* view of self and world and/or question himself, "Who am I," "What am I doing?" and the like. Similarly, we note that faith, also, is taken for granted when the "situation is normal." Then, in times of social change, of challenge and crisis, man becomes self-consciously aware of "having faith" in the context of the possibility of "losing faith." Developmentally speaking, *the* time of the more or less self-conscious identity-crisis, adolescence, is also *the* time of ideological unrest, religious doubt, and conversions. Erikson has a continuing interest in various "great men" who merge their crises of identity and integrity with the larger questions of cultural and human meaning. He finds that these people and, to some degree, all deeply, personally, religious people are "forever adolescing." They plumb the depths of existential crisis and identity and do so with extraordinary self-consciousness.

Erickson's core definition of the sense of ego-identity is "the accrued confidence that one's ability to maintain inner

[5] Erik H. Erikson, *Childhood and Society*, 2d ed., rev. (New York: W. W. Norton & Co., 1964), p. 251.

[6] Erikson, "Identity and the Life Cycle," *Psychological Issues*, 1, no. 1, (1959), p. 118.

sameness and continuity (one's ego in the psychological sense) is matched by the sameness and continuity of one's meaning for others."[7] That identity is a kind of dialectical relationship between the self and the other is also suggested in other definitions of it. A person "feels most himself where he means most to others," where these others are those who "mean most to him." Ernest Becker's work on identity emphasizes the life-long dynamic of this valuing aspect. He refers to the necessity of continued "self-esteem," the "warm feeling of self-righteousness,"[8] and of the reinforcement by the social transaction of the conviction that one is an "object of primary value in a world of meaningful action."[9]

Both Erikson and Becker emphasize that the individual's own action and response, the exercise of his gifts, is also vital to his sense of identity.[10] The person "chooses and creates his environment of others even as he is chosen and created by them."[11] He must have some sense of being master in his own house of experience, of it being *his* experience, with a sense of the reality of his own unique powers. Thus, an adequate identity is not merely passive, at the mercy of the recognition of others. Rather, it is "*self-realization* coupled with a mutual recognition."[12] Angyal's formulation agrees when he sees two complementing directions of "autonomy" and "homonomy." "How . . . to do what one wants to do and be loved for it" is the human dilemma. He sees the two sides, "for oneself" and "for others," merging. "The human being is both a unifier, an organizer of his immediate personal world, and a participant in what he conceives to be the superordinate

[7] *Ibid.*, p. 89.
[8] Becker, *The Birth and Death of Meaning* (New York: The Free Press of Glencoe, 1962), p. 79.
[9] *Ibid.*, p. 81.
[10] Erikson has especially developed this side of the story in his recent essay, "Psychological Reality and Historical Actuality" but he has spoken of it consistently. See chap. 5 in Erikson's *Insight and Responsibility* (New York: W. W. Norton and Company, 1964).
[11] Erikson, "Late Adolescence," *The Student and Mental Health: An International View*, ed. D. H. Funkenstein (World Federation of Mental Health and International Association of Universities, 1959), p. 76.
[12] Erikson, "Identity and the Life Cycle," pp. 113–14.

whole to which he belongs. His striving for mastery is embedded in his longing for participation."[13]

Erikson continually sees a mutuality of individuality and participation. The individual life cycle and man's corresponding social institutions have evolved together.[14] To become socialized and to become an individual are two aspects of one developmental process whose climax is "integrity." In "integrity," becoming socialized is climaxed in the fullest realization of one's concern for and participation with humanity as a whole; and becoming an individual is climaxed in that this same participation is a self-realization, and the concern is a "detached" concern.[15]

This polarity of self and other is based upon man's capacity to relate to himself as an object within a larger context by means of his powers of symbolization in language including memory, imagination, and the cultural and symbolic ritual. He is not a mere body behaving in immediacy; he *has* experiences, *has* a body, *has* a past, *has* a future. He "locates" himself self-consciously in relation to other persons and things in time and space. All of this is focused in his name, the central symbol of his existence. His name is the location of his definiteness in the midst of the indefiniteness of physical experiencing. It is the locus of perceiving, feeling, acting and being acted upon, valuing and being valued. One's name is inseparable from a definite way of "doing and undergoing" in the world. It is part of a style recognizable to oneself and to others, a developing pattern, a unique gestalt, which focuses one's experience. It is part of a self-central image, which places one in relation to all other images of reality. Also, just as symbolization and communication are two aspects of one process, so too are individual identity and group identity. We establish ourselves as identities always in reference of sociohistorical groups. By means of images of "good" and

[13] Andras Angyal, *Neurosis and Treatment: A Holistic Theory*, ed. E. Hanfmann and R. M. Jones (New York: John Wiley and Sons, 1965), p. 29.

[14] Erikson, *Childhood and Society*, p. 250.

[15] Erikson, *Insight and Responsibility* (New York: W. W. Norton & Co., 1964), p. 133.

"evil" portrayed in word and ritual, we share with some, we repudiate others.

Thus, "identity and ideology are two aspects of the same process."[16] Self-image and world-image, phenomenal self and phenomenal world[17] are interrelated. The "way life is," as viewed, supports the "way of life," as lived. Erikson defines ideology as "an unconscious tendency underlying religious and scientific as well as political thought: the tendency at a given time to make facts amendable to ideas, and ideas to facts, in order to create a world image convincing enough to support the collective and the individual sense of identity."[18] This "doctrinal logic" is united with a certain ritual and discipline of behavior, supremely expressed in what Erikson calls a "militant system with uniformed members and uniform goals."[19]

He notes the arbitrary nature of the ideological process as it is viewed by an uninvolved outside observer. Our feeling of inner freedom is always tied up with the acting out of the patterns which *happen to be* the limited historical content of our culture. Truth is an intensely subjective "truth for me," for my existence. Thus, Becker speaks of the "cultural fiction" and the "joint theatrical staging"[20] which characterize the effort of human symbolic behavior to establish a coherent and predictable context for valued, meaningful action. We are "on stage," acting out with utmost seriousness the only parts we know. Here we are confronted with the necessity and the power, but also the fragility and risks, involved in man's being a symbolizing animal. In this light we have a fresh glance at "the power of the word," as it were, to "make alive" or to "kill." The apostle Paul rightly calls preaching both foolishness *and* wisdom.

The fragility and danger of the ideological process lie in its propensity occasionally to lose touch with the real feel-

[16] Erikson, "Identity and the Life Cycle," p. 151.
[17] Arthur W. Combs and Donald Snygg, *Individual Behavior* (New York: Harper and Brothers, 1949).
[18] *Young Man Luther*, p. 22.
[19] *Ibid.*, p. 41.
[20] *Birth and Death of Meaning*, pp. 108–9.

ings and tensions of the person. Identity should be, ideally, "a pattern of verification which pervades one's whole being."[21] Becker finds that one's symbols may become "disembodied," separated from "organismic orientation." One may become schizophrenic in attempting to maintain the coherence and logic of the symbolic framework.[22] Meaning must be grounded in experience, the "answers" must be "behaved" in directed engagement with life.[23] One's identity, ideally, is being actualized in its self-expression in "vocation." A "whole" identity, where ideology and experience are united, is always a lived identity. It includes the verification of the reality of one's own powers, in relation to verifying encounter with the reality of things and with the real reactions of persons. The symbolic valuing must be intrinsically related to the experience. "Transcendent" schemes of meaning must have a referent "where the action is." Otherwise, they will be shipwrecked on the need of the person to be valued where he feels vulnerable, and on the need for his everyday ups and downs to have meaning and prudent ordering. Ideally, symbol and experience constantly enrich each other; in fact, for human beings, each is lost without the other.

Erikson has a sure grasp of this holistic view of man's nature. Some may see man as basically an "animal," who "becomes human" when he has enough culture "grafted on to him." Some posit an almost metaphysical self-actualization principle in man. It is blocked, distorted, released, and developed by culture. For Erikson, however, the "ground plan"[24] of body experience shapes culture and, in turn, through developmental "crises," culture completes physical experience. Man is never just animal. He is human and social "from the word go." Without culture he can not even "be" and survive physically. The basis for this assertion is Erikson's observation about the nature of human "instincts." They are not like

[21] Erikson, *Insight and Responsibility*, p. 172.
[22] Becker, *The Revolution in Psychiatry* (New York: The Free Press of Glencoe, 1964), p. 33.
[23] *Ibid.*, p. 14.
[24] Erikson, "Reflections on Womanhood," *Daedalus*, 93 (Spring, 1964): 592.

the animal's instincts, which are complete, which have built in patterns of completion, self-preservation, and interaction with other segments of nature. "Tradition and conscience" must organize man's drives.

> As an animal, man is nothing. It is meaningless to speak of a human child as if it were an animal in the process of domestication; or of his instincts as set patterns encroached upon or molded by the autocratic environment. Man's "inborn instincts" are drive fragments to be assembled, given meaning, and organized during a prolonged childhood by methods of child training and schooling which vary from culture to culture and are determined by tradition. In this lies his chance as an organism, as a member of a society, as an individual. In this also lies his limitation. For while the animal survives where his segment of nature remains predictable enough to fit his inborn patterns of instinctive response or where these responses contain the elements for necessary mutation, man survives only where traditional child training provides him with a conscience which will guide him without crushing him and which is firm and flexible enough to fit the vicissitudes of his historical era. . . . The human child learns to exist in space and time as he learns to be an organism in the space-time of his culture. Every part function thus learned is based on some integration of all the organ modes with one another and with the world image of their culture.[25]

Thus man cannot find the "fittedness" with reality, taken for granted by the animal world, and cannot be a whole individual apart from relationships. Every step and crisis in the development of the ego is transcended only by the person's taking into account or including in his phenomenal self a larger segment of social reality. Achieving identity is at the heart of this development.

As I sum up the observations of Erikson and of the rest of ego psychology about identity, I find three interrelated dy-

[25] Erikson, *Childhood and Society*, pp. 95–96.

namic aspects in it: unity, continuity and mastery. The unified, consistent, and masterful "face" of personal recognition, and the world-image of ideology with its "cosmic wholeness," "providential planfulness," and "heavenly sanction"[26] relate to these aspects. Such recognition and ideology reinforce these aspects in the unique image or gestalt of identity, which transcends and ties together all the conflicting identifications of one's social history. They should provide a consistency of context which bridges the discontinuities of internal developmental and external historical change, supporting the ego's thrust to provide a succession of experimentally relevant and interrelated images and a "longitudinal logic" for one's life career.[27] They should challenge and draw forth the ego's capacity to "be on top of," to master, its experience, to "have dominion" of one's own time and space, to live and to die actively, and not to have the "feeling that life is happening to the individual rather than being lived by his initiative."[28]

The unity, continuity, and mastery of experience, more or less guaranteed by the animal's instinctual mechanisms, is, for the human, a matter of social, symbolic transaction. The strain of this open-system transaction with its attendant contingencies and normal developmental anxieties is accentuated in our time of rapid disruption of social, political, technological, geographical, and religious patterns, expectancies, and relationships. Thus, today, people are more often confronted by the "Medusa" of identity-anxiety, the "horror of facelessness" before them and within themselves. This threat is potentially more horrifying and devastating than that of physical death. It is a kind of "real presence" of nonbeing. It is not just an imagined and vague possibility in the dim future but a nonbeing *experienced now*, a living death of having life and yet not living it oneself. Thus, Erikson says, "In some periods of his history and in some places of his life cycle, man needs (until we invent something better) a new ideological

[26] Erikson, "Identity and the Life Cycle," p. 158.
[27] Erikson, *Insight and Responsibility*, p. 207.
[28] Erikson, "Identity and the Life Cycle," p. 126.

orientation as surely and as sorely as he must have air and food."[29]

Identity is a psychological process that dovetails with the social process called ideology.[30] Together, in the movement of time, they are a part of the historical process. Identity is a constant becoming: "The overriding meaning of it all, then, is the creation of a sense of sameness, a unity of personality now felt by the individual and recognized by others as having consistency in time — of being, as it were, an irreversible historical fact."[31] Identity cannot be fabricated. It happens. It grows in the historical process in interaction between the individual and his world, including all of the events and images of reality that become *him*. Literally, identity is always a gift of "providence," because whatever has happened in his existence has "provided" for him, has served to make him who *he* is. As Bernard Loomer has said, the events and thoughts of the past give rise to the thinker in a becoming of continuity, an identity which is an unchanging style of changing.[32] Obviously, this process does not occur automatically, apart from the person's uniquely real participation and mastery. There tends always to be active *"ideological seeking* after an inner coherence and a durable set of values"[33] with an "I'd rather do it myself" quality. There are inevitable decisions for the individual, "cutting off" some possibilities of one's history, affirming others. There is a continual focusing and a centering of self within the factors of one's experience, which involves continual reinterpretation of one's changing self within a changing context:

> The process of identity formation emerges as an *evolving configuration* — a configuration which is gradually established by successive ego syntheses and resyntheses throughout childhood; it is a configuration gradually

[29] *Young Man Luther*, p. 22.

[30] Erikson, "Youth: Fidelity and Diversity," *Daedalus*, 91 (Winter, 1962):15.

[31] *Ibid.*

[32] Class Lectures in "Constructive Theology," Divinity School, University of Chicago, Spring, 1961.

[33] Erikson, *Insight and Responsibility*, p. 125.

integrating *constitutional givens, idiosyncratic libidinal needs, favored capacities, significant identifications, effective defenses, successful sublimations, and consistent roles.*[34]

Identity is a consistently identifiable image or pattern of changing in the midst of change. It is a continuity of personal development, which includes continual ideological reinterpretation of one's context. It involves symbolic processes, perceiving, remembering, forgetting, and imagining.[35] This process involves a constant reinterpretation of experience, which enables the ego to live with the shocks of reality, "to make the most of it," as a unity, a continuity, and a mastery.[36] Erikson sees such ego-strength as related to the inner strength of faith:

Luther's strong emphasis on the here and now of the spiritual advent, and on the necessity of always standing at the beginning, is not only a platform of faith, it is akin to a time-space quality dominating the inner state which psychoanalysts call "ego-strength." To the ego the past is not an inexorable process, experienced only as preparation for an impending doom; rather, the past is part of a present mastery which employs a convenient mixture of forgetting, falsifying, and idealizing to fit the past to the present, but usually to an extent which is neither unknowingly delusional nor knowingly dishonest. The ego can resign itself to past losses and forfeitings and learn not to demand the impossible of the future. It enjoys the illusion of a present, and defends this most precarious of all assumptions against doubts and apprehensions by remembering most easily chains of

---

[34] Erikson, "Identity and the Life Cycle," p. 116.
[35] Erikson, *Insight and Responsibility*, pp. 203–204.
[36] A particularly clear and self-conscious illustration of this encounter of the ego with a man's history is Soren Kierkegaard's self-revelation, *The Point of View for My Work As an Author: A Report to History*, ed. Benjamin Nelson, (New York: Harper Torchbooks, Harper and Brothers, 1962). See also Leland E. Elhard, "Faith and Identity," Unpublished Ph.D. dissertation, University of Chicago, 1965.

experiences which were alike in their unblemished pres-
entness. To the healthy ego, the flux of time sponsors the
process of identity. It thus is not afraid of death (as
Freud has pointed out vigorously); it has no concept of
death. But it *is* afraid of losing mastery over the negative conscience, over the drives, and over reality. To lose
any of these battles is, for the ego, living death; to win
them again and again means to the ego something akin
to an assumption that it is causing its own life. In theological terms, *creaturae procedunt ex deo libere et volun-
tarie et non naturaliter*: what lives, proceeds from God
freely and voluntarily, not naturally, that is, not by way
of what can be explained biologically.[37]

Some Contributions of the Identity Concept to an Understanding of Faith

The concept of identity lifts up things in relation to the concept of faith which theology has been groping for and hinting
at but has not been able to discern "perspectively." Put side
by side with the concept of faith, identity helps us see familiar
things about our experience from a slightly different angle
and with two eyes instead of one. Thus it illuminates the
intricacies and shows the deeper unity of the various aspects
of the faith experience.

We use a metaphor to describe this illumination and integration. The four words used to characterize identity: perva-
siveness, relationship, tension, and change, may be united in
the metaphor "living." First, "livingness" is pervasive in
something that is alive. Second, being alive depends on relationships. Third, life literally runs on tension. Fourth, being
alive means constant development and change. At these four
points of illumination, identity shows that real faith is always
integrated "living faith."

Faith and Pervasiveness

Tillich has already incorporated into his definition of faith
the implications of identity as a sense, an overall attitude,

[37] *Young Man Luther*, p. 217.

which pervades all elements of the personal life, including conscious and unconscious aspects.[38] We also may regard faith as Erikson has described identity, a "way of experiencing accessible to introspection." Living faith has always been linked with experience. This faith-experience is an "inner testimony," unique to the individual, which confirms for him that he has faith. Furthermore, this "sense of faith," so to speak, pervades the whole life of the believer. Whether or not he confesses a faith, his actions inevitably express it. As one behaves in the style of his identity, he also behaves in the style of his faith. The presence and style of works indicate the presence and style of faith in unique "gifts of the Spirit." Faith, as an attitude of the whole person is observable in the "test and analysis" of "fruits." As Luther says, "It is thus impossible to separate works from faith — yea, just as impossible as to separate burning and shining from fire."[39]

Thus the pervasive character of identity supports Ebeling's contention that to speak of faith is not to point to some separate capacity or discrete step on the road to something more. Faith, per se, describes the whole Christian history, experience, and life. On that basis Ebeling writes a brief dogmatics with the various doctrines as components of faith.[40]

Faith and Relationship

We have seen that man's need to avoid the "living death" of identity-failure pushes him to make a "total reorientation" out of a "given stage of partial knowledge." This need helps to explain why faith is "ultimate concern," in which man tends to relate absolutely to some relative, finite aspect of existence as if all existence depends upon it — because, for the ego, it does! Here also are illuminated the dynamics of H. Richard Niebuhr's statement that "to be a self is to have a god,"[41] when he explicates the tradition of Luther and Schleier-

---

[38] *Dynamics of Faith*, p. 4.
[39] Harry Emerson Fosdick, ed., *Great Voices of the Reformation: An Anthology* (New York: Random House, 1952), p. 122.
[40] Ebeling, *Nature of Faith*, pp. 106–7.
[41] *The Meaning of Revelation* (New York: The Macmillan Co., 1960), p. 80.

macher. "Trust and the faith of the heart alone make both God and idol. . . . For the two, faith and God, hold close together. Whatever then thy heart clings to . . . and relies upon, that properly is thy god."[42] Niebuhr concludes that God is the "being on whom the self feels wholly dependent for any worth as well as any existence it possesses."[43]

One has no sense of being real without identity. One has no identity without relationship. One has no identity in ultimate terms, in other words, one has no faith, without relationship to some version of the ultimate. In Christian terms, one's existence as a self-in-God is the gift of God's relating to him. Ebeling notes that, as far as man is concerned, the Holy Spirit and faith are one and the same. "When we affirm concerning the Holy Spirit — that he sets free, makes alive, makes men into sons of God, that he is the source of sanctification, and so on, . . . all this can likewise be affirmed of faith. . . . faith and the Holy Spirit are the two aspects of the one event, namely, of that which has become new in the relation of God and man in virtue of Jesus."[44] Regin Prenter's exposition of Luther's pneumatology finds the Holy Spirit creating the new man of faith ex nihilo, "out of nothing," by virtue of his creatively recognizing presence and word.[45] Turning to therapeutic psychology, we find that Andras Angyal describes most acutely the fact that relationships of personal recognizing and valuing call us into being as selves, ex nihilo. Others who care about us satisfy our "unquenchable longing to come into existence."[46] Angyal asserts that he really means it, not as "poetry" but as "earthly reality"; that this is the "most specifically human" feature of our existence.

> The struggle for existence at this level is for meaning and significance of our person. To be, to exist on this level, *is to mean something to someone else*. On the physi-

[42] *Ibid.*, p. 42.
[43] *Ibid.*, p. 24.
[44] *Nature of Faith*, pp. 106–7.
[45] Prenter, *Spiritus Creator*, trans. John M. Jensen (Philadelphia: Muhlenberg Press, 1953), p. 185.
[46] Angyal, *Neurosis and Treatment*, p. 19.

cal level we have only to maintain what we already clearly are. On the second level [occupational] we have to actualize the direction of our pursuits out of an initial state that is given to us merely in the form of vaguely perceived multiple potentialities. On the third level we do not start even with potentialities. We start with nothing. We are nothing within ourselves, nonexistent. To be is to mean something to someone else. This existence we cannot directly create for ourselves; it can only be given to us by another.

The true human problem is this: in a sense that matters to us above everything else, we are nothing in ourselves. All we have is a profound urge to exist and the dreadful experience of nonexistence. A poem written in a language that no one can read does not exist as a poem. Neither do we exist in a human sense until someone decodes us. A man in the most crucial way is a symbol, a message that comes to life only by being understood, acknowledged by someone. Otherwise, his existence has no more meaning or reality than an inscription on a rock on an uninhabited planet. William James said that there could be no worse punishment for a human being than to be unnoticed by everyone. Starting with the small child who urgently wants to be noticed, we all want to have a life in the thoughts and feelings of others, to have them reflect our individual existence, and reflect it in an understanding affectionate way.[47]

Similarly, Gabriel Marcel's study of hope, which he sees as inseparable from faith, concludes that hope arises from love and communion.[48]

Identity most richly intersects with faith in its illumination of the thought of Soren Kierkegaard. In his difficult classic, *Sickness Unto Death*,[49] he says, "The self is a relation which

[47] *Ibid.*, p. 18.
[48] Marcel, *Homo Viator*, trans. Emma Craufurd (London: Victor Gollancz, 1951, from French edition: *Homo Viator*, Fernand Aubier Editions Montaigne, Paris, 1951), p. 67.
[49] Trans. Walter Lowrie (Princeton: Princeton University Press, 1941), p. 17.

relates itself to its own self." This is a statement about identity. First, the sense of identity consists, in part, of a relation relating to itself. It is an inner image, which relates to and patterns the diversity of one's experiences, one's limitations and possibilities, but it is also a *relating to that image* in an attempt to be consistent with it. It is a self-realization but also a continual checking and recognizing oneself in terms of that self-realization. Second, Kierkegaard indicates that this relation, which is the self, is always a "derived, constituted relation," constituted by relation to another.[50] This is a statement about the second part of identity. Identity, as a relation to a relation to oneself, is possible only in the context of a relation to another. We mean most to ourselves where we mean most to others. Our self-realization is coupled with recognizing ourself in the context of being recognized by others, whom we recognize.

Kierkegaard then defines faith as the situation in which, "by relating itself to its own self and by willing to be itself the self is grounded transparently in the power which constituted it."[51] Faith is the self constituted by God's relating to it. In this normative definition faith and identity coincide. Here, the relationship of God with a man uninterruptedly forms man's relationship with himself. God's recognition becomes the self-realization and self-recognition of the self. I mean most to myself when I mean most to God when God means most to me. Negatively, the condition of despair or sin is the opposite of faith. Despair, as lack of faith, is either asserting one's old self, unaffected by the God-relationship, or failing to be the new self possible in the God-relationship.

Based on this dialectical relation of self and other we find that "The self is potentiated in the ratio of the measure proposed for the self, and infinitely potentiated when God is the measure. The more conception of God, the more self."[52] The incarnate Christ, the "paradox," is the greatest measure of

---

[50] *Ibid.*
[51] *Ibid.*, p. 19.
[52] *Ibid.*, p. 129.

God, affecting proportionately the identity of the believers. Paradox is here understood as a contradiction not merely of logic but of "personal logic," of the "reflectively organized common sense of mankind, including as its essential core a sense of life's values . . . The self-assurance and self-assertiveness of man's nature in its totality."[53] The situation of the paradox is best described by Kierkegaard in the following:

> Christianity teaches that this particular individual and so every individual, whatever in other respects this individual may be, man, woman, serving-maid, minister of state, merchant, barber, student, etc., — this individual exists before God — this individual who perhaps would be vain for having once in his life talked with the King, this man who is not a little proud of living on intimate terms with that person or the other, this man exists before God, can talk with God any moment he will, sure to be heard by Him; in short, this man is invited to live on the most intimate terms with God! Furthermore, for this man's sake God came to the world, let himself be born, suffers and dies; and this suffering God almost begs and entreats this man to accept the help which is offered him! Verily, if there is anything that would make a man lose his understanding, it is surely this! Whosoever has not the humble courage to dare to believe it, must be offended at it.[54]

The self face to face with this Christ is confronted with becoming a radically altered identity, "a self potentiated by the prodigious concession of God."[55] His unity, continuity, and mastery are radically altered by God's intense involvement in him. The most vivid portrayal of this transformation is the "young man" in Kierkegaard's *Training in Christianity*[56] who was captured by the image of Christ.

It is a mistake, however, to think that the unique partic-

[53] Kierkegaard, *Philosophical Fragments*, trans. David F. Swenson, (Princeton: Princeton Univ. Press, 1962), p. 222.

[54] *Sickness Unto Death*, p. 137.

[55] *Ibid.*, p. 186.

[56] Trans. Walter Lowrie (Princeton: Princeton Univ. Press, 1941).

ularities of one's history are evaporated, "infinitized" by the God-relationship. One is really meant to be himself before God, as a "perfectly definite something."[57] Faith is really saying "I" in the presence of God, finding all the experiences, part-identifications, and images of the past given unity, continuity, and mastery in the living encounter with God's love in Christ. Kierkegaard's own life may be viewed as illustrative of this definite character of the faith-identity. The "spyish" characteristics of his life were employed in the God-relationship in the image, "The spy in a higher service."[58]

To summarize both this section and the basic contention of this essay: both faith and identity are relationship concepts. We tend to view faith as the "Godward pole" of the relationship and identity as the "manward pole." Ordinarily, in this scheme, we think of faith as a *resource for* identity. Usually, this is how our religion is useful to us. With the help of Kierkegaard's strictly normative definitions, however, we also see that identity and faith merge. Ideally, both point to the self-in-God, where one is fully God's self and fully one's own self at the same time.

Faith and Tension

To continue with our model, life as a biological process is characterized by continuing transaction and tension between necessary processes, such as anabolism and catabolism. The process of identity also is a continuing crisis between achieved identity and "identity-diffusion." The concept of identity as applied to faith indicates how a number of polar tensions also characterize faith.

We have already spoken of the polarity between the individuality of the historical self and the recreating personal action of God in the faith-relationship. We found that, ideally, individuality and relationship are not contradictory, either in identity or in faith. In this relationship, one's individuality is not destroyed but affirmed. Kierkegaard expressed this cogently in the illustration of the mythical "knight of faith"

[57] Kierkegaard, *Sickness Unto Death*, p. 56.
[58] Leland E. Elhard, "Faith and Identity," see footnote 36.

who, after relating fully to the infinite, received fully again the finite.[59]

A number of other interrelated polarities are evident. First, individual faith exists always in conjunction with the faith of the group. Identity affirms this fact but also accentuates the vivifying tension in both the group and the individual that results from the person's being a "successful variant" of the group. In his own serious progress of faith, he differs from the group tradition enough to indicate that he has really participated in its faith enough to work out his own personally relevant version of it. The tradition of the group is continually renewed by its various members' appropriating and redirecting it in terms of their ongoing experience.

This brings us to another tension. The concept of "meaning," as a way of understanding the "livingness" of faith, arises out of a polarity between concrete event and abstract symbolism, experience and context, the "embodied" and the "disembodied," event and interpretation, spontaneity and ritual, "spirit" and "word." Ernest Becker recalls us to the necessity of participation in everyday reality for a sense of meaning to develop. He calls for the primacy of the "engaging act" over the "symbolic construction." He questions the reality of the self purchased at the "bargain counter" of religion, with its fictional "eternity of duration." The answers to the common human problems, he holds, can only be "painstakingly, daily fabricated in the encounter of self and interpersonal world."[60] Here we interject that Christianity has focused its decisive meanings in terms of "interpersonal relationships" with God and other human beings, a faith "painstakingly fabricated." As Luther says, "I did not learn my theology all at once, but I had to search deeper for it, where my temptations took me. A theologian is born by living, nay dying and being damned, not by thinking, reading, or speculating."[61]

We note with Becker that human experience is at its richest

[59] Kierkegaard, Fear and Trembling, trans. Walter Lowrie (Princeton: Princeton Univ. Press, 1941), pp. 48–51.
[60] The Revolution in Psychiatry, pp. 70–71.
[61] Erikson, Young Man Luther, p. 251.

in dialectical polarity between event and symbolism; between the stimulating, distracting disunities and discontinuities of moment by moment experience, and the transcendent unities, continuities, and anticipations of the symbolic framework. Kierkegaard saw that a man could become equally lost in the "finite" or the "infinite." The locus of meaning is neither "in the action" nor above it but in polarity between the two. On the one hand, no identity, no meaning is possible without some sort of continual ideological structuring that gives coherence and predictability to the confusion of immediate experience, and that gives a perspective from which to view the sensing-feeling-thinking landscape. As Kierkegaard points out in his "aesthetic" authorship, experience on the surface level of contingency and wish fulfillment, the "aesthetic sphere of existence," proves meaningless. It has no adequate inherent unity, continuity, and mastery. At some point, meanings rooted only on this level inevitably break down, and, as Erikson indicates, "Any span of the cycle lived without vigorous meaning, at the beginning, in the middle, or at the end, endangers the sense of life and the meaning of death in all whose life stages are intertwined."[62]

On the other hand, a rigid framework, which loses touch with the energies and realities of experience, also fails to produce an identity with *real* mastery of experience and real unity and continuity *in* the experience. An outgrown ideology, a faith which is "dead," produces not meaning but disgust. It is, indeed, a "faith" which, in its lack of "works," is shown up to be no faith at all. Kierkegaard calls faith an Archimedean point beyond the world by which one can move the world.[63] It is not an escape from the world of experience and its disruptions; it is the point from which one is on top of one's very real experiencing, actually "overcoming the world." Faith, therefore, cannot be separated from vocation, as the

[62] *Insight and Responsibility*, p. 133.
[63] Kierkegaard, *The Gospel of Suffering and the Lilies of the Field*, trans. David F. Swenson and Lillian Marvin Swenson (Minneapolis: Augsburg Publishing House, 1948), p. 29. Also see *The Journal of Soren Kierkegaard*, trans. and ed. Alexander Dru (London: Oxford University Press, 1938), pp. 249–50.

realization of one's identity in its unceasing development of unity, continuity, and mastery *in* experience.

Gabriel Marcel finds the same polarity in hope, viewed as faith facing the future. He finds that the transcendent aspect of meaning is not an "import" foreign to experience, but that it arises in encounter. "We might say that hope is essentially the availability of a soul which has entered intimately enough into the experience of communion to accomplish in the teeth of will and knowledge the transcendent act — the act of establishing the vital regeneration of which this experience affords both the pledge and the first-fruits." [64]

Another polarity in faith is that between self-activity and self-passivity. A synergism is not here intended. That we exist in response before God has already been affirmed. Nevertheless, the activity of faith is man's total self-active involvement as it has been called forth by God's total involvement in man. Faith is all God *and* all man. This involvement has a dialectic of passivity — or "receptivity" — and activity. On the one hand, one "receives himself" from his relationships, concrete, symbolic, social, and historical. Erikson finds this passivity actively exercised, as an "undergoing" in the name of "doing," in the "regression in the service of the ego." [65] Here a receiving of the flood of undifferentiated experience enables the ego to reorganize its focus of experience in order eventually to master it.

But, on the other hand, a person must also affirm himself. He "receives himself"; he also "grasps himself." He is shaped; he also shapes. He is a creature; he also creatively "exercises dominion." Even the most theocentric versions of faith concede some response, some measure of mastery by a man in his own destiny, because response is inseparable from the human identity. For a man to be real for himself, he must in some way self-consciously *live* his life, not have it *lived for him*. No matter how much his worth is potentiated by the valuing of the other, it is not actualized apart from *his* participation, his *own* valuing. The electric livingness of faith

[64] *Homo Viator*, p. 67.
[65] *Young Man Luther*, pp. 103, 208.

occurs only when the poles of other-participation and self-participation are connected, even if the one is a "negative pole." Faith must always flow through my center, must be *my* faith. Faith always participates, even when it participates "in the omnipotence of God."[66] Ebeling has appropriated this contribution of the identity concept to the tension of faith:

> Even at that point where St. Paul, looking at the believer's life, simply abolishes the life of the human I as subject, he says, characteristically, "It is no longer I who live, but Christ who lives in me" (Galatians 2:20); but he does not say, and could not say, "It is not I who believe, but Christ who believes in me." For the believing that takes place in my own I *is* the change in mastery and guidance which concerns my whole existence, my life as a person. We must therefore say that both are alike essential to faith: both its divine character as a gift and its being always my faith, being really faith when it is a responsible action and commitment of my person, in a faith which is my own and nobody else's. To confess one's faith is part of faith, and to commit oneself personally is the meaning of confession.[67]

We concluded the consideration of identity with a quotation from Erikson, in which he related to the freedom of God the mastery of the ego in the midst of its determinisms. This reference introduces the tension between freedom and determinism from the ego's point of view. Ebeling has appropriated this tension in describing faith as participation in the omnipotence of God. Faith is freedom, a sense of freedom from care and anxiety about oneself. The believer knows that he receives himself from outside himself. In faith, he appropriates the "determinisms" of his life as gifts of a gracious providence. In faith, one's admitting his powerlessness is his freedom, and is possible because of the faith relationship.[68] This does not constitute a hidden, egocentric, and "bargain

[66] Ebeling, *Nature of Faith*, p. 111.
[67] *Ibid.*, p. 112.
[68] *Ibid.*, p. 136.

basement" mastery, where one projects his need for centering his world solely in himself onto God and then "borrows" God's great egocentric identity by being one of "His boys." Rather, this omnipotence that faith sees is the omnipotence of the Cross, where it perceives God's free power to love. It is the power of God to triumph as "suffering servant" *in the midst* of human experience. It is the power to turn everything in the flux of experience into a sponsorship of meaning and identity. It is the real mastery of the world by being *in* the world, not a cheap mastery in splendid isolation above the world. It is a perfect union of the poles of experiential and symbolic meaning. Faith discerns and participates in this omnipotence of God as the ultimate power and pattern of real existence. As H. Richard Niebuhr says, "We discern in the contemporary confusion of our lives the evidence of a pattern in which, by great travail of men and God, a work of redemption goes on which is like the work of Christ." [69]

Thus, faith is a way full of meaning, in tension with the real possibility of meaninglessness. This way grows in the "ego-strength" of unity, continuity, and mastery in the continuing process of winning the battle against meaninglessness. As Ebeling says:

> It is a way, indeed, which has certain similarities with Nihilism, because it appears as a way into darkness and nothingness and yet it is the one real opposite of Nihilism: for it is life lived in the great affirmation, which never deceives, but fulfills all reasonable expectation, *is itself fulfillment.* . . . Faith that is really faith knows that it is the victory which has conquered the world, in which the apparent superiority of the world is weakness and the apparent weakness is the superior power. *Faith and the power of faith, faith and the victory of faith are identical* — even if they seem to the onlooker to be as widely separated as death and life, hell and heaven, nothingness and God [italics mine].[70]

[69] *Meaning of Revelation*, p. 125.
[70] *Nature of Faith*, p. 132.

Ideally, then, faith is the centering of all the tensions of faith in the revelation of God in Christ. Christ is the living image that encompasses all our personal and group experience and ties our worlds together.[71] He is the adequate center for our experience.

Faith and Change

There remains one more dialectical tension, that between past and present. The ideal centering is never achieved; it is always "on the way." As soon as a gestalt of experience appears, the discontinuities of living experience make it inadequate and necessitate a new thrust toward a more adequate gestalt. The life of identity and faith is a tension and alternating between "centering down" on a given center and "centering out" beyond it to gather some of the nagging "leftovers" of past experience and the surplus of new experience into the possibility of a more adequate center. Even as we receive ourselves from the past, we constantly recreate our past in the light of the present to achieve identity. In *The Meaning of Revelation*, H. Richard Niebuhr discusses the accentuation of this natural process of identity reformation brought about by normal personal and historical change. Revelation is this accentuation. It is the radical reconstruction of our images, by which we discover meaning, by which we "reason with our hearts" in order to bring unity, continuity, and mastery into historical personal existence. In this book Niebuhr takes remarkable cognizance of the phenomena we have viewed in terms of identity and he relates them to his description of revelation and faith. Space does not allow elaboration of this observation beyond the concerns of "faith and change."

Faith is never an "empty sack," a sheer capacity apart from content. It is always a content, a limited, particular history, in some aspect of which we invest and pattern ourselves, "relating absolutely to the relative" in an attempt to make "one story" out of our confused experience. Every new experience forces us to change and rationalize a little to keep the

[71] Niebuhr, *Meaning of Revelation*, pp. 120, 184.

story straight. Niebuhr sees the revelation of Christ as a continual impact on our life stories. The event of Christ continually calls into question our idolatries, and impels us into a permanent conversion of our faith.[72] The "forever adolescing" character of our religious human nature is supremely accentuated by the event of Christ. We have already touched on this in the effect of Kierkegaard's "paradox" on the faith-identity. The limited, self-centered, and contradictory characteristics, the "evil imaginations"[73] of our self- and group-images, with their attendant inner division and social conflict, are continuously grasped and overcome by the event of Christ in our lives. In this encounter our histories are transformed. We remember and forget according to our self-images and world perspectives. In the new self-image we have in Him, our memories are transformed, and our individual and collective life histories begin to "make sense." As He becomes a common memory of groups of people, they are bound together in a common identity and life. From the point of view of faith, He is ultimately the unifying image of all peoples.

Decisively in Christ, faith experiences the unconditional valuing by the infinite self for whom all souls are valuable.[74] In Him we discover that the principle of being is the principle of worth, "That whatever is, is good."[75] This "basic trust" overcomes all our limited "conditions of worth" and leads to a faith which is "simple thankfulness."[76] In His consistent favorable valuing of us in forgiveness, He overcomes the "identity diffusion" caused by the guilt of the past. Before Him, one is free to be himself. Ultimately, faith is an utterly nondefensive experiencing in the midst of all the past and present threats to one's selfhood, "having all things as having them not." As an absolute relating to the absolute, it is the simplicity and wholeness of identity in God, which "wills one

[72] Ibid., p. 191.
[73] Ibid., p. 108.
[74] Ibid., p. 151.
[75] H. Richard Niebuhr, Radical Monotheism and Western Culture (New York: Harper and Brothers, 1960), p. 32.
[76] Ibid., p. 126.

thing." It sees all things for what they are, relates to each person as a "Thou," loves the enemy. Thus, faith and love become the one act we have described in Luther's "fire and burning" description of faith. We turn once more to Kierkegaard's "young man" to exemplify this patterning of the self in Christ, its painful progressive character and its eventual destiny in the completely internally congruent way of life. It should be remembered that this picture of faith that Kierkegaard paints is not the imposition of an unworldly abstract framework upon experience. Rather, this faith "occurs," as it were, in unending experience with the forgiving, freeing, unchangeable love of God. Faith is the identity that continually discovers itself in God, Who is the unchangeable Whom Kierkegaard likens to a spring of water. Unchanging in its refreshing coolness, it does not stay in one immovable location but is available always in the midst of the vicissitudes of experience. This spring "seeks out the traveller, the errant wanderer: who has ever heard the like of any spring! Thus thou art unchangeably always and everywhere to be found. And whenever any human being comes to Thee, of whatever age, at whatever time of day, in whatever state: if he comes in sincerity he always find Thy love equally warm, like the spring's unchanged coolness, O Thou Who art unchangeable." [77]

Thus we view the end of the permanent revolution of our identity, of our "way of life," as living faith. The first Christian believers were identified as "followers of the way." With Niebuhr we, too, refer to Augustine, "I do not say to thee, seek the way. The way itself is come to thee: Arise and walk." [78]

[77] Kierkegaard, *Edifying Discourses, A Selection,* trans. David F. Swenson and Lillian Marvin Swenson, ed. Paul L. Holmer (New York: Harper Torchbooks, Harper & Bros., 1958), p. 264.
[78] *The Meaning of Revelation,* p. 191.

7

Pastoral Counseling as Christian Perspective

LeROY ADEN

Pastoral counseling as we know it today had its inception with the rise and development of depth psychology. Obviously, pastoral counseling as part of the church's ministry to individuals existed before Sigmund Freud's time, but with the advent of depth psychology it was innervated by a new and heuristic force. Since then it has been in the process of realignment, seeking to assimilate the theoretical and therapeutic discoveries of dynamic psychology. In this process different questions have come into focus at different times, in a pattern not unlike the epigenetic one of Erik Erikson's developmental tasks.

One especially pressing question today concerns the nature or the identity of pastoral counseling. Serious discussion among pastoral counselors almost always touches this question. How does pastoral counseling differ from the other helping professions? What is its distinctive character? What function does the pastoral counselor perform on a healing team? These questions indicate that pastoral counseling is in a period of adolescence, where the question of "Who am I?" takes on primary importance. The present paper addresses this question. While it does not pretend to be definitive, it is seriously concerned with the distinctive character of pastoral counseling. It seeks to set forth and develop one possible position in regard to it, a position that seems fruitful on both a theoretical and an operational level.

The reader should note that our primary focus is pastoral

counseling rather than pastoral care. Pastoral care is a broader and more generic term referring to the church's entire ministry of helping or healing, of caring or curing individuals or groups. Pastoral counseling, a specialized activity within pastoral care, is a ministry of helping or healing through intensive attention to the individual and his life situation. This difference can be illustrated by the methods of each. Pastoral care confronts us with a multitude of methods. At different times and in different circumstances it has used confession (public and private), anointing, saints and relics, charismatic healers, exorcism, prayer, spiritual letters, sacraments, scriptural reading, religious literature, "holy" conversations, discipline, and other activities.[1] In addition, the church functions of teaching, evangelism, worship, and preaching have been used at times to serve the purpose of pastoral care. Such diversity does not hold for pastoral counseling as we know it today. Pastoral counseling tends to be characterized by a single method, that of conversation. It seeks to accomplish its task by talking about the life situation of the individual. It may at times employ rites or readings or actions, but by and large the process of pastoral counseling evolves by means of verbal exchanges between pastor and parishioner.

Common Conceptions of Pastoral Counseling

How can we define pastoral counseling in order to highlight its distinctive identity? To answer the question, we will explore the assertion that *pastoral counseling is a Christian perspective*. This assertion is new in the history of pastoral counseling, though the writings of other men, especially those of Seward Hiltner, prepare the soil for it. But it will be helpful first to set forth alternative ways in which pastoral counseling has been conceived. These are the central and often unexamined ways in which the novice in pastoral counseling tries to pinpoint its amorphous identity. Each way, of course, em-

[1] See William A. Clebsch and Charles R. Jaekle, *Pastoral Care in Historical Perspective: An Essay with Exhibits* (Englewood Cliffs: Prentice-Hall, 1964). Also recommended is John T. McNeill's classic, *A History of the Cure of Souls* (New York: Harper & Brothers, 1951).

bodies a degree of truth, and can therefore be considered a limited disclosure of the identity of pastoral counseling.

First, pastoral counseling has often been identified according to its subject matter. This position says, in effect, that pastoral counseling deals with certain material to the exclusion of other material. Accordingly, pastoral counseling takes place when pastor and parishioner center on certain Christian ideas or employ Christian concepts. This means that talk about a parishioner's faith in Christ is considered pastoral counseling, but talk about his inability to trust his wife, for example, would not qualify. In actual fact, however, the distrust of his wife may be a pivotal aspect of his present predicament, including the moral and spiritual dimensions of that predicament. In this sense, the identification of "religious" content as the real essence of pastoral counseling is a false and misleading use of the distinction between the secular and the sacred. Material that does not seem to be spiritual in any explicit way may be decidedly spiritual, or at least it may be very relevant to the spiritual on an implicit and deeper level.

No matter where the line is drawn, content is, finally, an inadequate way by which to define pastoral counseling. It recognizes the fact that counseling between pastor and parishioner may deal with certain content more often than with other content. But if we use content as a way to define pastoral counseling, we soon end in an artificial and segmented world, where preliminary concerns are cut off from ultimate concerns, a world in which the pastor as counselor quickly becomes irrelevant to the needs of the parishioner.

Second, pastoral counseling can be identified with methods or procedures so that counseling is considered pastoral if the counselor employs particular techniques or performs particular activities which are considered especially appropriate to religious purposes. This position is the least feasible of all, and its inadequacy is clearly seen when, for example, a pastor is either authoritarian or passively nondirective because he believes that one or the other method is the only one that really implements the spirit of the Christian faith.

It is true that some methods tend to be more compatible with the concerns of pastoral counseling and the basic attitudes of the pastor than others. For example, Carl R. Rogers' client-centered therapy, with its belief that the counselor must enter the client's world with love and respect, seems to be more in line with the Christian faith than any method of counseling which would propose that the counselor enter as master, judge, and final authority. But pastoral counseling cannot be defined at the level of methods, for the same end can be achieved by any number of methods, as expressed, for example, by Ludwig von Bertalanffy's principle of equifinality.[2] Further, in an activity such as pastoral counseling, methods are merely an outward form of something much more important, namely, the counselor's inward attitude.

Third, pastoral counseling can be defined by a particular office in the church. A recent book states this position boldly when the author is content to say that "pastoral counseling means, simply, counseling by clergymen."[3] The simplicity of this definition is unrealistic, but the general thrust of it is rather prevalent in the history of the church, for pastoral counseling and pastoral care have frequently been identified with the office or person of the pastor. Seward Hiltner clarifies this point when he states that since the Reformation the term "pastoral" has been used in both a functional and a structural sense.[4] The first sense defines pastoral as a functional extension of the noun "pastor." It was assumed that "functions followed from title," so that everything done by one called a pastor was considered a pastoral act. Obviously, then, a social worker or a psychiatrist would never be seen as doing pastoral counseling, for they are not ministers of the church.

The truth, and error, of this position follow quite naturally from its chief emphasis. That certain persons are especially

[2] Von Bertalanffy, *Problems of Life: An Evaluation of Modern Biological and Scientific Thought* (New York: Harper Torchbooks, Harper & Brothers, 1960), pp. 142ff.

[3] Douglass W. Orr, *Professional Counseling on Human Behavior: Its Principles and Practices* (New York: Franklin Watts, 1965), p. 11.

[4] *Preface to Pastoral Theology* (New York: Abingdon Press, 1958), p. 15.

trained and set aside to perform specialized activities is true, but this does not necessitate an inevitable connection between activity and office. Not all persons holding the office of pastor, for example, are qualified to do pastoral counseling. In fact, a psychiatrist in some cases may offer more effective pastoral counseling than someone called a pastor. We do not find in any of our three definitions or in any combination of them a decisive clue to the distinctiveness of pastoral counseling. There is, we believe, a fourth way to define it, one that also, points more effectively to its unique identity.

Our contention can be put in the form of a thesis: *Pastoral counseling is a Christian perspective which seeks to help or to heal by attending to the life situation of the troubled person.*[5] Obviously, the several assertions composing the thesis would have to be explored in some detail before the full meaning of the thesis could be explicated, giving us a fairly complete description of the nature of pastoral counseling. Owing to limitations of space, however, we will focus here on the first portion of the thesis, that *pastoral counseling is a Christian perspective.*

The Matrix of Our Thesis

Before clarifying and attempting to establish this contention, it will be helpful to turn briefly to the theoretical matrix from which it comes. The background that deserves our special consideration is the thought of Seward Hiltner.[6]

Basic to the whole of Hiltner's thought is field theory,[7] taken from physics and used to highlight several principles

[5] The thesis implies but does not intend to support the idea that pastoral counseling is necessarily limited to those who stand within the Christian faith.

[6] Hiltner's theory of pastoral counseling is elaborated in *Pastoral Counseling* (New York: Abingdon-Cokesbury Press, 1949); *The Counselor in Counseling* (New York: Abingdon Press, 1950); and *The Context of Pastoral Counseling* by Seward Hiltner and Lowell G. Colston (New York: Abingdon Press, 1961). For his closely related theory of pastoral theology, see *Preface to Pastoral Theology* (New York: Abingdon Press, 1958) and *The Christian Shepherd: Some Aspects of Pastoral Care* (New York: Abingdon Press, 1959).

[7] Hiltner, *Preface to Pastoral Theology*, pp. 57ff.

which are crucial to his theory of pastoral counseling. First, in field theory there are no compartments or categorical divisions in a given field. All forces in a field are interrelated with one another and form an ordered totality at any given time. Second, although the field has no sharp division, a distinction between core and periphery or between figure and ground can be made. The focus (whatever it might be) is the dominant and organizing core, and provides the criterion by which forces in the field are evaluated. Third, the field is fluid and dynamic, changing as a new force becomes the focus and thus dominates the field. Consequently, one must evaluate the relevance of any new datum according to its relation to the existing focus rather than to some preestablished norm.

The influence of field theory is reflected on various levels in Hiltner's theory of pastoral counseling. On one level, pastoral counseling is a focus within a field, having both unique and shared dimensions in relation to other helping professions. Elaboration of these two dimensions would set forth Hiltner's complete theory of pastoral counseling, but our primary concern calls for the elucidation of only the first.

Hiltner has twice attempted to define the uniqueness of pastoral counseling, his second attempt being the more thorough and therefore the more significant. The first is embodied primarily in his book *Pastoral Counseling* (1949), and is epitomized in what he calls the pastor's "focus of function." By this phrase, Hiltner refers to the pastor's role and the pastor's faith as they contribute to his unique identity. His more mature attempt appeared in 1961 under the title *The Context of Pastoral Counseling*. Here the pastor's distinctiveness is summarized and defined by what Hiltner calls "context." The context or distinctive identity of pastoral counseling consists of four factors:

(1) *Setting*. Setting refers to the *total* environment in which the pastor usually carries on his counseling, although its particular reference is to the church. The church as setting carries with it many things that also belong to the setting of pastoral counseling. Tradition and symbols, such as "art

forms, pulpit and Bible, prayer, liturgical music, altar or communion table, and others,"[8] are part of the total setting that is associated in the mind of the counselee with the pastor as counselor. As Hiltner points out, this setting may be positive, negative, or a mixture of both to the counselee, but it cannot be simply "neutral ground." Just as a medical center has a distinctive tone, so the church and its various symbols connote something unique to the person who enters it for counseling.

(2) *Expectation.* The clerical role often invites projections of various sorts from parishioners. These expectations manifest themselves in various forms, deriving possibly from personal acquaintance with the pastor, or from "the parishioner's generalized conception of any pastor's role, function, and convictions."[9] They may be fairly explicit and realistic, or they may operate implicitly and be in sharp contrast to the pastor's own image of himself and his function. Whatever the form, the expectations of the parishioner are generally unique to the pastor's office or person and are therefore distinctive ingredients of pastoral counseling.

(3) *Shift in Relationship.* The pastor does more than simply counsel. He carries out a variety of activities which put him in close contact with his people. Unlike other kinds of counselors, the pastor often knows the counselee before and after the counseling situation. Pastoral counseling, therefore, involves a "shift" in relationship, which creates "out of a previous, general pastor-parishioner relationship a special and temporary relationship . . . with the recognition that, upon conclusion of the special and temporary relationship, the general relationship will be resumed."[10] Other professional people who do counseling, such as teachers and physicians, may also have to navigate a shift in relationship, but "none to so marked an extent and so uniformly as the clergy." In some cases this shift in relationship may be absent; mostly, however, there is involvement before and after counseling, a

[8] Hiltner, *The Context of Pastoral Counseling*, p. 32.
[9] *Ibid.*, p. 30.
[10] *Ibid.*

feature of the relationship desired by both pastor and parishioner.

(4) *Aims and Limitations.* In *Pastoral Counseling*, Hiltner posited a twofold division of the aims of the pastoral counselor. On the one hand, pastoral counseling has the same aims as the church itself. On the other hand, pastoral counseling has its own special aim, namely, "the attempt by a pastor to help people help themselves through the process of gaining understanding of their inner conflicts." [11] There is a decidedly psychological ring to this description.

This early formulation is reflected in a later one. In *The Context of Pastoral Counseling*, a twofold division is again posited, this time between the general aim of the pastor's total ministry and the specific aim of his counseling ministry. The aim of the pastor's total ministry is said to be the salvation or redemption of the "total person." But in this second formulation Hiltner is not as explicit about the aim of the pastor's counseling ministry. He says the pastor should have "self-imposed professional limitations" with regard to time and skill. His time is limited because he has other pastoral functions to perform. His skill is limited because he is not trained to enter into the deep, intrapsychic problems of a parishioner and to free him from repressed childhood experiences, which influence and distort his present reactions. He should, instead, limit himself to problems "in which a more or less integrated person — with no deeper inner conflicts than most people have — nevertheless requires special help." [12] Qualified in this way, the aim of the pastor's counseling ministry still retains the psychological ring we noticed in the first formulation.

These four factors are together called the context of pastoral counseling. They are, however, only one side of Hiltner's total theory. As we have seen, pastoral counseling is both related to and distinct from all other kinds of counseling, and this dipolar feature is essential for an adequate representation of Hiltner's theory of pastoral counseling.

[11] *Pastoral Counseling*, p. 19.
[12] *The Context of Pastoral Counseling*, p. 28.

Pastoral Counseling as Christian Perspective

A Critique of Hiltner's Theory

Seward Hiltner's contextual analysis, more than any other present-day theory of pastoral counseling, has formulated some crucial and often forgotten ingredients of counseling. His analysis, however, does not exhaust the distinctiveness of pastoral counseling. To his four factors we would add a fifth, one that is far more integral to the pastoral counselor himself. For we believe that the pastor, as pastor, possesses and is committed to basic "frames of orientation and devotion." This framework, we contend, is an integral and vital dimension of pastoral counseling, and a dominant ingredient of its distinctive identity.

In his first formulation, Hiltner maintained that the pastor's unique "focus of function" derived from two sources, his pastoral role and his Christian faith. In his mature formulation of pastoral counseling, we find Hiltner elaborating its distinctiveness in terms of the pastor's role but not of the pastor's faith. Thus, of the four factors, the first three — setting, expectation, and shift in relationship — are obviously marks which derive from the pastor's role. The fourth factor, the aims and limitations of the pastoral counselor, could be derived from the counselor's faith, but Hiltner's development of it has never moved very far in that direction. At this point he prefers a psychological rather than a theological direction.

Hiltner seems hesitant for two reasons to consider the pastor's faith as a distinctive mark of pastoral counseling. The first is his acceptance of the doctrine of the priesthood of all believers, which maintains that no special priesthood is necessary to mediate between God and man. We wish to add, however, that the Christian faith is the dominant concern in the pastor's profession, whereas in most other helping professions it is of secondary concern. We therefore consider it one of the distinctive marks of pastoral counseling.

The second reason is Hiltner's guard against an "encapsulated gospel," a gospel closed in upon itself, cut off from human knowledge in general. Against this viewpoint Hiltner insists that man's understanding of the Gospel is always related to his concrete situation. Although both point out areas of potential danger, they do not convince us that the Christian faith should be eliminated as one of the unique ingredients of pastoral counseling. Instead, we believe the Christian faith *is* a unique mark of pastoral counseling in a precise and particular way, and we will develop this approach through our contention that *pastoral counseling is a Christian perspective*.

Pastoral Counseling Is a Perspective

Stephen C. Pepper once said that behind every philosophy or world hypothesis there is a root metaphor or basic analogy.[13] Such a metaphor lies behind our assertion of perspective in counseling, namely, that man never perceives from a universal and unbiased position. The French existentialist Paul Ricoeur elaborates this insight in a systematic way. As part of his philosophical anthropology, Ricoeur's interest in the finiteness and fallibility of man leads him into a discussion of "my body." He maintains that the first meaning of "my body" is that it is "an openness." By its various modalities of sight, sound, taste, smell, etc., my body is a "mediator 'between' myself and the world."[14] It not only "opens me to others insofar as it displays the interior upon the exterior" but also it allows the world to be experienced by me and to become a part of me. In this sense, my body is first of all an "openness onto the world."

But my body is not simply openness. It is finite and limited, a fact which, for Ricoeur, becomes apparent in a modality like perception. The perceiving body always perceives from somewhere. As an existing totality it perceives from a certain angle and in a certain way. In short, its "view of" is always a perspective, "a *point of view* on." As Ricoeur writes, "My body is the center of orientation, the zero origin, the 'here from where' I see all that I can see."[15] Perspective or point of view

[13] Pepper, *World Hypotheses: A Study in Evidence* (Los Angeles: University of California Press, 1942).
[14] Ricoeur, *Fallible Man: Philosophy of the Will*, trans. Charles Kelbley (Chicago: Henry Regnery Co., 1965), p. 30.
[15] *Ibid.*

is, to Ricoeur, one of the primary and unavoidable characteristics of finite man.

Ricoeur's elaboration of perspective can well be applied to counseling. Recently I have had the opportunity to observe counselors from various helping professions as they discussed and analyzed interview material. That they did not come to the material with an unbiased concern, that they in fact perceived the client from a certain stance or point of view, was so visible that it was initially shocking and then highly instructive. One discovers what one should have known all along — that all counselors see their clients and perform their therapeutic maneuvers from particular perspectives. It may be Freudian or Rogerian or Jungian, but in every case it is a perspective, a point of view. Furthermore, the counselor is unable to escape the perspectival nature of his existence, although he may shift perspectives, or he may hold a particular perspective more or less flexibly.

Pastoral counselors are also inevitably perspectival. They can shift but they cannot eliminate the "here from where" nature of their perceptual attentiveness. And though this perspectivity is a manifestation of their finiteness, it is also an expression of their distinctiveness.

Pastoral Counseling Is a Christian Perspective

Once the perspectival nature of pastoral counseling is acknowledged, our inquiry moves forward: From what stance or point of view does the pastoral counselor perceive and respond to the troubled individual?

Since the advent of dynamic psychology, clergymen and other counselors have often accused pastoral counseling of sharing with the psychotherapist a perspective which is dominantly and finally psychological. There is much truth in this accusation, and my recent experience with various groups of pastoral counselors have reinforced this impression. Very often the perspective of the pastoral counselor cannot be differentiated from that of the psychotherapist, at least not in terms of basic orientation. The pastoral counselor, unlike the psychotherapist, may not delve deeply into the parishioner's intrapsychic and genetic problems, but, like the psychotherapist, his primary and perhaps final concern has often been confined to a Freudian or a Rogerian or some other psychological viewpoint.

The value of the psychological sciences for pastoral counseling cannot be denied. Knowledge of the thought of Freud, Rogers, and other personality theorists is a vital prerequisite for much of the work and concern of pastoral counseling. Without such knowledge, pastoral counseling would become a crippled and even a barren enterprise. What our thesis questions is the practice of making a psychological bias the final or basic concern of the pastoral counselor. The assertion that "pastoral counseling is a Christian perspective" implies that man's moral and spiritual struggle is its final and basic concern. Professional knowledge of this struggle is not the exclusive possession of the pastoral counselor, but it is the focal and thus the distinctive concern of his perspective.

The words "final" and "basic" are pivotal terms. The word "final" is used in a longitudinal sense, pointing to that which is ultimate for man from a developmental or long-term viewpoint. It refers to that which is the end or climatic point of a process. "Basic" has a cross-sectional reference, pointing to that which is ultimate for man in the present moment, to the depth dimension of a particular moment of time. Pastoral counseling as a Christian perspective may now be defined in a very precise and limited sense. Its vision of the client's basic or final struggle differs from the vision of psychology. Like most forms of counseling, it maintains that the counselor should deal with and be centered on the immediate verbalizations of the client, that he should be concerned with what the client is struggling with at the moment. But pastoral counseling has a different guiding image of man's plight and rescue, and therefore it often perceives in the client's verbalizations a different struggle and end-point.

For example, as a Freudian therapist explores the life situation of a patient, he will see the patient's final or basic struggle as one with repressed impulses of infantile sexuality. A Rogerian counselor will perceive in the client's verbaliza-

174

tions a struggle which basically or finally revolves around the client's denial or distortion of his "total organismic experiencing." The final concern of each therapist may not show through at any particular point in the therapeutic process; but whether implicit or explicit, it is the underlying concern of much of what the therapist says and does.

If we were to cut into the therapeutic process and take a section of either a Freudian or a Rogerian psychotherapeutic relationship, their final or basic concern probably would not be very evident. There is, after all, a good measure of the client's life situation to which all therapists must attend, without referring it immediately to their own underlying bias. This means that therapists from the various orientations generally have more in common than they care to admit. Only at crucial points and only as one takes a sustained look at the therapeutic process does the therapist's underlying perspective become manifest.

Three Marks of Christian Perspective

While the pastoral counselor may make use of either the Freudian or the Rogerian interpretations — or both — he cannot accept either as an exhaustive description of man's ultimate struggle. In contrast to these, we contend that the pastoral counselor sees the client's basic or final struggle as concerned with one of three problems that are pivotal in man's moral and religious self-affirmation. These are (1) the problem of finitude, (2) the problem of alienation, and (3) the problem of guilt. The first is a struggle with life's limitations, the second, with it's meaning, and the third, with it's fulfillment.

In what sense do these particular concerns define and exhaust a Christian perspective? We maintain, on the one hand, that the Christian faith points to them as vital ingredients of any Christian position. A serious study of man indicates that finitude, alienation, and guilt are pervasive issues in human life and belong to the deepest dimensions of existence. Christian theology addresses itself to these concerns and sees them as central to man's moral and religious self-affirmation.

As Augustine's dictum "I believe in order that I may understand" implies, the Christian pastoral counselor is committed to a basic position out of which understanding arises. That position is the Christian faith, which gives him a decisive clue to the client's basic or final struggle.

But, on the other hand, we maintain that these concerns are not specifically Christian unless they are seen from a Christian point of view. Existentialism, process philosophy, Marxism, dynamic psychology, and phenomenology are just a few schools of thought that pay some attention to one or more of these problems. They belong to and form a Christian perspective only if understood from within the Christian life. Although the Christian faith is not uniform in its expression, it does have its own specific understanding of man's predicament and rescue. It is a Christological interpretation of life, revealing how fallen man is lifted up and recreated by divine love. Therefore, it understands man's struggle with finitude, alienation, and guilt in the light of the revelation which is disclosed and embodied in Jesus the Christ. This understanding constitutes the ultimate goal of Christian pastoral counseling, giving us the ideal outcome of man's moral or religious quest.

The Problem of Finitude. Man is limited, finite, a child of nature. He is constituted by and is subject to the laws, vicissitudes, and necessities of the natural order of existence. He becomes ill, he can tolerate only certain variations in the supply of heat, food, and oxygen, and he is an unrelieved prisoner of eventual death and decay. But man is also unlimited, infinite, a spirit. He possesses the ability to transcend himself and to make his ego both subject and object. His mind can move back and forth in the dimensions of time and space, he can put himself into the world of another person, and he can anticipate the fact of his demise and can even imagine its possible circumstances. This two-sided, tensional conflict in man constantly requires of him some kind of response, some kind of resolution. Ideally, of course, the two sides of this polarity should be brought together into a workable and harmonious synthesis, but in actuality the polarity often causes a basic and pervasive disruption in the life of the troubled client. The transcendent pole of this conflict may and often does cause serious difficulty, but generally it is the opposite side of the conflict with which the client carries on an intense and prolonged struggle. For this reason we have chosen to call the first concern the problem of finitude. It does not intend to obscure the pole of transcendence, and the client's struggle with his own transcendence.

The problem of finitude manifests itself in numerous ways in the verbalizations of a client. It is experienced not only in one's own life but also as reflected in the lives of other people. On an absolute level it is a concern with the *fact* of one's existence in the world, that is, when and in what circumstances one will either die or lose a loved one. On a relative level it is a concern with the *mode* of one's existence in the world, that is, with the style in which one will dwell in the world — as sick, healthy, handicapped, adequate, etc. Clinical examples of the absolute concern are a client's struggle with the fear of death, the reaction of grief and bereavement, the feeling of helplessness, or the sense of being nothing. Clinical examples of the relative concern are a client's struggle with the fear of sickness or of life's vicissitudes, the feeling of inadequacy, and, in some situations, the feeling of failure.

As pastoral counseling attends to the problem of finitude (however it is expressed by the client), its goal is to help the individual move toward a Christian resolution of that problem. The resolution lies in the existential disposition of courage, and its meaning can be stated in Tillichian terms. Courage refers to the "self-affirmation of being in spite of the fact of nonbeing," because one is in "the state of being grasped by the power of being-itself." [16] Therefore, pastoral counseling seeks to help the client move toward the ability to affirm his life in the face of its limitations, because he is rooted and grounded in the source and sustainer of life, namely, God.

[16] Paul Tillich, *The Courage To Be* (New Haven: Yale University Press, 1952), pp. 155ff.

The Problem of Alienation. In discussing the first problem we proceeded from general principle to clinical example. Here we will reverse the procedure in order to illustrate that both directions are equally possible.

Miss Tad, as we will call a certain thirty-three year old single woman, came to the pastoral counselor because her life was "falling apart." Increasingly she found herself in a world of confusion, bitterness, and doubt, without being able to put her finger on a definite reason for the feelings. About four months after Miss Tad started counseling, she came for her regular appointment one evening in a very pensive and discouraged mood. She opened the session with the comment, "I don't know what's happening to me anymore. I'm going around in all kinds of circles, and the circles never seem to meet anywhere." Miss Tad went on to elaborate the statement, indicating that she had been struggling all week with an intense desire to destroy, maybe even to kill. Near the end of this discussion she said:

> This wanting to destroy has been such a strong feeling all week. All week long except one night, I've — I don't know, it was just as if I was deliberately building up — the attitude: "I don't care. I want out of it. I just want everything to end." And that's the way it went until — I guess it was last night when we had the fog, and I was looking out of my window and — ordinarily I can see all the lights in the Hart and the Y.M., and, oh, a lot of other buildings. And I can always see a number of cars on the street. [Slight pause] I don't know quite how I felt or what I did, but all — all the lights that were visible at all were the car lights, and they were very dim, and — I couldn't even stand it. I pulled down the shade and walked away.
>
> *Pastoral Counselor:* What feeling did this seem to arouse?
>
> *Miss Tad:* Well — panic — more than anything else. I don't know, I guess it was utter isolation. Nothing above, nothing below, nothing around me.

These remarks can be used to lift up the second ingredient in man's moral and religious struggle. Miss Tad's struggle is with alienation, with being isolated and cut off from the world above, below, and around her. After living for a week in a desert of hostile isolation, in which she is ground down to the thought, "I want out of it. I want everything to end," her climactic experience with the isolation of the fog is a dramatic example of a sense of aloneness. This aloneness can be understood from the genetic and interpersonal concerns of a psychological perspective, but it is probably not exhausted by that concern. There are also moral and spiritual and ontological dimensions to her struggle with alienation, to which the perspective of pastoral counseling can and should respond.

Loneliness and isolation are not the only manifestations of alienation. The problem appears in other forms, chiefly in a sense of rejection, a sense of hate and disgust, a sense of dependency and self-alienation, and a sense of emptiness and despair.

The Christian antidote to man's situation of alienation and unrelatedness is love or, more precisely, *agape*. Through the gift of *agape*, man is reunited with self, others, and God. Reinhold Niebuhr has spoken of grace as power, as *agape*, shattering the self as it seeks to realize itself solely through itself, and empowering the self to seek fulfillment through the law of its essential being, that is, through loving relation to God and others. In this sense, the gift of *agape* both fulfills and negates man's penchant toward self-realization. It negates, for "every actual self-realization is partly an egotistic and therefore a premature closing of the self within itself." [17] Yet it also fulfills, for the freedom of the self, which is the "essence of man," is implanted in a power which can give genuine newness of life. However we put it, love remains the existential and spiritual disposition that Christian pastoral

[17] Niebuhr, *Faith and History: A Comparison of Christian and Modern Views of History* (New York: Charles Scribner's Sons, 1951), p. 179.

counseling seeks to nurture in the face of man's struggle with the problem of alienation.

The Problem of Guilt. Guilt presupposes a norm or an expectation in relation to which the individual is found "wanting," as well as some degree of responsibility in relation to both the norm and the failure to measure up to the norm. Guilt is therefore a discrepancy between potentiality and actuality in the context of man's "respondability." It refers, on the one hand, to the norms and standards which come to us as a result of our socialization and acculturation, the failure to obey laws and expectations which originate from outside us but which may have been interiorized by us. On the other hand, guilt refers to the inner "gestalt" of the individual himself, to the norms and demands of his own "essential being." In this case it refers to the individual's failure in the moral sphere of his own self-affirmation, and is the deepest and most important kind of guilt. It suggests a "discrepancy between what man ought to be and what he actually is, a discrepancy for which man himself bears some responsibility." [18]

When experienced at the level of feelings, guilt can appear as a sense of failure and shame, a sense of hopelessness, a sense of unworthiness, a sense of rebellion and disobedience, and a sense of pretense. For example, Miss Tad, who became pregnant out of wedlock, decided to undergo an induced abortion, an experience in which "I saw what would have been my child." Her consequent struggle with intense guilt is exposed when she says:

> It's like I can never go past this — It's just like this is some kind of gate or — something. I can't cross it. I'm guilty; therefore I'm condemned, and — that's it. I — when I first came back, I just very literally had to shut myself in my apartment, not go anywhere, not see anyone, not do anything, because if I had seen anyone — the desire — to tell everyone, to — I don't know, in a sense be forgiven because I couldn't forgive myself for what I had

[18] LeRoy Aden, "Distortions of a Sense of Guilt," *Pastoral Psychology,* 15, no. 141 (February, 1964): 17.

done. I knew if I saw anyone, I'd start talking and — I couldn't afford to do that.

Miss Tad provides an example both of the problem of guilt and of the sense of forgiveness that Christian pastoral counseling accepts as the proper resolution of guilt. Forgiveness is the Christian answer to man's struggle with guilt, not because it wipes away all guilt, but because it assures men of being "accepted in spite of his being unacceptable."[19] Pastoral counseling, therefore, in attending to the client's struggle with guilt, seeks to help him move toward the existential and spiritual disposition of forgiveness or, more correctly, toward the acceptance of forgiveness.

Conclusion

As a concluding remark we can go a step beyond our thesis, for the thesis speaks of pastoral counseling simply as a therapeutic endeavor. The validity of the thesis may not be limited solely to therapy. Freud found himself in a similar position when he discovered that psychoanalysis, as a "method for the treatment of neurotic disorders," was at the same time a method of investigation and data-collecting. Pastoral counseling as a Christian perspective offers the same advantage. It is also a method of research which offers us a close and sustained look at an individual's struggle with the problems of finitude, alienation, and guilt.

An examination of the therapeutic hour in pastoral counseling should uncover data that is relevant to the deeper dimensions of man's moral and spiritual life. In this way, pastoral counseling as Christian perspective is a vital part of theological study. It contributes to that enterprise, not by standing outside it and bringing the resultant findings back to it, but by standing within it, perceiving the client's struggle as basically and finally spiritual. More specifically, this method of inquiry could be called a theological phenomenology. And this data, if collected and organized, might help to give us a more adequate theological anthropology.

[19] Tillich, *The Courage To Be*, p. 164.

8

Psychology of the Dream:
Dream without Myth
LEIGHTON McCUTCHEN

Introduction

Why is it that we do not share dreams fully and regularly? Why does dream-telling in public seem shameful and out of place? Why does it seem exhibitionist to wonder aloud about the meaning of a dream, and to invite others' suggestions?

These questions may reflect my own background more than pose a problem of general interest. Few of my own dreams have found their way into public discussion, even that connected with counseling. As a parish minister I found myself using dream interpretation as a part of pastoral counseling, though sparingly and with a sense of being out of bounds.

After all, are there not times and places in which we tell dreams? What about the cocktail hour, that peculiarly "liquid" and transitional institution? There one can hear echoes of the previous night, or at least of the dreams already recounted before "my therapist." The frequent use of shallow, stereotyped interpretations in such a context obscures, however, the potential at issue — a depth sharing of dreams.

The more likely answer is in theater or religious "witnessing." In both these cultural forms, public reference is made to dream. An example of the former is Osborne's play *Inadmissable Evidence*.[1] Within explicitly religious contexts, the

[1] John Osborne, *Inadmissable Evidence* (New York: Grove Press, 1965). The play begins with an overt dream sequence with the anti-hero Maitland at the dock on trial for unethical practices. There is a sudden reversal to waking reality — his office as barrister. As the play presents evidence to corroborate his plea of "not guilty," we find a

183

appeal to visions located in dreams in the night is still made by those wishing to lend objectivity to their particular conversion experiences. Though distinguished from vision, and often interpreted minimally and selectively (separating from the rest those elements giving portent of divine revelation), the dream remains a bulwark to some groups within the Christian fellowship; in it lie authentic words from God.

Despite these cultural forms of dream-telling, and with a sense of having my query informed by them, I am not convinced that they represent significant dream-sharing. The thrust of both the theatrical and the religious use of dream-telling is ulterior; in drama and "witness," interest in what *is not* dream deflects attention from what *is* dream. The response of the audience or the hearer is to judge the normalcy of the person dreaming, not to wonder about the dream itself.

Sigmund Freud's masterpiece, the *Interpretation of Dreams*, met with an indifferent response at its first publication. Despite the almost commonplace status of some of the ideas in this book, a status lending itself even to stereotypy, there is still, in the present day a silence in our culture about the phenomenon of dreams. Dreams are the property of esoterics and experts; they receive no public airing.

Hypothesis. This essay points to such a gap, a lack of public dream-telling, and attempts an explanation of why this is so. The reason for our silence is twofold: we do not share dreams because to do so requires, first, a desire to think through private feelings, to apprehend the self, to "logos" the psyche,[2] to search for the soul; second, this process, manifest enough in a culture dominated by "psychological men" in other areas,[3] is blocked with respect to dreams, because

---

dream-like quality more and more unmistakable. At the conclusion, he drops off at the telephone, asleep and dreaming. We are, as an audience, put in the position of Alice on confronting the sleeping king.

[2] Logos is used here as a verb in an attempt to convey manifold actions, including (a) speaking and making words about, (b) structuring and constructing in a reasonable way, (c) playing against the noun logos, which assumes stasis and substantive permanence.

[3] "Psychological man" means the image of man permeating our culture with a personalistic, healthy, hedonistic, careful, and analytic ideal. Philip Rieff's construct "the therapeutic" is similar in intent; I assume

to think publicly about dreams is to reason about myth. In the popular extrapolation from psychology, myth is either foolishness or it is holy. Either way it is unavailable to reasoning. To the positivist side of psychological man, myths must be extirpated by reasoning, which limits itself to observable, partial, controllable data. Myths drain the individual's energy away from the difficult chore of problem-solving. To the mystifying tendency of "psychological man" (and we should not be surprised at the coincidental union of extreme reductionism and romanticism in our society), myths are the gateways to the unspeakable mysteries, to the unnamable wholeness which *must* be experienced as ineffable. Reasoning is called into question and cannot helpfully touch mystery.[4]

A certain definition of myth will be used in this essay. Myth is a description, an imaging, of the centers of uncanny power and absolute authority. To reason about myth is to come out of Eden, to lose our "dreaming innocence," which is wont to locate the "centers" simply and straightforwardly. Without the conjoining of reason with myth, power and authority lie merely outside man — as in the transcendent heavens — or merely inside man — as in technology, the gospel of immanental unfolding.

There is a resistance to finding a complex origin, a double source, for power and authority, one that is both inside and outside in some sense. To "logos" myth is to waken, to be responsibly appreciative of the complex origin and consequence of mythic centers and images. On the basis of this sort of resistance, reasoning about myth is hard to achieve. Hesitation in public dream-telling is one form in which the difficulty is reflected.

Myth and Dream. The connection between myth and dream is subtle. The lines of the argument are as follows: the process of dream-telling is contiguous with the process of

---

Rieff's contention that this ideal is, indeed, "triumphant" in our culture. See Rieff's *The Triumph of The Therapeutic: Uses of Faith after Freud* (New York: Harper & Row, 1966).

[4] There is a "mystifying" tendency in some schools of the History of Religions. The old discipline of Psychology of Religion is an instance of the former positivism.

mytho-logizing, that is, reasoning about myth. Though different in many respects, dreams and myths are linked in at least three ways: first, similar thought processes are used in appropriating them; second, both manifest centers of agency and authenticity of peculiar relevance for selves and cultures; third, both dream and myth have intercourse with wish.

Wishing is the central psychological category, borrowed from Freud, used in this essay. Energetic and related to bodily gratification, wishing is a pervasive psychic fact, linking conscious to unconscious, past to present, possible to actual. It is the only single category that can point to the common motivation for dreaming dreams and living myths, namely, wish-fulfillment.

The subtitle "Dream without Myth" comes from a reflection upon the title of Schubert Ogden's work *Christ without Myth*.[5] Though there is no identity of motif, it will be necessary to treat his argument at several points. Ogden argues against exempting the "Christ" from demythologization, which he suspects Bultman of doing.

> Christian Faith is to be interpreted exhaustively and without remainder as man's original possibility of authentic existence as this is clarified and conceptualized by an appropriate philosophical analysis.[6]

There is to be strict adherence to the two criteria for Christian theology. One criterion is that, in contrast to mythology, everything asserted about God must be equally applicable to assertions about man. Bultmann holds back here by failing to develop within anthropology a theory of analogy that will allow us to say something objectively about God without falling into mythology.

The second criterion is "the revealed word of God declared in Jesus Christ, expressed in Holy Scripture, and made concretely present in the proclamation of the church through its word and sacraments."[7] All theology must, therefore, be true

[5] *Christ without Myth: A Study Based on the Theology of Rudolf Bultmann* (New York: Harper and Brothers, 1961).
[6] *Ibid.*, p. 146.
[7] *Ibid.*, p. 138.

to this particular Christian image by seeing that possibility of faith in Jesus Christ is a strictly human possibility under any condition of being human whatsoever. Again, Christ is "demythologized" in the sense of being seen as the disclosure of human possibility, *coram deo.*

The definition of myth at work in Ogden's analysis is not identical with the one with which we are presently working. If, with Ogden, one uses philosophical anthropology as the knife that pares away the covering of first-century myth (which is as far as Bultmann goes), one cannot keep from allowing the incrustation of the Christ element of that myth to suffer the same destiny as any other element.

My meanings are slightly different, though related at crucial points. Presently I am going to say "as with dream, so with myth," in the sense that to possess the possibility of dream-telling is to possess the possibility of reasoning about myth, understanding all the while that the absence of dream-telling comes from a hesitation about demythologizing. Ogden's thesis runs, "as with myth, so with Christ," in the sense of affirming Bultmann's program of demythologizing, and simply desiring to take it further by delineating the ontology underlying the anthropological meaning of the kerygma. So far as I know, Ogden does not treat the dream and its connection with myth; and he is innocent of psychological intentions in his philosophical critique.

The intimate connection between the way we deal with dream and with myth is central to the present analysis. Contradicting the spirit of Ogden, I assume that modern man is *not* ready to enter fully into demythologization. The prime evidence for this is the contrast between what is known theoretically about dreams and the lack of public practice concerning them. Contrary to Ogden, I assume a certain autonomy to myth, and to dream, for that matter. Neither dreams nor myths need protection or encouragement. We need no will to dream, no will to make myths. I do advocate that a definite care be taken of dream and myth. But, unlike Ogden, I desire no reduction of myth's influence, only a qualification of its meaning. We will go on dreaming and

187

having our myths whether or not we reason about either one. The emergence of these phenomena is a given in human experience.[8] Myth and dream have a complex origination. No single "source" is set forth in this essay. The whole creative process, of which man's self-understanding is but a part, breeds those experiences and phenomena best interpreted as myth and dream.

More narrowly, I find that the ubiquity of wishing has guided my thought here. Wishing is, singularly, both flexible and persistent enough to catch the subtle mental transition involved in reasoning about myth and dream. Being central to both myth and dream, it is the proper bridge toward understanding them.

Although dream and myth are born out of the whole creative process of which man is but a part, I hold that the way men receive and prepare for both dream and myth conditions the constructiveness and destructiveness with which they emerge. Both dream and myth can undo us if they are not properly cared for; if reason — in the sense of tender, careful concern for what is going on — does not find a way of noticing them and coping with them. Dreams and their associates — impulses, habits, phobias, hallucinations, visions and mystifications — can delude us from within if they are not given the proper respect. Myths and their associates — insights,

[8] Contemporary research suggests a need for dreaming. If subjects are deprived of "dream-time" during sleep by awakening them at the start of dream-connected physiological changes (such as Rapid Eye Movements — REMs — characteristic EEG patterns, kinesthetic changes, hormonal balance shifts, and apparently, penile erections in men) they will attempt to dream more often and more quickly on falling back into sleep. If interruptions to normal dream sequences are halted, the subject gets in "dream-time" sooner on interruption-free nights. Continual interruption produces a variety of negative reactions on the part of the subject if pursued drastically. Cf. Norman MacKenzie, *Dreams and Dreaming* (New York: The Vanguard Press, 1965) especially the chapter on "Sleep and Science." Calvin Hall, in *The Meaning of Dreams* (New York: McGraw-Hill Book Co., 1966), has challenged this inference of a need to dream on the basis of his distinction between the meaning of the repeated dream and the physiological associates of the dream. See also Nathaniel Kleitman, *Sleep and Wakefulness*, rev. ed. (Chicago: University of Chicago Press, 1963) for original and definitive work in this area.

mystiques, rituals, cults, theophanies, disorientations — can, in like manner, confuse us with illusions from without.

The loosening insight I seek to follow is the *ubiquity of wishing*, the concrete fulfillment of which is the goal of both dream and myth, and the pervasive energy on which reason runs.

A Dream Specimen

There is nothing like trying to share a dream publicly as a way of discovering why we do not do more of it. The following dream was subjected to such an attempt. The person who originally had the dream offered it as part of his contribution to the life of a group, one located in a Christian church. The group was designed to offer the conditions whereby several church members, each of whom had particular concerns that had brought him or her to the pastor for guidance, could find a common resource in each other and in the faith.

The problem of dream-telling seems to be, whose dream shall be told? To be a real test, it must come from someone present. Literary dreams are protected by the absence of their authors, as the readers of this essay will doubtless point out. I can only urge you to try the experiment yourself.

The Dream: "The Note of Hope." "I am in the balcony of my home church, there to sing my usual solo. There is a small group with me, like a choir. It is a festival service, something like Christmas eve midnight carols. The ritual moves on closer to the appointed time. I am struggling with the recall of both words and tune.

"I consult with members of the group in the balcony; they coach me. I am asking myself, 'Why didn't I prepare completely? Why wait until the last minute? But maybe I can bring it off anyhow — No: it is impossible.'

"Sometimes the song is fixed in my mind — what it is that is expected of me. At the next moment, I do not know what is to be done; panic. The group tries to rehearse me, and even to create a song from the start to fit the occasion.

"The struggle mounts to an intense agony. The time is too short. Then something happens on the floor of the sanctuary, like a cry of fire — or a general disgust at what is going on. People begin to get up angrily and move toward the exit.

"The panic of ambivalence is irresolvable. The place is emptying. I open my mouth to sing. In a voice that is both silent and clear, a monotone and monoword sings out — 'hope.' I hold it till almost out of breath. Then I awake."

Free Associations and Wishing. The psychoanalytic interpretation of dreams, as set forth by Sigmund Freud, will give us a conceptual framework. An insight and a method link together. The insight is that the dream is a wish fulfillment; its motive is a wish that is latent, and its content is the work of condensing, representing, symbolizing, and elaborating this wish.

The method that fits the insight is free association. One trusts mental connections, no matter how absurd, contrasting, or jolting. The mind runs free, noticing the chain of contiguity displayed by ideas. Free association is a kind of mental playfulness, itself a wishing that breaks down the screens set up by the censor and reality principle to hide the underlying, enduring wish.

To change the metapor, in free association, the dreamer watches the fleeting wish as it wings along through the mind's pathways, now dipping to alight, now soaring in a crescendo of meanings, now diving toward its prey, at last to perch and sing its own song. The bird-watching metaphor is useful if it connotes the variety of forms the wish takes, the sense of organic wholeness despite partial glimpses, and the ethologist's sense of lazy watchfulness of a bird on its own ground, in its own territory. It fails if a compulsive counting of species or "taking" of a rare find is implied.

Let us see if we can recognize the wish, the "bird," of the dream specimen by putting together several glimpses it gives to us. Following Freud (and as Bakan has suggested, Freud was following in a transformed way the older method of exegesis of textual elements),[9] several elements in the

---

[9] David Bakan, *Sigmund Freud and the Jewish Mystical Tradition* (New York: Schocken Books, 1965), see the chapter "Techniques of Interpretation."

dream will be noted, and some of the associations connected with them cited. The dream element will be italicized, with a few of the individual's associations about each element included within the quote. The dreamer gave some of these in the context of the group's life, and some of them personally to the pastor. My own interpolations lie outside the quoted material.

"*I am in the balcony of my home church.* The first acceptance given me by adults for something I as a child could do — sing. Many times I stood in the balcony of churches for a Christmas solo. The church wants me, as person, as worker. It captured my family, most of them in 'full-time Christian service.' But being a preacher comes later; I can only promise it. The song is here and now; it's something I can do which I greatly enjoy, and they like it.

"First acceptance — first rejection; I remember a little boy standing on the porch of an Indian missionary house. He is alone, scared — in his belly. He looks out from under an overhanging roof, mounted by thick vines, and sees an empty pathway running the length of the village. Nobody. He looks up, and there in the sky, looming over the edge of the encroaching jungle, are three gigantic animals — pink, blue, and green. There is an elephant, a giraffe, and a smaller, nondescript one. He is frozen with fear."

The story behind this combination "screen-memory" and hallucination is a long one. Part of the essential elements include a series of accidents eventuating in disease for the mother, death for the father, and abandonment of the dreamer. The mother's accidental injury refuses to heal. The father, just recuperating from fever, too quickly leaves his bed to ready transportation "in case it's needed." He is bruised, blood poisoning sets in, and death comes three days later. The mother experiences a radical depression, and the dreamer is left in the care of a loving, but frightened, friend.

The singing from a balcony seemed to carry with it a reversal of the old image; by it he is looming over the totem animals (which were linked with an early memory of the first piano instruction book, carrying on its initial page just such

191

a group of animals). Thus far, the wish underlying the dream seems to point in the direction of longed for strengths, talents, that will give security to the dreamer. It is as if he wanted to stand above it all, above the conflict over vulnerability, with their strength.

"There is a small group with me, like a choir." The dreamer is, as noted above, in a small group of laymen and pastor, called a "Growth Group." The juxtaposition of "small" and "growth" leads to, "I always wanted to grow up tall, like my father. In the Growth Group I am finding some comfort for the rejection given me by the men of the church which I am trying to lead. Most of the men think I am too radical in pushing for integration with another race. My support of the guaranteed annual wage also offends many of them. It's really the first time a group within the church itself has rejected my ideas."

The support and communication within a small group, however, did give the dreamer a transitional structure. Heretofore, his work in music had been warmly received. Now he was trying another tack, and receiving outright hostility in place of acceptance. In the face of the adults' rejection, the group gave him a "clutch" of brothers and sisters seeking to grow. As an only child himself, this felt good to him.

"The ritual moves closer to the appointed time. Control of breathing is one of the most difficult parts of solo work. Anxiety left me panting and breathless. Butterflies in the stomach; aren't butterflies a symbol of death or something? Rebirth? At times I would pray, 'Just this one song, God.' "

The control reflected in public singing was a problem to the dreamer in other dimensions as well, but reflected an overall bodily conflict, described in the Freudian literature as anal in quality. Daily bowel movements were a combination of retreat from family, fantasy spinning, dalliance, and delay. But the other side was severe straining throughout childhood, leaving a tendency toward minor hemorrhaging. Similarly, adolescent sexual experimentation was caught up in the same pattern; erotic excitement was used to dull the fear of loneliness, but it was calculating, prudential, and mechanical — without a move toward genuine risk of sharing.

"Sexual to sacred ecstasy; the midnight service moves toward a midnight climax. Two joys, one religious — having the hymn of praise coming just at the right time; the other secular — the moment of awakening on Christmas morning to find all the presents there. Santa Claus and the Christ Child. And if the former comes, perhaps the latter will too! Though I have seen through the secret for longer than the adults know, and play it to the hilt. It is a shame for them to know that I know what is there in the package. So smile and act surprised." The dreamer appears to be wishing to be genuinely and delightfully surprised.

"*I am struggling with the recall of words and tune.* Funny mixture of words and music; new words to an old tune, or old words to a new tune — leftovers and beginnings. The last time in the church I didn't sing. Someone else did. I hadn't gone back since changing from being a minister of music to being a teacher. But in that same church a long time ago I had begun this very shift, from singing to talking and listening. My first public address was there. A terrific struggle preparing for it, whether to write a manuscript or speak out of the moment's inspiration. Could I talk and lead a discussion, listening to others, and not feel overwhelmed?

"*Then something happens on the floor of the sanctuary.* Spilled milk, spilled blood. I get furious when the children spill carelessly. They fill their cups too quickly and too full. 'Come, fill the cup slowly.' That phrase from my mentor."

The dreamer has become aware of the danger of rushing pell-mell into life, willing to sacrifice everything for too meager a prize. He felt that his father had in some sense sacrificed himself needlessly. There had been panic among the faithful at his death; God had taken away His most promising servant. The son is left as the only one who remains faithful to his memory; devotions themselves had been a matter of addressing the deity alongside the father in heaven. The wish now takes the shape of a desire to be comforted and to bring comfort, to gather the spilled drops together again.

"*. . . like a cry of fire — or a general disgust.* Curious combination; fire, heat. Animals are 'in heat' and humans get 'hot' with love-making. When a farm animal was described as a 'bitch in heat' sometime during childhood, I liked it, liked entering into this direct language freely and openly. Then the promiscuous 'fall-down dance'; everyone dancing to a lively tune, then the music shifts to langorous mood, everyone falls down and feels each other. Disgust and arousal. Accustomed to approaching sex as a 'holy' thing.

"*The place is emptying.* Urgency mounts; I must fill the hall with my voice before it completely voids. The sounds, the words, must cover the action. Talk about sex without the family circle began to cover the acts of seductiveness between people, both inside and outside the family."

The dreamer often was called upon to fill the void of the oldsters of the family by singing after supper. Most of the songs were love songs of an era of a generation that was long gone. The tunes evoked the past for the old ones, but dulled the present for him.

The wish now appears to be one of wanting to respond to the occasion, but not in the same old way. Some breakthrough to genuine bodily preference, some escape from pretentious control by the past is wanted.

"*In a voice both silent and clear.* A contradiction, like having to run without moving. But in this case I feel a closeness to the voice of conscience; an internal voice that speaks without sounding. The voice of God too? Once it came through an angelic choir, 'heard' only by shepherds and visible only to the 'eyes of faith.' The voice in the dream is mine. I can talk to myself or sing to myself without fear of carrying a secret against someone. I can resist the temptation to tell mother all!"

The dreamer's mother had evidently called for more intimacy than either she or her son could explicitly face. In hearing the voice of the dream, the dreamer was gaining some ground toward an appreciation of something weak, but persistent, within himself. He linked this "sounding" with the deafening silence of the screen-memory when once again there is external quiet but inward beating and panting. At times of being left alone, later in childhood, he would try to "blend into the woodwork" when left alone in a house, making no sound, so that "if" an intruder should come in, he would hear beforehand and be able to flee. In the dream, he is making a sound that fits the silence. He wanted not only to be comforted but to give courage and resource out of himself for others.

". . . *hope*. This is my word, the only virtue to which I cling. It is a frequent word in our group, one that carries with it the tradition of the faith, and yet leaves some room for the future.

"The good ship Hope, a mission of mercy from our country; another memory of a bright ship filled with darkness — the ship bringing us home after the death of father. Twenty years later I took another ship-trip, which brought me, after only three days, nausea and 'thanatos.' Finally the parallel emerged; I was sailing back in the direction of fear, back to the country with the grave, back into the source of my chaos.

"The thing that frightened me most as a child was eternity — living on, and on, and on, and on — each lifetime punctuated by a comma. I would run to a grand-aunt and hide my face in her lap when the cycles of eternity would obsess my mind. Afraid of death? No, rather, afraid of the magic power of death to pass into endless life, repetitious, boring. I feared the power of life to take its toll in suffering again and again."

There is some indication that the dreamer, experiencing the loss of his father during the period of life usually marked by unusual conflict of love and hate toward the father, was facing in this dream his fear of his own desire to kill the father, a desire once too patently powerful. Hope would be some sort of transition, recognizing the fear of death-dealing and consequent punishment (in heaven) but also desiring to give death time to come. The dreamer is coming to terms

with impulsivity, which in his case meant rushing death
(either his own or his loved ones). Now he could, in some
incipient way, affirm life as full of time. If hope springs eternal, *he* does not have to! He stands up in the dream, in contrast to seeking the ample lap in which to bury his head. And
he shouts the word, until his breath runs out. Then it is safe
to awaken.

The Wish: What is it? According to Freud, the key to
dreams is wish-fulfillment. A dream is a hallucination, manifesting the actualization of at least one central wish that has
heretofore been denied or repressed. This wish, most clearly
present in the latent dream, is "worked" on in order to elude
total repression; it is disguised. The dream is thus not exactly
what it appears to be, and yet more is accomplished through
it than meets the eye. We shall look closely at the process of
"dream work" in a moment. Granting this, however, what
wish has been fulfilled in this particular dream? What underlying yearning of the dreamer can be detected in the inter-
weaving of dream per se and associations?

Hope is overcoming the false-note of fear. That is, I believe,
the wish. Hope's deformation is fear — the pseudo-hope for
safety in numbers, the preoccupation with protection against
a premature death, the compulsive pleasurable eroticism, the
sacrificed ego expression reduced to the one mode of singing.

Hope can be an authentic word (in the sense of an appropriate *logos* — word, spirit, and structure). It can keep oneself
open to oneself, giving one the motive for other relations, for
specific others whom one has loved and hated.

Hope is often seen as ambiguous in its consequences. The
Pandora myth is sometimes told in such a way that hope, the
last daemon out of the box, gives surcease to those afflicted
by the other pestilences. But often it is hope itself that is the
most distrusted of the daemons, since it gives man the capacity to proceed with living against any reasonable cause. It
can be either the balm to heal the wounds of history or the
ultimate insanity of merely holding on to a senseless life,
better cut short by the Fates.

Erikson catches this essentially good, but existentially ambivalent, quality of hope in the following definition:

> Hope is the enduring belief in the attainability of fervent wishes, in spite of the dark urges and rages which mark the beginning of existence.[10]

For him, hope is the virtue (one of those combinations of "strength, restraint and courage")[11] first experienced and last to be called into question. It is the rock bottom, without which nothing exactly human can continue.

The dream sets forth this wish, to have a hope that is genuinely specific for this dreamer; it calls him back into the early maelstrom, in which any kind of hope was radically threatened. It ends with a transition into awakening to the concrete present. Yet hope is the bearer of the very mark it comes to erase. At the dream level, the wish for hope is a wish for genuine bodily appetition. The dreamer tries to transcend, without destroying, the hesitation of ambivalence and to move with the flow of time, the flux of space.

Note that without the associations, without the attempt to uncover the latent dream, hope could have been seen as fatuous. It could have remained at the level of growth reflected in the self-pity of a middle-aged man acting like a choirboy! It had to find its root in the personal history of the dreamer, catching up the old argument in his life about who was guilty for the father's death, and who responsible for his own generation. But it rephrased this argument, giving it a new twist; now the son is in the position of fathering himself in the sense of seeing the continuity but distinctness of his life style as compared with his father's. The hope felt is concrete, drawing to itself a manifold of kairotic concerns. And it is part of a process, leaning into the next-coming moment like the last relaxed breath of the high-diver a moment before the plunge.

[10] Erik H. Erikson, *Insight and Responsibility: Lectures on the Ethical Implications of Psychoanalytical Insight* (New York: W. W. Norton and Co., 1964), p. 118.
[11] *Ibid.*, p. 113.

197

The Dream Work

Some readers may feel that my interpretation of the dream is far from complete, or that it lacks the evocation of an intuitive appeal. Both are possible. We meet one more barrier to dream-telling, that in public intercourse, consensus is the first assumption and the last achievement. There are many loose ends to dream-telling. By no means all of the associations connected even with this dream are present to the reader, much less the other sorts of clinical indications usually relied upon.

A partial help comes from a study of what Freud called the "dream-work." After the initial shock of dream-telling has worn off, it is possible to notice genuine regularities, patterns, themes. I am not referring here only to what Calvin Hall refers to as the thematic unity of "dream series." [12] Important as the thematic unity in dreams may be, however, the kind of patterning of more interest to us is in what Freud called the "mechanisms" of the dream work, including condensation, elaboration, representation, and symbolization. I will discuss only symbolization here as one of the ways by which the dream work disguises the wish. This way seems to me more relevant to our concern with the connection between myth and dream.

Dream symbols are those elements held constant between the dreams of a single dreamer or between dreamers over time. They form a rudimentary dream language sufficiently unclear to escape conscious repression, and sufficiently clear to be "understood," if properly approached (that is, through free association).

Symbols come from at least three territories: from the body as the location of broad-gauge sexuality; from the long

[12] Hall, *Meaning of Dreams* (see footnote 10), xvi. Hall eschews free associations in favor of massive collections of dreams from single individuals over long periods of time, a method identical with some of Jung's ways with the dream. Hall uses content analysis on these dreams, however, in order to establish the sorts of themes manifest in them. This approach lacks any appreciation for the "dream-work," however, and moves to a level of generality which obscures most of the drive toward seeing the specific meaning of dreams, carried in this essay.

dependency of the child and the consequent enhancement of such acts as games, play, and imagination; and from the general or collective unconscious, the "residue" of the common experience of the race. In speaking of territories, I do not mean areas that do not touch each other. On the contrary, each symbol is a synthesis of at least two such territories, or areas, in my view.[13]

Symbols are marks of disguise; they are ambiguous. Without the freedom of the individual dreamer to see the symbol and *not* know directly what it means, the individual could not control the gradualness of the break in the wall of repression. And without this control, he could be wounded by an onslaught of wishes coming into consciousness too soon and too fast.

It follows that I would oppose Hall's method of studying dream symbol exclusively by their comparative value. Symbols are specific; or rather, without specific appropriation on the part of the dreamer, there is no check on the nuance of meaning, on the subtlety of timing which is their essential quality.

In the dream-specimen, the fire and disgust embody sexual intensity. The animals are totemic, embodying the phallic father, the womblike mother, and the unformed child. The balcony captures the nurturing breast on which the dreamer clings for support and on which he can, later, stand. The voice is his, God's, conscience's. But of what meaning is such a list of symbols apart from an accompanying list of the disguising elements also associated with them, or apart from the set of associative relations between them, relations that come to light only as the dreamer "works" them over in a "playful" way?

[13] I take responsibility for this loose paraphrasing of the whole scope of Freud's compass about symbols. "Broad-gauge sexuality" is my term for the perennial controversy over the meaning of the libido in Freud; the "long dependency of the child" is closer to Freud's own manner of speaking, though "games," "play," and "imagination" are not directly linked together by him in just this way; finally, the idea of "collective unconscious," though underlined by Jung, is clear in Freud as well in his "The Poet and Day-Dreaming," *Collected Papers*, vol. 4, trans. Joan Riviere (New York: Basic Books, 1959), p. 182.

The symbol is a moving feature, though it appears to be static. It is not only sexual, not only childish, not only unconceiving (unconscious). Properly approached, the symbol sets in motion insightful movements of the mind between all three of these features within the personal life.

Myth and Dream: Mirror Images

What is the parallel to the dream-work's efforts on the cultural level? It is myth. That is, it looks as if the kind of mechanisms which the dream-work uses to construct a dream are the reverse-image of the mechanisms used to demythologize a myth. While the dream-work condenses, we try to expand the time and space referents of a myth. The dream-work represents parts for wholes, a yes for a no; in mythology we try to reason dialectically, to see the patterns hinted at, to fit in the missing pieces.

Discussing the nature of dialectical thought in understanding myths, Altizer writes:

> Genuine dialectical thought, in its various expressions, revolves about the crucial principle that ultimately negation is affirmation, that the opposites coincide, that the acts of radical negation and radical affirmation are finally two poles of one dialectical movement.[14]

The dream work elaborates, makes something fairly coherent out of a jumble of impulses; whereas in demythologizing we try to analyze historically, to translate the "story-line" into its various elements and meanings, its sources and influences.

Clearly, if the above is true, then symbols cap the climax. For as the dream seeks to symbolize, the myth presents symbols as fait accompli. The study of dream and myth coalesces at the point where both are concerned with indispensable symbols, with irreducible disguises on the part of dreams and dreamers, with irreplaceable recognition of the limitation and mystery of myths.

[14] Thomas J. J. Altizer, Mircea Eliade and the Dialectic of the Sacred (Philadelphia: The Westminster Press, 1963), p. 82.

With symbolization necessary, it seems evident to me that myths will be ubiquitous. Not that those who wish to demythologize necessarily state that the day of the myth is over, but they move in that direction when they assume contemporary man's readiness to accept only a gospel shorn of myth. As Ogden points out, if Bultmann's denotations of the meaning of myth are followed, his argument has less inconsistency than otherwise. First, myth in the history of religious sense means "that manner of representation in which the unworldly and divine appears as the worldly and human — or in short, in which the transcendent appears as the immanent."[15]

> The second definition is more explicit. Myth is an event in which supernatural or superhuman powers or persons are at work; hence the fact that it is often defined simply as history of the gods. Mythical thinking refers specific phenomena and events to supernatural or "divine" powers that may be represented dynamistically or animistically or even as persons, spirits, or gods. Thus it excludes certain phenomena and events and also certain realms from the known and familiar and controllable course of worldly occurrences. . . . Myth objectifies the transcendent and thus makes it immanent. In doing so it makes it disposable, as becomes evident from the fact that cult more and more becomes a procedure for influencing the deity, for avoiding its wrath and for obtaining its favor.[16]

Holding aside for the moment the question of demythologizing, notice the ways in which symbol is to dream what the "divine" is to the myth. It is a point of transition, of movement between boundaries, of bridging heretofore separated (in appearance or in experience) qualities of existence.

Without presenting the case fully, some theorists concur in the linkage of dreams and myths, apart from the specific point about symbols. Both Freud and Jung are at one in seeing that myths are in some sense cultural dreams. Freud says:

[15] Ogden, *Christ Without Myth*, p. 24.
[16] *Ibid.*

The study of these creations (myths, legends and fairy-tales) of racial psychology is in no way complete, but it seems extremely probable that myths, for example, are distorted vestiges of the wish-phantasies of whole na-tions — the age-long dreams of young humanity.[17]

Jung concurs: the considerations of the Freudian under-standing of wish-fulfillment "tempts us to draw a parallel between the mythological thinking of ancient man and the similar thinking found in children, primitives, and in dreams."[18] In summing up the work done on myths, Jung denies that they are infantile, but rather finds them to be mature products of young humanity. Myths perpetuate not the every-day events of a culture, but the universal thoughts of mankind.

We are not yet ready to be drawn into the question of what we actually do, or should do, with myths. Though to that issue there has been reference. Rather, the point has been the reverse-image relations between the two phenomena when symbols are in view, and the overall linkage when individual and culture are held together. In time I will suggest that rea-soning about myths is cognate with thinking about dreams, and that dream-telling exists on the boundary between the dream per se and the interpreted myth. Let us take a step further into the psychological context in which Freud placed his insights about dreams, and see where this leads mytho-logically.

Psychodynamics of the dream. What is the psychic context of the dream and its wish? What is the structure which sup-ports the life of wishing? For our purposes we will limit con-sideration to the question of psychodynamics, that is, the perspective which seeks to elucidate energetic psychological struggle, or internal conflict. From his own viewpoint, Freud

[17] Freud, "Metapsychological Supplement to the Theory of Dreams," in *Collected Papers*, vol. 4 (see footnote 13), p. 182.

[18] Carl Jung, *Symbols of Transformation*, vol. 5 of *The Collected Works* of C. G. Jung, ed. Herbert Read, Michael Fordham, and Gerhard Adler, trans. R. F. C. Hull, Bollingen Series 20 (New York: Pantheon Books, 1956), p. 23.

has wounded modern man precisely here: for the process of self-knowledge contaminates itself, since it carries with it hidden resolutions of disguised conflicts, itself motivated by archaic struggles between illusion and reality, pain and pleasure, life and death. Freud's thoroughgoing, even pessimistic, energetic dualism makes him the keenest commentator upon the vicissitudes of the interior life.

For Freud, there was, if not a way out, a way beyond a short-circuiting of the life-and-death struggle. The "individual protects his own way towards death" (one definition of the "death-wish") through use of the weak but persistent voice of reason. While tending explicitly to absolutize the meaning of reason, Freud implicitly amplified it greatly. He restlessly created a welter of perspectives, which modern man could use to throw light on the understanding of his action, despite the wound to his consciousness. We cannot follow Freud here, only because it would involve an exposition of his whole thought. But we can take on the implications of one crucial perspective, that of psychodynamics. Readers familiar with Freud's work in the seventh chapter of *The Interpretation of Dreams* can refresh their own memories of the details of Freud's so-called "picket fence" model of the psychic apparatus.[19] This model is made up of a number of distinct and critical conflicts, several of which will be simply noted.

(1) Perception and memory are necessarily split apart from each other. But memory can properly function only when it enhances perception of the currently actual. (2) Ideas come from hallucinations. Through them the apparatus is freed from the totally impulsive quality of energies, but it is so only in order to seek more permanent gratification of these very impulses. (3) Thinking is "trial action with small quantities of energy" (a very pragmatic definition for an alleged

[19] Freud, *The Interpretation of Dreams*, trans. and ed. James Strachey (Reprinted New York: Avon Books, 1965), pp. 571–88. The model is used in this context to facilitate the discussion of regression. Later spatial models, notably the tripartite one of id, ego, and super-ego, are more satisfactory in making subtle distinctions in the energetic conflicts of the psyche. But for brute strength, the "picket-fence" is best.

irrationalist!). (4) Mnemic traces that are "forgotten" are the wishes, or instincts. (5) The role of the censors is a balancing, managing one. There have been several norms suggested for this apparatus, but the correct one probably lies with the ego-psychologists, who see in the censor the incipient egosyntonic principle of adaptation. (6) Consciousness amounts to a highly selective attending to pathways of energy. Sophisticated consciousness presumably breaks through the first censor and makes that which guards the unconscious per se semipermeable (though never totally transparent).

"To Sleep, To Dream . . ." These psychodynamics bear relevantly on the nature of sleeping and dreaming. Sleep, viewed within the model of energetic conflicts, is not the result merely of fatigue. It is the wish to paralyze innervation and consciousness, to lull the censoring functions, and to regress. If waking life is progress, sleeping life gives the one step backward for the two forward.

In sleep, energy flows backward, over the conflicts buried under repressive consciousness. Instead of a search for stimulation and innervation — or eros — the individual withdraws his cathexis (his energetic transactions with the environment) as the wish to return to primitive states, even inanimate ones, gains acendency — thanatos. Energies flow backward into the deep unconscious of the earliest state of human existence, the womblike resting on primal stimuli without perception.

The second inference we can draw is about dreaming. *To dream is to reason while asleep.* Dreams function to express the unconscious wish without at the same time ending sleep. But in order to do so, disguise of the wish is necessary. Dreams fulfill the double wish, to wake and to sleep. In them the individual attempts to change the regressive direction of the wish for prenatal peace, but he does not really make it all the way back. The dream hangs in the balance of the conflict between eros and thanatos.

The nature of sleep itself is subject to considerable rethinking on the basis of recent physiological experiments. We can appreciate Freud even more, in spite of both confirmation and discrediting of aspects of his dream theory by current research, for the reason that he presented a psychological theory of dreams. Too often, inferences drawn from current research are pseudopsychological, as when dreams are identified and reduced to the physical correlates, such as REM (rapid eye movements).[20]

Nevertheless the current excitement over dreams cannot be gain-said. To support Freud's contention that dreams guard sleep, some point to the seeming connection between light sleep and wakefulness to dreams, and deep sleep to non-dreaming. Others disregard Freud's emphasis, on the basis of discoveries of at least three stages in sleep itself (and perhaps more), of a possible cultural learning about how and when to stay awake, and of the physiological state of dreams, which resembles emergency situations more than relaxed, wakeful ones.

Freud is responsible for these physiological investigations, however, through his predisposition for energetic models of the psyche. So be it. I would only point to the consonant relation between one use of feed-back models for understanding sleep and the Freudian notion of the reduction of cathexis as the result of a wish. That the laboratory experiments stop short of postulating a correspondent to Freud's notion of wish may be a result of their preoccupation with detail, a disavowal of speculation, or a *lacuna* which other interpreters have a right to fill.

According to Freud, dreaming makes use of infantile and primitive forms of memory and thinking. Original mnemic traces clump together into apparently meaningless patterns, but these patterns always betray an underlying unity of intention. These intentions are immediate and illogical gratifications left over from acculturation. Necessity, that mighty taskmistress, is deceived, and her handmaidens, reality and delay, are duped.

[20] Hall, *Meaning of Dreams* (see footnote 10), pp. xii–xiii.

205

Whether these intentions are regressive in the strictly pejorative sense of that word is open to debate. That they were infantile in the main, showing forth aspects about oneself which, though perhaps embarrassing, still insisted that they be manfully owned, may characterize Freud's view. Erikson has challenged this view of dream-interpretation, using Freud's own dream analysis. He and the ego-psychologists, following Ernst Kris, have generalized the point, so that they speak of "regression in service of the ego" to include another, more coping, future-oriented way of including the infantile wish. In the dream-specimen above, it was the latter that prevailed, though, I trust, without falling into some of the illusive romanticism which Freud so cleanly punctured.

Forgetting the Wish

We resist remembering dreams, or remember them scantly, if the resistance to the dream's wish was great in the first place. The same censoring that makes us forget a dream upon awaking is the one that the dream was designed to fool. Necessity brings the censor into play as one awakes. Depending upon the cleverness of the dream, the censor is or is not successful in reinstating the original repression of the wish.

Notice that one forgets for the same reason that one began to think in the first place, that is, not to be fooled by illusion! In order to cope with immediate wishes, one learned to forget some of their disturbing aspects. This made thinking easier. But easy thinking is vulnerable to its origins; when some wish threatens its mode, it must be forgotten unless one's customary mode of thinking itself is to be called into question and change.

We reach a difficult dilemma: *if one could not forget, one would be flooded by hallucinations; if one cannot remember, one can be sabotaged by the "return of the repressed."*

Our dreamer *could not* remember, could not deceive his censor, without a number of allies — The Group, the pastor, the *possibility* of paying attention to dreams, and the development of his own mature skills and loves. Prior to a confluence of all these forces, he had to forget, to keep from being drawn back. He would have been preoccupied with threatening fears of hopelessness, impotence, reduction of powers, and the like, if he had not forgotten the dream and its wishing.

What this does is to recognize the developmental facts of life as they effect remembering and forgetting. The direction of growth calls for forgetfulness, until a time of reversal. The dream becomes the point of return, or of no return. If early childhood experiences are kept in mind, it is as if there is a "second time around." Personal history is both linear *and* cyclical as each developmental stage comes to focus. If this inference is correct, it seems dubious, at the very least, to try to collapse one into the other; either a highlighting of nothing but rational progress, depending as it does on ignorance, or the accenting of irrational regress, depending as it does on recall of a progress, is untenable.

One form that such reductionism takes is what is above called "sabotage." Just at the point where either too much remembrance or too much forgetfulness is seen (in clinical terms, a manic tendency or a depressive one) the specific wish that is fighting to cross the barrier of repression exerts an influence indirectly. The cost of its return is higher than the psychic balance can stand. "Neurosis" or "psychosis" are costly forms of such returns. Mental illness can be understood as originating in wishes that must be so thoroughly disguised that inordinate amounts of energy are tied up in them, and dysfunction results.

The dilemma suggests that the problem is one of forgetting successfully, without too high a price for the (inevitable) return of the repressed. If we could not forget, we would never wake up, either after a night's sleep or in the process of growing up, of moving toward individuality. But if we cannot remember, we are at the mercy of what is defensively forgotten.

Remembering the Wish

Placing Dreams. Dreams take their place as one of the several ways in which the unconscious wish expresses itself. Properly understood, they can be aids in the reckoning of one's development. But how far can we go in this "proper understanding"? An understanding of the function of dreams has unquestionably given fresh insight into the nature of psychopathology and psychotherapy. Can we suggest a concomitant insight on the side of health? In order to do so fully, it would be necessary to take account of those issues already clarified within the field of mental illness.

Karl Menninger, in *The Vital Balance*,[21] suggests a way of viewing mental illness holistically, and provides us with a point of limited departure. He makes contiguous the varieties of psychopathology, discriminating orders of dysfunction that range from everyday coping devices through to suicide. At each point on the "line," the struggle between "Eros" and "Thanatos" (to use Freud's last descriptions of the dual-drive theory also important to Menninger) has a peculiar character. These are the points of balance. At no "point" is the dualism overcome. Each level has within it a defense against further forms of dyscontrol and consolidates what it can of Eros. Each form of suffering bears the mark of energies for incipient renewal and return to modes of endurance less drastic.

I suggest that dreams, though obviously emergent in a personality finding itself at various levels of dysfunction, are most appropriately seen to belong in the midrange of normal expressions of vitality. They provide a balance point between the direction toward healthy expression of life, transcending mere coping devices, and the direction toward impulsive aggression and eroticism that leads to the pathological intensity of the higher "orders" of dysfunction.

Freud suggested in an offhand moment that "to love and to work" were the goals of life; add to these, as an implication of his work and loves, the appropriate form of dream-telling as the fitting use of sleep, that great, quiet third of human existence.

Sleep can add its weight to a form of forgetting that costs too much in terms of hatred and impotence; it can simply

[21] By Karl Menninger *et al.* (New York: The Viking Press, 1963).

move the individual toward the flood of hallucinations. Or, worse still, the individual can generalize from sleep to life (unconsciously), can never wake up (as in suicide), can be sleep-walking (as in Menninger's fourth level of dysfunction) or day-dreaming (as in his second level of dysfunction).

Or an individual can use dreams to begin really to wake up, to let sleep restore, through regression "in service of the ego," the vitalities useful in loving and working. The wishes discovered in dreams, when integrated into free association, symbols and interpretations between two or more people, can be used to enhance the actualizations of life.

Having said this, it is also necessary to point out the conditions under which dream-telling functions constructively. In an excellent chapter entitled "From Dreams to Waking," Bruno Bettelheim presents the ambiguity of listening to and telling dreams.

> When they first wake up many children are eager to tell us their dreams, but this presents several difficulties. For one thing, we are naturally interested in whatever has upset the child during the night. We want to help him with the fears which the dream, for example, may not only reveal but may actually have aggravated. We also want to help him to recognize and work through his unconscious desires, anxieties, and so forth. But while these and many other reasons speak in favor of our listening to the dreams of some children, there are equally valid reasons suggesting that other children should not be encouraged to prolong their irrational phantasies because it may only make it harder for them to approach the new day realistically. . . . Such newly recalled or associated material may often heighten the child's anxieties and have such a devastating influence on the rest of the day that he is powerless to come to grips with reality. . . .
> . . . In any case it is not easy to decide whether a child is strong enough to handle the residues of his unconscious as they reveal themselves in his dreams (and should therefore be encouraged to talk about them); it is

equally difficult to know that another child is too insecure
to go ahead with the tasks of living after he has just faced
in broad daylight what lay buried in his unconscious.
Such decisions can never be made in a general way.[22]

We must take seriously Bettelheim's caution against over
generalization. Again we have met with a limitation inherent
within dream-telling; it is an individual matter, embedded
in the concrete realities of personal history and current relations with other people.

Nevertheless, three functions of dream-telling can be suggested.[23]

(1) The first is *recollective*. Dream-telling implicates our
personal history with other histories. Dreams touch other
selves before interpretation of them is made. But with the
telling of them, the line between public and private life is
erased; the center of "propriate striving" and the periphery
of "role enactment" are linked together.

In the dream specimen, the dreamer brings together the
disgusting yet erotic feelings linked with public sexual displays — the "fall-down dance." Part of the disgust lies in a
fear of losing his own sense of sexual identification, bought
at the price of isolated sexual experimentation and overcon-
trol. The dream also puts together the role enactments of the
dreamer's life — the little lost boy, the obedient son, the cultural hero, the man of wisdom. These had to be juxtaposed by
the dreamer with some sense of finding a centering principle,
a "thread" on which to string these "beads."

Such a course may be dangerous. In a time when genuine
privacy is a state to be defended, exhibitionism is a sign more
of weakness than of strength. And yet dream-telling can be
selective. It can reflect a greater amount of wisdom in the
choice of one's intimates, a greater sophistication in the level
of communion with them. Instead of permanent loss of the

[22] Bettelheim, *Love is Not Enough: The Treatment of Emotionally
Disturbed Children* (New York: Collier Books, 1950).
[23] I owe a debt to Erik Erikson's discussion of dreams in "The Nature
of Clinical Evidence" in *Insight and Responsibility*.

self in the "other," dream-telling can be used to enhance the rhythm of loss and renewal.

Recollection is a private need and a human privilege. As a need, it arises in the later years of life to a higher degree of urgency than previously. But as a privilege, it is a way of entering into the benefits of the transmission of culture from generation to generation. I see no reason why our culture cannot use more story-tellers. Not more substitute novelists or playwrights; not more pseudodirectors of movies. But more story-tellers, especially among the elderly, whose sense of vocation is deeply threatened.

(2) The second reason for dream-telling is *predictive*. Dreams do foretell the future, or rather, with dreams the future, insofar as it is going to be influenced by personal wishes, is clearer. The immediate set of forces peculiarly one's own comes to light through the process. These forces are, to be sure, wishes, and thus no guarantee is offered for their successful actualization. It is a matter of allowing the wishes to play into the hands of our "destiny" (as distinguished from our "fate"): we are partially active, partially passive, in the light of our wishing; we are partially private and partially public because of the direct recognition of hopes.

At this point, notice the controlling attitude which is embodied in the dream specimen. What is at issue for the dreamer, even upon understanding something of the meaning of his dream, is the tendency to manipulate his own feelings through attempts at predicting to himself what is going to happen. In the dream, it is clear that he is comfortable only in getting "on top of the situation," so to speak. One thread, missed by the dreamer, is that of shouting with such power that the congregation is finally driven away. That is, it is a point of some ambiguity whether the dreamer's hope is a compulsive attempt to wrest for himself the final say, or to allow himself to feel his strength even when compulsive fatigue has set in. It is along these lines that his own psychological understanding had to proceed. This was the issue that determined a good number of his future relationships; could he finally relax into something of a harmonious balance with the object of his service, or would he continue to fight it out, even with sublimated and refined techniques?

A dangerous implication could arise here. Magical wishes are Janus-faced; they can give one the red badge of courage to support a dead cause. Dream-telling can be an unhappy, unlucky, and damaging practice of augury. Observation of bird's flight, untangling the pattern of guts poured out of the sacrificial animal — these were the basis of speculation in other times. But there was still interpretation by the priest or shaman; correspondingly, the dream must be told within a relationship with another. *And* the response of the seeker to the augury was crucial; often it went so far as to present to him a riddle, which his own intuition had to meet, and with which he wrestled in a very problem-solving way.

Within psychotherapy, dream-interpretation is placed in a context which is at once protection against excessive errors of interpretation and at the same time the ground within which these interpretations are validated. Some such *conditional prediction* must be found outside psychotherapy per se, so that the propensity toward doctrinaire speculation can find some meaningful substitute.

(3) The third reason for dream-telling is *heuristic*. The power tapped by dreams is that which is allied with the energy moving creativity, art, and higher forms of human expression. The dream is sometimes the direct source for literature and poetry (Blake, Coleridge), painting (Bosch), to say nothing of the visions of philosophy (Descartes), and religion (Jacob-Israel).

In a more mundane fashion, however, dreams can simply move a person toward the "fullness of life" side of the health-illness continuum; it can provide an indirect source for one's own definiteness, identity, and maturity. I have in mind things like story-telling, material for contemplation, and the expansion of our range of sensibilities. Dreams can, like that playful pedagogue Peter Pan, help our imaginations to soar.

That this is more than trivial can be seen if placed against one view of contemporary life: the view that it presents us with a vacuum, that contemporary young adults, in particular, are plagued by feelinglessness. Whatever the assessment of the fad over ingestion of LSD and other "psychedelic" efforts, these are, at the very least, attempts to provide intensity of feeling. Many persons do not feel anything; might this be addressed by eliciting their dreams, in which spontaneity of feelings appears as a hallmark?

To the extent that dream-telling does enhance the range of feeling, it is allied with other forces that intend to move our culture to a more hedonistic orientation. Norman O. Brown is the most obvious spokesman for this point of view.[24] Briefly, and too cavalierly put, my objection to Brown's viewpoint is that when the dream is everything, dream-telling loses its point, contrasts are obliterated; and with the end to repression, there is a final end to dreaming too. The disgorging of all wishes at every moment is pleasurable only when someone is repressing; dream-telling is fun only when one is awake.

The dreamer of "hope" often moved more toward unrepression and hedonism than his fellow group members liked. For a time, dreams preoccupied him. He recounted them to the group with frenzied excitement, as if each were a new revelation. For a time, he frequently missed many of the richer clues of his dreams, clues noticed by his peers, because he did not reason them out. He did not, in some sense, "awaken" until he had disgorged himself of a kind of compulsive spontaneity characterizing the behavior of many repressed people just after feeling some of their deeply repressed motives.

And I hold that not only do we want to awaken from fancies at various points and moments, but that life at the cultural level, where myth is important, depends upon keeping the dream a dream, the myth a myth, as well as seeing the "internal relations" between sleep and wakefulness, myth and faith.

Dream without Myth?

What, then, of myth as the cultural cognate of dreams? If there is a proper, if somewhat conditional, way of appro-

[24] Norman O. Brown, *Life against Death: The Psychoanalytical Meaning of History* (Middletown, Conn.: Wesleyan University Press, 1959).

priating dreams, is there also a way of appropriating myth? Or is the difficulty in taking a "proper" attitude toward myth part of the difficulty in dream-telling? Is it possible to have dream without myths? Or do we inevitably have to construct myths, or something very like them (such as Oedipus complexes, "picket-fence" models) in order even to understand dreaming?

First, let us mark off two aspects of myth — myth as formally established, and "mythodynamics." Formal myth is linked with cultus and history as our earlier definitions have shown. Thus the mythos of the "three-storied universe," exercised frequently in the debate over demythologization, is part and parcel with Near Eastern religious cults and propitiatory sacrifice, with prophetic revelation, and with historic cosmologies. So, too, the Greek mythological pantheism furnishes a borderline between explanations of historical occasions and institutions, and frameworks giving justification to religious cultic practices and personal piety.

"Mythodynamics" might be thought of as the motivation for myth; it could be defined as *the wish to have our wishes cared for without caring for them ourselves*. There is always the possibility for selves and societies to seek dreaming innocence, to look back sentimentally to simple and beautiful origins, in the hope that these will magically transform present conflicts. Mythodynamics, like psychodynamics, recognizes a continual conflict in the desire to locate power in agencies and frames of authenticity. One side of the conflict emphasizes sanctions and justifications from the "outside"; the other anchors power and vitality "within" selves or cultures. One side lures one toward participation in pure strength; the other chastens one toward perfect genuineness. Within this maelstrom of competing locations or centerings, the temptation is always on the side of simplicity. Either/or thinking, which is frequently the best one can do, makes for myths.

The problem is one of continually readjusting the balance between the proper distance from the gods and the appropriate intimacy with our peers. Myths are continually born out of the lure to distantiate ourselves from, and yet remain in contact with, our wishing. From this dynamic struggle there emerges formal mythos; in it, the fundamental wishes of a person or a people gathers consensus. Formal mythos attracts the loose ends of individual wishes and makes them concrete.

In the dream specimen, the intrusion of formal mythos is clear. Through the symbols, and all that they entail, there is no dream without myth. Myth, insofar as it manifests itself as part of the wish being fulfilled, is always indirectly present in dreaming. And even in the interpretation there is myth, in the form of the lurking Oedipus complex, or the synthetic "model" of repression, consciousness/unconsciousness. The elaboration of the nature and vicissitudes of "the wish" also tends in this direction.

The critical turning point comes in detecting the presence of informal and dynamic myth. In the dream specimen, this has been expressed in the fulfilled wish of hope. It could be stated in a number of ways, none totally free from connection with formal myth, and yet all relatively close to a direct apprehension of distance and proximity. The feature of informal myth to be noticed is its quality of being a *process*, a *transition*. Something is shifting; whereas in formal myth, something is repeated. In the dream, the informal mythodynamic might be, "Shut up except to sing if you want to be saved: shout out of your hoping." The colon represents the shift. Another form of it might be, "Self-sacrifice and all else will be given you: self-strengthening comes through delimitation."

The thrust of this essay suggests that we can make a move from formal to informal myth more often than we realize. Dream without myth would be the effort to move out of formal myths by their use in interpretation and understanding. Synthetic myths, such as the "models" or the myths we hold "as if" they were true, can make allowances for this.

The real question comes as to the usefulness of formal myth itself. Is it the case that contemporary man is now ready to do away with mythology, or at least with the older mythol-

ogies? Or must he, by the nature of things, allow for contemporary myth as long as he knows how to handle it?

Myths originate in the impossibility of owning up to one's
wishes all at once. They come from the psychic impossibility
of destroying the boundaries, the points of transition, between the conscious and the unconscious. Symbols, essential
to both myth and dream, are ineradicable as a species. But all
this does not gainsay the contemporary theological understanding that, in some sense, man has "come of age," is readier,
at some level, to exercise more responsibility for himself, to
demythologize, to care (in terms of this paper) for his own
wishes.

Why, then, the hesitation to demythologize, a hesitation
either felt in our theological roots or conditionally advocated
by a psychological analysis? Principally because it feels like
a loss of mythic agencies. An inability to believe in a literal
and eternal framework of justification threatens our culture
with a loss of self. For so long, the myth of self, unrecognized
though it was, shored up the mythic gods. The loss of one
leads to the loss of the other. Western man has not yet gotten
over the wound to his narcissism which Freud inflicted; for
behind the belief that we were masters in our own psychic
house lay the belief that the mythic gods were masters in
theirs as well. To hesitate at the opportunity to move from
mythos to mythodynamics, from literal to "as if" with reference to mythology, is, in my view, the last vestige of contemporary man's owning up to the psychological construct.

It is this attitude of hesitation, I maintain, that paradoxi-
cally keeps us from public dream-telling. Let me refer again
to Ogden's final construction to make the point clear. At the
end of his argument in *Christ without Myth*, Ogden makes
two points. In the first, he faults Bultmann for not speaking
as objectively about God as he has about man, while accepting
much of Bultmann's argument for the need to reassess "objectivity" in the light of Heideggerian analysis. In the second,
speaking of the second criterion of Christian theology as at
once an authentic possibility for all men *and* revealed in Jesus
of Nazareth, he concludes,

What confronts us in Jesus is not, in its first intention, a "world-view" addressed to our intellects, but a possibility of self-understanding that requires of us a personal decision.[25]

Now what happens to the need for "objectivity" or the possibility of "self-understanding" when we use the idea of myth-odynamics — wanting someone "else" to care for our wishes? First, the desire for objectivity itself becomes suspect; not finally, but at least temporarily. Any kind of objectivity must take into account not only the propensity to distort wishing, but the equal likelihood of coming to terms with deep wishes. Objectivity with respect to the gods or to man is never without the tendency to mythologize, nor should it be. We must, nevertheless, try to interpret dynamically. Failure to keep this dialectic going is always present in the growing fatigue that accompanies it. The more deeply the restlessness of the dialectic is perceived, the greater the temptation to stop it. It is no wonder that there is a hesitation even to begin it, and thus a hesitation to demythologize.

Second, self-understanding itself builds on symbols (or myths, even) and cannot proceed without such symbols. In this sense, Jesus is subject to the wishes of the believer no matter what is done to keep the symbol secure or protected. It is likely that the symbol "Jesus Christ" does tend to collect some of the deepest and most fervent wishes or hopes of individual people (to say nothing of whole cultures). It is another step, and to some a jolting one, to allow that the concrete wishes of the individual, those born out of his own peculiar history, are precisely those lying closest to the "holy" wishes surrounding the Christ figure.

To make the point as sharp as I can: we hesitate to allow for a free give and take between the enduring wishes fastened tightly about the mythological symbol of Jesus Christ and the seemingly evanescent plural wishes linked with the symbolic interpretation of our last night's dream. But our hesitation confirms the point of this essay, regardless of the special cases

[25] Ogden, *Christ without Myth*, p. 162.

in which dream-telling is allowed. We do not make room for it publicly because to do so would be to open the door to discovering the initial equality of influence between the motive for our religious myths and that of our private lives. To bring "the Christ" and "my dream" into such contiguity seems taboo.

Notice that I said equality of *influence*, and not of status. Myth and its symbol of Christ will no doubt be the more permanent, although last night's wish will get the greater charge of immediate energy. The mutual influence of myth-wish and dream-wish is to be recognized without *reduction* of one to the other (as is done in psychologizing all theology or in theologizing all psychology!).

There is no dream without wish, and no dream-telling without owning up to one's wish. There can be dream without formal myth; it is unlikely that there can be dream without informal myth. If myth must be protected, or rather if it operates in order to establish the secrecy of our hidden wishes, then it serves to inhibit dream-telling, it blocks the move toward mythodynamics. To resist dream-telling, properly undertaken, is to fear demythologizing.

But as a culture, we may still need to hesitate. Perhaps we are waiting for a "new" myth of the self that will protect us against too directly owning up to our wishes. Perhaps a synthetic myth is emerging that will make dream-telling more enlivening.

Take Care of Your Wish

John Ciardi tells the story of a little boy who wants a puppy for his birthday.[26] His father puts a cryptogram on the dresser as he goes to sleep which says "TAKECAREOFYOURWISH," and tells the boy to find his "wish tree" in his dreams. The boy does, and gradually comes to see that he must be selective of his wishes, must shepherd the one most important and care for it.

If we refuse to share dreams, we seem to like to protect myths, not to take care of our wishes. Rather than look upon

[26] John Ciardi, *The Wish-Tree* (Crowell-Collier Press, 1962).

our wishes as nemesis or unessentials, we can see them as partners, as emergents out of the center of ourselves and of our race.

To take care of your wish means to be reasonable — not simply rationalistic, without appreciation for mystery, novelty, or unknowns, but, rather, allowing our reason to be reborn every morning as it comes dripping wet from the hallucinations of our dreams. By letting ourselves share and think about dreams, and thus wishes, we complete the cycle once begun in the development of reason, instead of repeating it mechanically, mythically.

9

The Archetypal Self:
Theological Values in Jung's Psychology
FRANK M. BOCKUS

Modern man's search for self-knowledge has evolved to the
point where he can appreciate, more fully than before, Carl
Jung's psychology of the self. Today he deserves widespread
interest, not only among students of human nature, such as
behavioral scientists and theologians, but among thoughtful
men generally.

Jung's psychology is centered on a conception of the *self*.
By focusing on the self in its many aspects, we can best utilize
his views for a contemporary understanding of man. But material on the self is dispersed throughout the many volumes
of his collected works. In this paper I intend to explicate his
theory of the self by abstracting from several writings, and
to indicate briefly its present-day relevance for an interdisciplinary anthropology and theology.

Such studies are needed at this time for several reasons.
First, with the publication in 1960 of *The Structure and Dynamics of the Psyche*, we gained access to Jung's own interpretation of the "system theory" philosophy underlying his
work. Such philosophical data are crucial for a theological
evaluation. The material in that volume clarifies the evolving
methodology of much of his earlier work and illuminates the
philosophical conflict he experienced with other psychologists
early in his career. To them, he seemed to work on alien problems and to hold inadmissible assumptions, whereas to Jung,
the assumptions and theories of other scholars seemed too
mechanical and reductionistic. Through his acquaintance
with field theory in microphysics and through the application

of this theory to psychology, Jung in his later writing clarified his philosophy in a more formal manner.

Second, self theory has come to the forefront of the modern study of man, and Jung's exploration of this issue affords a rich resource. His direct inquiry into such topics as the self-realization tendency, the mind-body relation, genetic bases of memory, and the self in culture, all drawn together in a self theory, offers a way of synthesizing many current threads of scholarship. In addition, the assumptions of his system theory are to be found in contemporary anthropology, particularly in the *organismic* view. Hence, our own most pressing issues and presuppositions enable us better to utilize Jung's work.

Jung's quest for mankind's common humanity, culminating in his theory of the *archetype*, led him inevitably into other disciplines. It was a consistent movement, which took him from his own most normative concept, the self, to a consideration of Christology, the normative concept of Christian theology. Jung held that Christ represents a concrete embodiment of the God-man relation inherent in the nature of all men. In this conception he offers a most provocative resource for current theological construction, and, as we shall see, the lines of his implicit theology are now being developed by philosophers and theologians.

Our purpose, then, is to make Jung's self theory more readily available, and through this exposure to suggest its integrative relevance for anthropology in general and for theology in particular. We believe that a general discussion of his ideas is necessary before their implications can be developed, and we are therefore inclined to focus more on the former task than the latter. The discussion will proceed cumulatively, first elaborating the self under its several aspects, but leading toward its relation to God and toward a methodological analysis, in which Jung's theological implications are extended.

The Origins of the Self: The Self-Realization Tendency

The individual begins his pilgrimage toward selfhood, according to Jung, millions of years before his birth. This statement is not as ridiculous as it may at first appear. Today it is commonly accepted that the newborn infant possesses inherited potentials of physical development. The child, subject to certain environmental factors of health or diet, possesses genetic predispositions of size, height, and contour. Jung sought to explore the inherited tendencies of psychological development as well. For some reason, many people find the idea of intrinsic systems of psychic functioning more difficult to accept. For Jung, man is born with inherited possibilities of psychic functioning, which characterize him as human. Such common characteristics predispose man to decidedly human mental states, as contrasted with other creatures. The child is endowed with inherent and collective potentials to be actualized anew during the course of his development, subject to certain environmental factors of human interaction and of social and cultural influence. Certain possibilities are realized more than others during the course of the individual's unique personal history. Jung writes:

> In view of the structure of the body, it would be astonishing if the psyche were the only biological phenomenon not to show clear traces of its evolutionary history, and it is altogether probable that these marks are closely connected with the instinctual base.[1]

The child's mind is a teeming reservoir of potential structures and dynamics of human functioning. Jung called this reality a collective unconscious — collective, because this base of the human mind is common to all men, unconscious, because the potentials have not been brought into conscious realization. The collective unconscious presupposes that the psyche of man, everywhere, at all times and in all places, functions as a human mental process. In some respects it is an archaic and primitive reality, bearing the entire ancestral heritage of man over the course of human evolution.[2] As such,

[1] Carl Gustav Jung, *The Structure and Dynamics of the Psyche*, vol. 8 of *The Collected Works*, ed. Herbert Read, Michael Fordham, and Gerhard Adler, trans. R. F. C. Hull, Bollingen Series 20 (New York: Pantheon Books, 1960), p. 200.
[2] *Ibid.*, p. 51.

it is a creative reservoir. Speaking of this primitive mentality, Jung says:

> Man's unconscious contains all the patterns of life and behavior inherited from his ancestors. . . . It contains . . . the accumulated deposits from the lives of our ancestors, who by their very existence have contributed to the differentiation of the species.[3]

The collective unconscious in the newborn exists in a state of diffusion, a grown-togetherness of indistinct and undeveloped structures and processes.[4] In the course of human development, these potentials of the self become differentiated into separate functions and structures, grouping into systems and becoming increasingly more complex, as the personality takes on the richness of its singular traits of individuality. But at this collective stage, the various systems of thought and rationality have not begun to reach levels of abstraction where some aspect of the self's experience can be isolated from its context. Systems of feeling are incapable of shades of valuing. Systems of perceiving are too diffused with surrounding objects and persons in the external world. In short, psychic functioning, both internal and external, lies in a state of concrescence.

In his studies, Jung found similarities between the dreams of children and the child folklore of various cultures and historical periods. Further comparison, as we shall see more fully later, revealed similarities with the cultural forms of man's ancestral history, including the folklore and mythology of primitive peoples. He also observed that such primitive states are characteristic of certain mental states in the dissociations of the mentally disturbed. These various, yet related, correlations prompted Jung to posit a collective base to the mind. Such a base is grounded in and emerges out of the psychological evolution of man, a state prior to an individual's personal history. Yet this common base links the individual

[3] *Ibid.*, p. 349.
[4] Jung, *Psychological Types*, trans. H. Godwin Baynes (New York: Harcourt, Brace & Company, 1924), p. 533.

to mankind in general. Every child begins with the psychic potential last attained by the human race.[5]

Since the newborn inherits both physical and psychological potentials of development, Jung held that the mind and the body are two aspects of one reality in a reciprocal and continuous relation to itself.[6] Neither should be subsumed into the other, as if one were secondary to the other. He rejected any suggestion of psychophysical parallelism, as if there were no interstitial connection between mind and body, but he also held that mind and body cannot simply be identified with each other.

Jung drew from physical concepts of light to illustrate his view of the connection between mind and body. Light is unified, but it contains infrared and ultraviolet aspects. So, too, it is with mind and body.[7] The collective unconscious, although ultimately a single reality, bears both an infrared or *ecto* psychic aspect in its relation to the body and an ultraviolet or *endo* psychic aspect, in which mental processes are separate from physical control. The physiological and biochemical aspect of this reality passes over in its most basic level into the body. At this level, mind is virtually analogous to the autonomous systems of the body. Mind is materialized, subject to biochemical and neurological processes. Likewise, the more physical the mind at this level, the more primitive, archaic, and instinctive it is.

For purposes of analysis, however, a "cut-off" line is required between mind and body, so that one can properly speak of the mind as a distinct system. At this point we find an important philosophical assumption of Jung, one having to do with the correlation between causality and indeterminism. We shall have more to say later about his thinking on this point, but we need to note here that, for Jung, the mind is free from causal control of the autonomous systems of the body to which it bears an "ultraviolet" relation. Instinct is transformed into psychic patterns of functioning. The col-

---

[5] Jung, *The Structure and Dynamics* . . . , p. 51ff.
[6] *Ibid.*, p. 17.
[7] *Ibid.*, p. 215.

lective unconscious in this phase bears the potential of producing images which operate as mental processes. Such images, arising from the depths of the mind, are represented in the cultural forms of mankind everywhere. They reflect mankind's universal and collective depths.

Basic to Jung's concept is the view that this collective base of psychological functioning conforms to laws and predispositions in essentially the same way that the body conforms to tendencies of physical development. Jung's concept of the *archetype* refers to the primordial images and mental patterns which originate in and remain partially governed by the collective base of the mind. Since these images recapitulate the evolution of mankind and the common human situations of all men everywhere, they reflect innate potentials of human development. Furthermore, when such images become operative in the mind, they provide the means by which the collective potentials can cease to be merely latent and can become effectively realized by the individual.

We can now speak more clearly of the self-realization tendency. "The meaning and purpose of the process [of self-realization]," Jung writes, "is the realization, in all its aspects, of the personality originally hidden away in the embryonic germ-plasm, the production and unfolding of the original, potential wholeness." [8] Self-realization is a natural and spontaneous process, through which the potentials of the self are made available to the individual through the depths of his own mind. It is as if the innumerable and ever-recurrent experiences and situations of mankind are indelibly fixed in the mind as a ready-made predisposition of human functioning. For example, the newborn child seems predisposed toward some form of response in relation to the mother. This is a prototypal situation, which, through constant repetition, has made a permanent impression on the collective base of the human psyche. [9]

[8] Jung, *Two Essays on Analytical Psychology*, vol. 7 of *The Collected Works* (1953), p. 108.
[9] Jung, *The Archetypes and the Collective Unconscious*, pt. 1, vol. 9 of *The Collected Works* (1959), p. 48.

Jung never analyzed the stages of human development as extensively as have contemporary thinkers. He did, however, attempt to identify the various aspects of self-development and the critical issues in the life history, and there is considerable similarity between Jung's understanding of the dynamics of the self-realization tendency and some of the prevalent contemporary theories of human development. Such current theory seems to hold that the maturing human being has infixed within his organism a sequential series of physical, psychic, and social potentials. These potentials gradually emerge, and interact with, and are codetermined by significant persons and experiences within his social and cultural environment.[10] Emerging potentials are reciprocally regulated, completed, and invested with meaning through interaction with the concrete setting of one's personal history.

Jung held a similar view, although, as we said, he did not elaborate it in such detail. He referred to the interaction between the developing child and his environment as a process of unconscious identification. Furthermore, the dynamics of this process relate the individual throughout his lifetime to his environment and to the social patterns and cultural assumptions of the community around him. Basically, it reflects an indiscriminate projection or introjection between internal states and external objects. The child of few years, particularly, is a reflection of collective and environmental influences, owing to this identification. The really significant point in Jung's view is that human relations and cultural forms are not merely secondary to the depths of the mind and its tendencies. Instead, culture expresses the depths of the self and is an avenue to those depths.

It is plausible, Jung believed, to hold that the collective depth of the mind itself has been modified through the course of human evolution. Man's potentials are themselves changing. Each generation of men "adds an infinitesimally small amount of variation and differentiation" to the accumulated,

[10] Erik H. Erikson, *Childhood and Society* (New York: W. W. Norton & Company, 1950), p. 33.

227

ancestral deposit of human experience.[11] Collective potentials are lived out in concrete embodiment in the real world, and this transaction between the self and the world probably alters the self.

The Structures and Dynamics of the Self: Systems in Movement.

We turn now from the origins of the self to the development of distinct structures and dynamics. This is, above all, a differentiating process, the realization of original, collective potentials. Our purpose here will be not to present a series of steps toward selfhood, but to offer an exposition of the interpretive framework by which Jung viewed the dynamic processes of the self.

Of course, we do not experience our daily life in the technical categories that follow, and no claim is made that we do. The events of everyday living are transacted in the folk idioms of ordinary human conversation. What Jung offers us is a conceptual way of viewing the processes implied in the normal course of living, providing us with a perspective for deeper self-knowledge.

We said earlier that Jung's work coincides with certain recent developments in the life sciences. To show more fully this correspondence, we need a concept that affords explanatory power to Jung's thought in particular and to the life sciences in general. Such a uniting concept is the *open system.*

The open system is a view of reality increasingly employed in the life sciences. Over against that biological view which reduces the organism to isolated organs or systems, the open system conceives of highly interacting, complex, and overlapping elements, related to each other contextually.[12] A system is itself composed of extensive subsystems to which it is the wider context, and all are in a state of perpetual transformation. Thus a system is something more than the sum of

[11] *The Structure and Dynamics* . . . , p. 376.
[12] Ludwig von Bertalanffy, "An Outline of General System Theory," *The British Journal for the Philosophy of Science*, 1, no. 2 (1950), pp. 143ff.

its components, and any system's functioning within its super-ordinate system is different from its functioning in isolation. Only by considering a system's constituent subsystems and its larger context can it be understood.

A system is both centered and segregated. It is capable of extensive differentiation and greater complexity. At the same time the system bears characteristics of unity and integration. It tends to be centered either on some point or on some function within its overlapping context. Being centered, it possesses degrees of autonomy and uniqueness.

Every organic system maintains itself by a process of perpetual change of components. In fact, its very existence depends on its capacity to receive materials into itself and thus to change. For such change to take place, there has to be an inflow and an outflow between the system and its field. A system is *open* when materials or influence enter or leave it. It is closed when such interaction or change does not occur. Though the open system may attain a stationary state, in which it seems to exhibit a noncontextual and time-independent persistence, closer examination reveals even here a process of perpetual change through the building up and tearing down of subsystems.[13] Since an open system receives materials from other sources, it is not dependent entirely upon its own components. Nor is it bound by a never-changing set of conditions. Hence, a system can reach the same state or function by several different routes.

We can also view the self as an open system. This self system, however, like any other organic system, must be regarded from several angles. From one point of view, the self is the *total system* of the psyche. It is the superordinate system in relation to which the various structures and subsystems of the mind stand. From a second viewpoint, the self is the *centralizing tendency* of the psyche as a whole. It is the central point and function around which are clustered and integrated all the structures and dynamics. As one moves toward selfhood, one moves toward greater integrity

[13] *Ibid.*, p. 155.

and individuality. One becomes a unique center of one's personal history. From yet another standpoint, the self is the whole within which and in relation to which progressive differentiation and complexity proceed. The distinct structures of the self must be viewed in relation to the larger ground to which all are related. From a fourth vantage point, the self can be understood as the *goal* of human development. But this goal, grounded in a collective base, can be reached from a wide variety of developmental histories. Finally, the self, in yet another aspect, is an *archetypal tendency* which predisposes man toward human development.

The self-system is comprised of these various aspects concurrently. Selfhood presupposes the development of each aspect and the mutual regulation of each in relation to the others. While the content of any individual life is the singular embodiment of its time and place in history and in the world, the structures of its self-system partake of these various aspects.

The concept of the self-system, however, reflects movement, interaction, and process. In fact, it is preeminently a dynamic conception; the open system is a process. An image from music provides an illustrative analogy. The movement of the processes of selfhood is like the flow of musical process in Igor Stravinsky's *The Rite of Spring*. In that work, various elements and movements, expressed and given musical form by the various instruments, all participate in one flowing process. New elements emerge out of the process. Flowing out of the whole but having an autonomy of their own, they stand opposed to one another at one point, merge into each other at another, harmonize at yet a third place, and flow into new concrescences of tone and form later. At no one moment is the work reducible to its antecedents. The work affords a sense of wholeness, of differentiated elements and developments, and of synthesis. There is throughout a sense of continuity and direction, even at moments of apparent discontinuity.

This understanding of process can clarify the meaning of some of Jung's more popular concepts. No two of his constructs were more misunderstood in popular psychology than those of extraversion and introversion. Recalling our definition of the steady state, we are prepared to grasp the way Jung employed these two concepts. Basically, they refer to relatively enduring attitudes or orientations of personality. A multitude of traits and processes become constellated so as to form a fairly constant tendency in the personality. Extraversion refers to the general propensity of the person to respond positively toward the environment. Introversion reflects a relatively enduring tendency to withdraw from the external world into one's internality.

While the given person's attitude may be slightly more developed on one side or the other, daily living for everyone entails adaptation to both external and internal reality. Everyone must function consistently in the world of work, of social systems, of family, and of cultural forms. At the same time, everyone must listen to internal states, to feelings, and to undeveloped resources within the self. Progression is the "daily advance of psychological adaptation" into creative interaction with the world.[14] Regression reflects adaptation to internal needs. Mental health requires adaptation on both inner and outer fronts.

Any moment in the self's development can be viewed from both a causal and a purposive standpoint. In this latter assumption, Jung parted company with many of his contemporaries. Any moment in the life history, to be sure, can be traced to its origins and initial conditions, to a sequential series of connections and antecedent causes. Fundamentally, however, this causal view of a psychic occasion is a closed system. Such an occasion is reducible to initial conditions which follow a causal sequence with no exchange of incoming influences.

The purposive or final perspective, on the other hand, considers the uniqueness of a psychic moment. Such a moment is a novel and unique configuration of the self, reflecting something other than the sum of a series of causal sequences. It is prospective and purposive, insofar as it possesses future

[14] Jung, *The Structure and Dynamics* . . . , p. 32.

intentions and directions. The self, from this purposive stand-point, arrives at any moment by way of paths that elude sequential analysis. Expressing this dual perspective, Jung says:

> It is customary to effect a theoretically inadmissable compromise by regarding a process as partly causal, partly final — a compromise which gives rise to all sorts of theoretical hybrids but which yields, it cannot be denied, a relatively faithful picture of reality.[15]

One consequence of this apparently contradictory view is that the self and its subsystems may both "run down" in a causal sense and "increase in energy" through progressive differentiation and openness. Also implied in this view is the compensatory and self-regulating tendency of psychic systems in relation to one another. Therefore, the differentiating, integrating, and self-regulating processes contain within themselves the risk of disintegration, dissociation, and self-alienation. Thus, in the process of self-realization — the progressive differentation into complex psychic systems and into relatively stable orientations — certain functions and attitudes inevitably become more developed than others, resulting in a degree of one-sidedness.[16] Whatever is excluded from consciousness remains in an infantile, archaic, or unconscious state, but retains its potency for the tasks of daily existence. Conscious adaptation inhibits and counteracts these unconscious complexes.

In this state of imbalance, the self is alienated from its total self. A mild form of such imbalance arises when the directions and orientations of normal living are opposed and compromised by equally potent moods, feelings, and needs of the unconscious. Such an imbalance can be viewed both causally, in terms of the elements and stages leading to conflict, and purposively, in terms of the potential transformations inherent in it. In one sense such imbalance reflects a moral prob-

[15] *Ibid.*, p. 6.
[16] Jung, *Psychogenesis in Mental Disease*, vol. 3 of *The Collected Works* (1960), pp. 234ff.

lem, inasmuch as it offers the individual an opportunity to assume responsibility for his total selfhood.

But even greater degrees of imbalance can occur, producing dissociation and disintegration. In this state, consciousness and the requirements of daily living are overthrown or even controlled by partial systems of the self, especially by the more archaic complexes of the unconscious. The self is alienated from itself both inwardly and outwardly.

With the promise of differentiation and self-realization, comes the risk of fragmentation and self-alienation. But in both degrees of imbalance, the forces that have clustered in conflict contain within themselves the possibility of their own transformation. They reflect not only where the personality has been but also where it is tending. Even the most chaotic crises contain the potential of radical conversion.

Archetype: Bridging the Self and Its World

We have seen how the structures and dynamics of the self develop out of an original wholeness common to all men. Now we turn to yet another aspect of the self, to those processes by which the individual's responsibility for his own potential is sustained over his lifetime. The self continues to transcend itself in a self-surpassing realization of new potentials arising out of its archetypal depths. In some respects, this is a humanizing process, as the individual becomes identified with his common humanity. Each person bears responsibility for identifying with and incorporating the deeply human sensibilities inherent in common humanity.

The goal of the early years of life, including young adulthood, is the development of a highly individuated self. This is the time for the differentiation of a highly conscious, directed, and outwardly adapted self. Establishing one's place in the world of work, and taking responsibility for marriage and parenthood, require successful adaptation to the external world. The processes of abstraction, rationality, and direction are at a premium. At the center of consciousness stands a subsystem, the *ego*, the "I," which directs, abstracts, and adapts. The ego is predisposed in the larger self and is differentiated out of it. The realization of consciousness and its functioning is a basic task of these early years.

In this new phase of selfhood now under discussion, self-realization takes on a new aspect. From this new vantage point, consciousness and the ego are partial systems related to the archetypal ground common to all men. The archetypal self, like an underground stream, continually inclines the self toward its common humanity, its intrinsic potential. Of this process, Jung says, "The inevitable one-sidedness of our conscious life is constantly being corrected and compensated by the universal human being in us, whose goal is the ultimate integration . . . the assimilation of the ego to a wider personality." [17]

The ego, while still the center of consciousness, ceases to be the center of the personality. Consciousness, confronted by its own limits, enters into a reciprocal regulation with the larger, unconscious self-system. It is a centering and integrating process. The individual begins to realize that the values of rationality and technical competence are insufficient for the full life. Yet this transaction between consciousness and one's common humanity is in reality two sides of the same personality.

> If we picture the conscious mind, with the ego as the center, as being opposed to the unconscious, and if we now add to our mental picture the process of assimilating the unconscious, we can think of this assimilation as a kind of approximation of consciousness and unconscious, where the center of the total personality no longer coincides with the ego, but with a point midway between the conscious and the unconscious. This would be the point of a new equilibrium, a new centering of the total personality, a virtual center, which, on account of its focal position between consciousness and unconscious, ensures for the personality a new and more solid foundation.[18]

[17] *The Structure and Dynamics* . . . , p. 292.
[18] Jung, *Two Essays* . . . , p. 219.

Never, however, should consciousness be overthrown. This is alienation from one's self as much as over-directedness and extreme rationality. One cannot live in the everyday world and be driven by some partial or irrational system of the unconscious. Assimilating the archetypal depths of the self, instead, involves fundamental shifts in the psychic economy, but without annihilating the values of conscious life.

How does the individual experience these deepest levels of the mind, and how does he make them an effective part of himself? As we saw earlier, Jung believed that *the archetypal depths of the mind are represented in images and symbols.* His intense study of culture, ethnology, and anthropology reflected his effort to explore the meaning of man's symbols as expressions of common bases of human nature. In this side of his work he was badly misinterpreted. To anyone reading fragments of his writing, without regard for his overarching purpose, his investigations of folklore, mythology, dreams, and cultural and religious forms seem archaic, occult, and mystical. His method, basically a *comparative* approach, offered a procedure for going behind historical and cultural material to the common bases of the self.

Jung held that the symbols expressing the universal and critical situations of human experience were not merely accidental. Such symbols appear in diverse cultures and in different historical periods. In short, comparative cultural material affords a rich analogy with the determinative moments in the life history. Furthermore, mankind's most profound sensibilities are represented in the humanistic forms of culture and religion. Such forms tend to cluster around basic motifs indicative of the deepest levels of the mind.

If the archetypal depths of the mind are expressed in cultural forms and images, then these same forms afford a bridge to these same depths. The aim of self-realization, seen from this point of view, is to incorporate the archetypal realities contained in the primordial images. In this process the collective self and its potentials move from unconscious, archetypal tendencies to assimilation and embodiment within the personality. The individual partakes of his common humanity.

235

The self is expressed in culture, and culture is an avenue to the self. Culture shapes personality, and personality, culture. Jung's views on the transforming power of culture are valuable for scholars of social psychology.

Briefly, two illustrations of these archetypal motifs can be given. One is rebirth, the transition from some moment or state in life to another. The self-transcending tendency of change and renewal is common to mankind everywhere, but the symbols expressing this process are infinite. Sometimes the theme is one of initiation from one state to another, or the death of one state and change into another. Usually, the agents of change are water or fire in these motifs. Sometimes the self is enlarged and sometimes diminished. Most often, rebirth reflects change in the internal state of the self or the self's transformation of its own structure.[19]

Centering of the self is a common motif. Jung called the motifs expressing this process *mandala symbols*. Here too, the tendency toward integration characterizes man as man, but the symbols are rich in their variation. In such symbols the center is represented by an innermost point, surrounded by peripheral elements. The cross, for instance, is a preeminent symbol of the centered self. The following dream is illustrative:

> On board ship. The dreamer is busied with a new method of taking his bearings. Sometimes he is too far away and sometimes too near: the right spot is in the middle. There is a chart on which is drawn a circle with its center.[20]

In this brief dream a moment in the life history is depicted. There is a definite sense of movement from past to future. There is direction and purpose. Self-regulation and balance are implied, as well as the peripheral points around the center. But the overwhelming value is centering and self-regulation. In filling in the content of the individual's life, the meaning of these symbols for him can be approached.

[19] Jung, *The Archetypes and the Collective Unconscious*, p. 119.
[20] Jung, *Psychology and Alchemy*, vol. 12 of *The Collected Works* (1953), p. 100.

The Archetypal Self

The Self and Christ

Inevitably, Jung's inquiries into the archetype of the self and into its manifestation in religious symbolism led to an interest in Christology. While he never wrote systematically or at length on the relation between the self and Christ, he did approach the problem indirectly on several occasions, for example, in his Terry Lectures at Yale University[21] and in his research into the symbolism of the self in *Aion*.[22] He did have some well-defined views, and here, drawing from several of his works, we shall abstract three principles for understanding his thought.

The God-Man Archetype: Origins of Everyman

The original fact of human nature is the God-man archetype. In view of everything that has been said thus far, should we not say that the archetype of the self is the original fact in human nature? The introduction of the archetype of the God-man here is not an inconsistency, but the elaboration of a new aspect of selfhood, its transpersonal extension. The archetype of the self presupposes an indefinite extension beyond the single personality.

Theoretically, no limits can be assigned to the self. In its collective aspects, in its emergence through evolution and its open relation to the world around it, the self is grounded in reality itself. Jung calls this correlation the cosmic correspondence,[23] a correspondence between the individual as microcosm and the world as macrocosm. The collective base of the self binds man to his world, yet at the same time it tears him apart from the world as a distinct and unique person. He participates in tendencies toward both a common humanity and an individuality.

The joint inherence of self and world is experienced as the

[21] Jung, *Psychology and Religion*, (New Haven: Yale University Press, 1938).

[22] *Aion: Researches into the Phenomenology of the Self*, vol. 9 of *The Collected Works* (1953).

[23] Jung, *The Undiscovered Self*, trans. R. F. C. Hull (Boston: Little, Brown and Company, 1957), p. 60.

237

life process, the chief symbol of which is "God." Symbols of God represent an intuition of the union of the self and its grounding in the processes of life, and are most powerful in the personality, centering the self-world correspondence and the self-realization tendency. Self-realization, in relation to God, is represented by such a symbol as the *Imago Dei*. This traditional formula affirms man's creation in God's own image, implying an intrinsic relation between the two. *Imago Dei* represents the self-world correspondence, binding man to a common ground and thrusting him toward individuation.

Both *God* and *Imago Dei*, therefore, symbolically point *within* the self and *beyond* it. They express those aspects of the self which are transpersonal and illimitable. At the same time they reflect those aspects of the self which are most immediate and personal. These symbols are found in all cultures and historical periods, even if they represent nothing more than an assumption of the unity and ordering of life. Jung felt strongly that psychology should explore so universal and powerful a symbol and its role in the personality.

Jung never restricted "God" to man's unconscious, although he did make other theological speculations. For example, he was convinced that, since the archetype of the God-man relates man to God, theology ought to construct a concept of divine relativity.

> "Absolute" means "cut off," "detached." To assert that God is absolute amounts to placing him outside all connections with mankind. Man cannot affect him or he man. Such a God would be of no consequence at all. We can in fairness only speak of a God who is relative to man, as man is to God . . . That kind of God could reach man.[24]

Self-realization, in one sense, is given from beyond the self, and at the same time it is an inherent tendency. Self-realization, viewed as Jung saw it, becomes a moral problem, insofar as man is responsible for the original potential with which he is endowed.

[24] *Two Essays* . . . , p. 233.

Jesus Christ: The Archetype Embodied

The life of Jesus Christ can be understood as the personal and historical realization of the God-man archetype. Jesus Christ lived a concrete and unique life, which had, at the same time, an archetypal character.[25] Ultimately, every human life is archetypal in its collective bases. Hence, the clue to understanding Jung's thought is found in a bipolar movement, from microcosm to macrocosm, from the "other" prior to the self to the "other" common with the self, from potential to actual.

In Jesus Christ, we find that the achetype as potential became actual in his life. The archetype as indefinite and illimitable became definite and concretely embodied in him. The archetype as universal became unique. As eternal, in the sense of an ever-present reality, it became unitemporal. The archetype as collective became individuated. We can speak of the self-transcending side of the archetype in Jesus Christ as the "Son of God." We can speak of the personal aspects of his selfhood as the "Son of man."

We are justified, however, in a reverse understanding. On the basis of the archetype of the God-man, we can say that Christ's divine nature refers to his actuality, definiteness, uniqueness, individuality, and unitemporality. Incarnation is, from this point of view, the movement of God into human nature, into embodiment. To enter history is to become actual and particular, conditioned by time and place in human experience. To understand fully the historical Jesus, we must consider the God-man relation to which Jesus constantly referred and which he sought to make transparent in his life. Anything less is poor history, if we seek to understand Jesus as he understood himself.

The archetype of the God-man requires, according to Jung, the doctrine of homoousia.[26] The movement from microcosm to macrocosm is a transition from two sides of the same reality

---

[25] Jung, *Psychology and Religion: West and East*, vol. 11 of *The Collected Works* (1958), p. 88.

[26] This classical doctrine held that God and Christ were of the *same* "substance" instead of *similar* substance. Also see Jung, *Psychology and Religion*, p. 193.

or "substance." Jung says, "it makes a great deal of difference whether the self is 'of the same nature' as the father or only 'of similar nature'."[27]

The Task of Modern Man: Withdrawing Projection and Discovering the Self

The archetype of the God-man must be withdrawn from projection onto the historical Christ and must be regarded as the original fact inherent in the nature of modern man. Projection is the transferring of a subjective content onto an external object. It represents a form of dissociation, since the person fails to recognize the content as a part of himself and to assimilate it into his selfhood. To the extent that the content remains unassimilated, the self is unrealized.

When an archetype is transferred onto an external person, the archetype becomes identified with the other and is dissociated from the self. When this happens, the other person is invested with values originating within the self. The process of projection is intensified if the other possesses qualities which stand as a lure for unconscious identification.

This, to Jung, is exactly the meaning of christological doctrines. The archetype embodied in Christ is also the archetype inherent in every man. When projection occurs, as it did in the early Christian era, the concrete and historical Jesus virtually vanishes behind the archetypal projections onto him.[28] He is absorbed into the surrounding religious systems of his time and becomes their archetypal exponent.

As early as 1937, Jung identified one of the crucial problems of New Testament scholarship:

> This character [the archetypal character of the life of Christ] can be recognized from the numerous connections of the biographical details with worldwide myth-motifs. These undeniable connections are the main reason why it is so difficult for researchers into the life of Jesus to construct from the gospel reports an individual

[27] *Symbols of Transformation*, vol. 5 of *The Collected Works* (1956), p. 391.
[28] *Psychology and Religion*, p. 154.

life divested of myth. In the gospels themselves the factual reports, legends, and myths are woven into a whole.[29]

If modern man is to assume responsibility for himself, he must withdraw his projections from the historical Christ. Under the condition of projection, modern man cannot become responsible for his own relationship with God, since God remains outside any connection with himself, and one's archetypal depths are not experienced as part of one's own selfhood. When the archetypal symbols are withdrawn from projections, however, they can be dealt with as disclosures of the original nature of modern man. Now the symbols can manifest the primordial reality of a common humanity. One can argue, in fact, that it was precisely these archetypal realities that Jesus sought to reveal to his fellow men.

When Jung calls on modern man to assume responsibility for his own depths by withdrawing his projections, he is *not* doing away with the archetypal symbols. Man continues to experience his original reality by means of symbols, the representatives of archetypal realities. The depths of the self are expressed in the symbols and images of religion, culture, and mythology. They possess a mediating character, mediating the original self to the immediate self. They are vehicles of psychic transformation. "Experience of the Mass," Jung says, illustrating the transforming power of religious symbols, "is therefore a participation in a transcendence of life overcoming all limitations of time and space. It is a moment of eternity within time."[30]

In this dramatic Christian liturgy, the eternal aspect of the God-man archetype is experienced in unitemporality, and a moment in present individual and communal history shares in the ongoing depths of a common, timeless humanity. Such symbolic quality in religion demands preservation. Returning to the gospels, Jung says that "they would immediately lose

[29] *Ibid.*, p. 88.
[30] *Psychological Reflections: An Anthology of the Writings of C. G. Jung*, ed. Jolande Jacobi, Bollingen Series 31 (New York: Pantheon Books, 1953), p. 324.

their character of wholeness if one tried to separate the individual from the archetypal with a critical scalpel."[31]

God, from Jung's point of view, seeks to become embodied in man's experience, to be incarnated in the world. When man knows his own depths, his inherent grounding in the divine reality, God becomes effectually and concretely present in human affairs and human experience. Modern man must take his potential for self-realization with absolute moral seriousness. Alienated from his own depths, he is alienated from God. And aliented from God, he is estranged from himself.

Discovering the Self: An Approach to Knowing.

It is possible for us now to look backward at Jung's psychology of the self, to examine the methodology implied in his work. Methodology, as used here, refers to the presuppositions, delineations of problems, and methods of inquiry in Jung's work. Since Jung refused "to play favorites" with various philosophical categories, his methodology appears, at first, to be filled with contradictions, which, when viewed as part of a whole system, are actually correlations of categories taken from different sources. Furthermore, his strenuous effort to preserve these correlations opened up avenues of inquiry which were to be recognized by others only later. To recall, we have observed his syntheses of mind and body, of causality and indeterminism, of the individual and the collective, of process and effect, and of the transpersonal and personal.

Basic to his study of man was a bipolar approach, which sought both *understanding* of the individual in particular and *knowledge* of mankind in general. The former concern left him throughout his career an avowed clinician, interested in the uniqueness of persons. The latter concern moved him toward a persistent investigation of common features of human nature, toward cultural anthropology, ethnology, and religion. In *The Undiscovered Self*, one of his last works and one where his methodology was fully explicated, Jung wrote:

[31] *Psychology and Religion*, p. 88.

There is and can be no self-knowledge based on theoretical assumptions, for the object of self-knowledge is an individual — a relative exception and an irregular phenomenon. Hence, it is not the universal and the regular which characterize the individual, but rather the unique. He is not to be understood as a recurrent unit but as something unique and singular which in the last analysis can neither be known nor compared with anything else.[32]

Failure to give complete recognition to the concrete individual renders a distorted picture of human uniqueness.[33]

Taken by itself, this viewpoint left Jung open to a one-sided criticism. Jung took the ideas and images of people seriously. Hence, some critics found him too relativistic. The fact that an idea or image exists in the mind, they argued, is no ground for its validity. Mental images must be subjected to criteria of verification, especially in the realm of religion.[34]

Curiously, the other side of Jung's method was concerned precisely with establishing an objective basis for mental ideas and images and for cultural and religious symbols. In fact, because Jung kept an open mind consistent with his phenomenal method, he refused to dismiss cultural and religious symbols, to be indifferent to them, or to assume that enlightenment would somehow eliminate them. Such universal symbols were, to him, the avenue for exploring mankind's common characteristic. Employing the comparative method, then, he sought the inherent tendencies, structures, and dynamics of the mind. His studies here led to the concept of the archetype. Interestingly, later in his career Jung often referred to the collective unconscious as the objective psyche, the common base of the self. Again, in *The Undiscovered Self*, Jung wrote:

[32] *The Undiscovered Self*, p. 9.
[33] This concept of *understanding* can be compared with Gordon Allport's theory of the *idiographic* method in psychology. See his *Becoming* (New Haven: Yale University Press, 1955), p. 19.
[34] Erich Fromm, *Psychoanalysis and Religion* (New Haven: Yale University Press, 1950), p. 15.

At the same time man, as a member of a species, can and must be described as a statistical unit; otherwise nothing general could be said about him. For this purpose he has to be regarded as a comparative unit. This results in a universally valid anthropology or psychology . . . with an abstract picture of man as an average unit from which all individual features have been removed. . . . knowledge of man, or insight into human character, presupposes all sorts of knowledge about mankind in general.[35]

Unavoidably perhaps, such views left Jung subject to criticisms from another side. He was too withdrawn, too introspective, and too occult, some scholars claimed. He was not interested in the ordinary events of everyday human affairs. Indeed, it must be acknowledged that Jung's writings in comparative religion and ethnology, read out of context, seem strange to the modern mind. But by now it should be clear that this was but one side of Jung's method, making use of the tools available to him at the time for investigating aspects of human experience which he deemed important.

Jung constantly disclaimed any formal "expertize" in philosophy and theology. In fact, he rejected philosophy as he understood it formally. But the case can be made that he worked with an implicit process conception of reality and with a theology of divine relativity. Movement and direction pervade his thought. We must conclude that he held to his assumptions about the holistic, dynamic, and purposive nature of life in the midst of opposing presuppositions held by the thinkers of his day. To stress effect as well as cause, future as well as past, mind and body as unified, collided, in Jung's time, with the then widely-held presuppositions of mechanism, reductionism, and reactivism. The lines of disagreement can now be recognized more distinctly.

Jung did understand science differently from many of his contemporaries. Once more, we find that in this theory of scientific objectivity he refused to play favorites. The in-

---

[35] *The Undiscovered Self*, p. 9. Again, compare this concept of knowledge with Allport's theory of the *nomothetic* method in *Becoming*, p. 27.

quiring subject and investigated object, to him, existed in a strict relation to each other. No doubt his understanding of scientific method was influenced by his personal acquaintance with the microphysicist Wilhelm Pauli. He became increasingly interested in the complementarity principle in physics, and applied its implications to psychology. This principle seeks to recognize and to allow for the effect of the observer on the observed. Reality, in this conception of scientific method, forfeits some of its objectivity. Personal and tacit aspects of the experimental situation are recognized as part of the scientific process.

In accordance with this principle, Jung viewed the researching psychologist as standing in a strict relation to the mind, his object of inquiry. In effect, this meant that the inquirer must study the human mind within the medium of the mind. The conscious mind may be able to make the remainder of the self an object, but so, too, can consciousness receive images from the depths of the mind, as in dreams. At best, a psychological conception is limited to gradations of probability within the multidimensional field of the mind.

This system-theory methodology is firmly established in the current life sciences. We are still in a time of transition in the philosophy of science, however, as indicated by this criticism of Jung written in 1962:

> For most of us scientifically trained Occidentals who worship objectivity and stress causality . . . this basically oriental approach to reality . . . stresses the *configuration* rather than the *sequence* of events. . . . Despite strenuous effort at understanding, much of Jung's writings simply do not "make sense" to us.[36]

Jung, we have said, held an implicit theology of divine relativity. God is related to man in his archetypal depths and is always seeking embodiment in human experience and human history. The archetype of the God-man consists, we saw, of transpersonal and illimitable depths, which are neverthe-

[36] William Douglas, "The Influence of Jung's Work: A Critical Comment," *Journal of Religion and Health*, 6, no. 3 (1962), p. 261.

less personal and immediate. Divine reality seeks concrete realization in man. One Protestant theologian writes of Jung's theology:

> The changes to which man is subject, his whole evolution, are in the last resort nothing less than a reflection of the becoming of God — the pattern of emergent Deity. . . . We can say with some truth, then, that this places Jung in a spiritual current whose representatives in philosophy are generally reckoned among the so-called "life-philosophers" . . . their theme is the changing and emerging God. . . . This doctrine is closely connected with the doctrine of the relativity of God; indeed, it is its necessary counterpart.[37]

We should not attempt to push Jung's conception of God beyond the point where he was content to leave it. But his view of God as both absolute and relative has parallel development, for example, in the contemporary theistic philosophy of Charles Hartshorne. Hartshorne's theory, elaborating and extending the process views of Alfred North Whitehead, has, in turn, greatly informed the work of several modern Christian theologians.[38]

In Hartshorne's thought, reality is a social system of interdependent and interpenetrating creatures, who exist and endure through the presence and influence of a dominant member. God is the supreme social creature, who co-ordinates all creatures into a complex society.[39] God influences his world in a supremely relative and social manner. As such, he is both absolute and relative. If God were only absolute, he could in

[37] Hans Schaer, *Religion and the Cure of Souls in Jung's Psychology*, trans. R. F. C. Hull, Bollingen Series 21 (New York: American Book-Stratford Press, 1950), pp. 214ff.

[38] See for example: Norman Pittinger, *The Word Incarnate* (New York: Harper and Brothers, 1959); Schubert Ogden, *Christ without Myth* (New York: Harper and Brothers, 1961); Daniel D. Williams, *God's Grace and Man's Hope* (New York: Harper and Brothers, 1949); and John Cobb, *A Christian Natural Theology* (Philadelphia: The Westminster Press, 1965).

[39] Charles Hartshorne, *Reality As Social Process*, (Glencoe, Ill.: The Free Press, 1953), p. 135.

no way increase in value, would be self-sufficient, and could be entirely independent of his creation.[40] If he were only relative, he would be perfect and supreme in no way and would in every way be subject to change.

But although God is perfect and complete in some respects, he is not so in all. God's enduring character, in this conception, is his infallibility of knowing, his perfection of loving and valuing, and his adequacy with respect to his eternal purpose.[41] At the same time, he genuinely lives and shares in the actual world of each creature, taking its concreteness into himself. He is supremely related to all creatures at all times and in every aspect of their being.[42]

It has been our claim that Jung's self theory offers a rich resource for integrating many developments in contemporary anthropology, including its theological aspect. No attempt has been made here to utilize Jung for a broader interdisciplinary theory, although an interpretive framework has been present throughout in attempting to show his relevance. In making this material available and showing its relevance, a necessary preliminary step has been taken.

[40] *Ibid.*, p. 155ff.
[41] *Ibid.*, p. 202.
[42] *Ibid.*, p. 135.

10

Order and Chaos in Psychopathology and Ontology:
A Challenge to Traditional Correlations of Order
to Mental Health and Ultimate Reality, and of
Chaos to Mental Illness and Alienation.

WILLIAM R. ROGERS

Among the concepts that may be fruitfully utilized in interdisciplinary discussion are the polar notions of order and
chaos. Investigating the interplay between the processes of
ordering and the processes of disordering or chaos in various
areas of academic investigation may be of mutual help in the
dynamic understanding of each. Certainly within psychology, the notions of order and chaos (or structure and fragmentation or balanced wholeness versus imbalance and
confusion) are fruitful organizing concepts when we are
looking at the process of personality disorganization and
corresponding notions of personality reintegration. In theology the concepts are also significant, both epistemologically
and substantively, in such doctrines as creation and salvation.
The following is an attempt to examine the interplay of forces
moving toward structure or order in personality, both individually and ontologically conceived, and the forces leading
toward disorder or chaos.

It has been customary for some time to speak of psychological dysfunction or breakdown in terms of disintegration
or disorder, and to speak of the process of restoration as a
process of regaining order or meaningful structure. It may be
even more cogent, however, to argue that personality dysfunction can be seen as a process in which an individual

attempts to order his experience too narrowly or too rigidly, so that he may avoid accurate, though perhaps disorderly, perception of events or feelings which would be too anxiety-producing. Chaotic and unmanageable feelings are ruled out through repressive processes of denial and distortion on the basis of these narrow, protective, ordering principles. The process of psychotherapy would be seen from this perspective as a way of facilitating a breakthrough in the rigid defensive order, by providing a psychologically safe setting in which the person can reincorporate the chaotic and conflicting elements of his real inner and outer world back into accurate awareness. But to do this, he must allow himself to experience something of his chaos.

Ontologically, attempts at conceptualizing order in the universe may also be deceptive and defensive, protecting us from the chaos (in Greek, "gap" or "yawning chasm," and in Hebrew, "formlessness") that separates man from an ultimately indeterminate God, a God free and unrestricted by any such conceptualizations. Salvation, too, may imply the unsettling recognition of such indeterminacy (the Deus Abscunditus), in spite of the discomfort that this brings our "oceanic feeling" (Freud), and feelings of absolute dependence" (Schleiermacher).

Order and Chaos in the Process of Personality Dysfunction

Any responsible attempt to deal with the process of personality dysfunction (or mental illness) must be based on (a) a broad recognition of the interaction of a person with other persons and the culture; and (b) a recognition of the sequential process of human growth and development. This is particularly true when we attempt to examine the way in which an individual comes to develop some meaningful order in his conception of his own life and the world.

In interaction with the culture, it is apparent that language is of extreme significance. Language is the primary tool that a culture provides to enable the individual to order experience. Language creates the possibility of distinguishing the significant from the insignificant in individual experience. And it is amply clear that some cultures enable persons to have a more discriminating order of experiences than other cultures do. The arts and humanities within a culture can be expected to give greater breadth to individuals within that culture for perceiving meaningful order. One problem that exists within modern Western cultures is that many functions of language in symbolization and communication have been undercut by our attention to individual autonomy in idiosyncratic communication (H.S. Sullivan's prototaxic mode [1]), the art and theater of the absurd, and the general heterogeneity of values. This has made it increasingly difficult for an individual to develop any profound sense of the truly meaningful. And it exaggerates tendencies to grasp at partial but narrow orders for understanding life, stressing some events and values but allowing no meaningful symbolization or recognition of other events. Indeed, the post-Freudian suspicion of any ultimately organizing conceptualization as being only an illusory security operation has ironically narrowed, for some, the realm of significant reality to the analytic experience itself, rather than broadened their openness to reality. But while the perceivable world thus becomes restricted, inevitably other events do break in. Because they cannot be dealt with, they create feelings of confusion, threat, anxiety, and perhaps despair, which severely impair the person's ability to function adequately.

In the study of developmental processes at the same time, a number of scholars have also given attention to the emergence of symbolization or imagination (image-making) and its function in ordering human experience. Jacob Bronowski [2] and Jean Piaget,[3] particularly, have dealt with the importance of this process. It has been clear that the scope of one's image-making capacity is restricted by psychological and

[1] Sullivan, *The Interpersonal Theory of Psychiatry* (New York: W. W. Norton and Co., 1953), pp. 28–29.
[2] Bronowski, *Insight* (New York: Harper and Row, 1964) and *Science and Human Values* (New York: J. Messner, 1956).
[3] Piaget, *The Construction of Reality in the Child*, trans. M. Cook (New York: Basic Books, 1959).

socioeconomic factors. For instance, the deprivation of parental love and support has led in some cases to autistic thinking and private symbols, which are personally relevant but socially incommunicable. And environmental and educational deprivation among the lower class has in a different way impoverished the capacity to order symbolically the world. This has meant that many people settle for a flimsy or restricted structure of life and the world. And the result, taken together with the restricting capabilities of the culture, is that an individual, when under conditions of stress, is frequently unable to incorporate the meaning and emotional weight of a new or complex event. When this happens, anxiety increases sharply, a person's instinctual mechanisms may become more difficult to control, and the individual feels an exaggerated sense of loss of identity, of helplessness, and of chaos.

It is this kind of process that we have traditionally referred to as personality "breakdown" or "disintegration." It has appeared to be a process in which the individual's normal way of interpreting or ordering life has been incapable of withstanding the shock of an experience that he cannot interpret or incorporate within his ordering system. This is true whether we interpret the ordering system in terms of an individual's "self concept," his "belief system," his "frame of orientation and devotion," or his "security operations." Whatever we call them, those principles by which the person normally interacts with his environment and with himself may at some point prove inadequate to the process of accurately assimilating and understanding his experience in conscious awareness. Mental illness in this scheme is viewed as chaotic, bizarre, dissociated, or delusional patterns, which are fragmented off from the normal and balanced course of human growth and development.

And yet if one looks carefully at the clinical pictures of most disturbed persons, what he finds is frequently anything but confused, chaotic, disintegrated, and unstructured lives. Rather, there seems to be a retreat into a narrow, personally *organized* world, which is carefully structured to protect a person from the threatening feelings and situations with which he has been unable to cope. The recognition that neuroses and psychoses involve a narrow and rigidly organized idiosyncratic frame of reference has come largely from the contribution of phenomenologists who have attempted to see what the inner world of the disturbed person was really like, rather than approaching him with preconceived categories and diagnostic schema.[4] When one enters into the personal and unique frame of reference of a patient, what one often finds is a highly ordered way of viewing the world, which maintains its gestalt by denying any experiences that do not fit this defensive frame of reference. We see this in everything, from what has traditionally been termed mild phobias and obsessive compulsive neuroses to exaggerated, paranoid, delusional systems and chronic depressive reactions. We see it furthermore in the evidence of brain-damaged individuals and retarded individuals who can cope with a limited environment but seem quite incapable of adapting themselves to strange situations, which would require powers of generalization and flexibility not exercisable from within the limited order of their system.

Perhaps the reason we have called these persons fragmented or disorganized is that their tightly structured world and "bizarre" forms of communication have seemed fragmented or broken off from the reality that most individuals experience. To call them fragmented or disordered personalities also reflects the fact that, in their restricted stance in life, they are broken off from their real potentialities of feeling and experience. Or, theologically stated, they are broken off from the power of Being, or the ground of Being. In each of these expressions, however, we are speaking about personality dysfunction from an *objective* or *essential* point of view. From the outside, viewing man as an object in relation to reality, we can interpret the dysfunction as a *disorder*. He is "out of

[4] See Rollo May, ed., *Existence* (New York: Basic Books, 1958); B. Kaplan, *The Inner World of Mental Illness* (New York: Harper and Row, 1964); Medard Boss, *Psychoanalysis and Daseinsanalysis* (New York: Basic Books, 1963); and R. D. Laing, *The Divided Self* (Chicago: Quadrangle Books, 1960).

order" with his essential nature and potential for wholeness. Psychology, theology, philosophy, and even physics *can* take such an objective perspective on man's disordered "predicament."

Viewed from the *subjective* or *existential* context of the person himself, however, we see the dysfunction as an attempt to achieve *order*; it is an attempt to achieve a personal, idiosyncratic order, which will enable one to feel more comfortable by avoiding accurate perception of events and feelings that might be disruptingly painful, anxiety-producing, or guilt-producing. Again the various academic disciplines, through their phenomenological and existential sensitivities, may be attentive to this subjective reality of the individual. And, indeed, to understand accurately the real nature of the person, it seems crucial that we do attend to this internal reality of one's private quest for order.

Ontological Order and Chaos

Such a switch in our perception of the functioning of ordering processes in psychopathology points up more ultimate questions of the ontological status of order and chaos. Is there an inherent principle of order in the universe, such as is testified to in Logos theology and in eighteenth-century Deism,[5] or is there inherent chaos in the universe, which even the most refined theological and physical conceptualizations cannot contain or specify?

The appeal of a notion of order in the universe is instinctive, Whitehead believes;[6] and it certainly promotes scientific dependability and personal security. The appeal of a notion of chaos in the universe is also instinctive, believes Berdyaev,[7] and promotes the affirmation that both personal freedom and the freedom of God are beyond all determination or definitive description. To break from the sustaining order of

[5] See for example Tom Paine, *The Age of Reason* (New Rochelle, N.Y.: Tom Paine National Historical Association, 1925).

[6] Alfred North Whitehead, *Science and The Modern World* (New York: Macmillan Co., 1926), p. 5.

[7] Nicolas Berdyaev, *Dream and Reality* (New York: Macmillan Co., 1950).

being may be viewed as man's fall into the demonic and Dionysian chaos of prideful self-indulgence (sin). Or, alternatively, to break from the restless and uncharted potentialities of man's freedom and creativity into some ordered retreat of conventional thought-forms and ritual behavior may be viewed as static security-seeking that cringes back from any response to an active God (also sin).

The debate between these dichotomous ontological perspectives has taken some interesting turns recently. Of particular interest have been the recent contributions by such diverse disciplines as nuclear physics and musical composition. The physicists have indeed informed us that there may well be a lever of indeterminacy beneath the sort of ordered regularity assumed by early nuclear investigators. Heisenberg has been specific in contrasting this to previous conceptions — typified, for instance, in Kepler's solar system theory — of a beautifully ordered universe.[8] And musicians have simultaneously struck us with the unnaturalness of highly mathematically ordered serial compositions, and allowed us to hear the chaos of the chance randomness of sound by presenting scores which, in some cases, simply call for the selection of any eleven notes at random below middle C.[9] Listen to the sounds in nature, they say, and you will notice no real order or predictability. Musical order is something we have merely superimposed on the chaotic noises of nature.

Psychology, of course, has stringently cautioned us against any facile escape into a comforting notion of order in the universe, which could neurotically defend us against the painful realities of concrete human existence. This is most noticeable in the writing of Freud and his followers. And, although Freud apparently did not recognize it, such cautions are also given in the prophetic dimension of the Judeo-Christian tradition. In Freud's argument, given most clearly in *The Future of An Illusion*, religious or philosophical attempts at ordering the universe may very easily be delusional systems, manu-

[8] Werner Heisenberg, *The Physicist's Conception of Nature* (New York: Harcourt, Brace and Co., 1958), pp. 79–80.
[9] See *Perspectives of New Music*, Fall–Winter, 1965.

factured by individuals and sustained by cultures, designed to protect men from the harsh realities of life. In so doing, however, such systems force men to repress significant aspects of their experience, which, when repressed, lead only to personal self-division, unconscious conflict, and, finally, neurotic or psychotic disturbance.

Existentialism has also reinforced the importance of the ontological significance of chaos. The attack on an ontology of order is expressed partly in an appeal to the radical particularity of every concrete moment and person over against the generality and nomothetic arbitrariness of all abstractions. It is expressed also in the concern for change. Berdyaev puts this in both a religious and psychological context when he writes:

> The hierarchical order of being from God down to beetle is a crushing order of things and abstractions. It is crushing and enslaving and there is no room for personality in it either as an ideal or as a real order. Personality is outside all being . . . outside unchanged order. . . . The spirit is not subject to the order of being; it intrudes upon it, interrupts it and may change it.[10]

The attack on order is expressed, too, as a response to the problem of suffering. Note, for instance, the way Dostoevsky shows Ivan Karamazov rejecting any notion of world harmony or world order on the grounds that this could not be reconciled with unmixed suffering, even in one tear of a tortured child. And it is expressed preeminently in concerns for both man and God's ontological freedom — the unlimited, boundless, undetermined potentiality to move in new ways undictated by any fixed structure and order.

Such emphases have had their obvious impact on theology, especially, perhaps, in Wieman.[11] They are spoken of more frequently as "process" metaphysical concerns, over against

[10] Nicolas Berdyaev, *Slavery and Freedom* (New York: Charles Scribner's Sons, 1944), p. 80.

[11] See Henry Nelson Wieman, *The Source of Human Good* (Chicago: University of Chicago Press, 1946).

static notions of structure or substance. But the concern seems similar throughout: to emphasize that which is open, active, dynamic, in tension, ambiguous, and free, in contradistinction to that which is closed, ordered, determined, and complete. I am suggesting, therefore, that this altered thrust is common to a wide range of contemporary thought forms, especially to these ontological and psychological perspectives, though we must push for an even deeper understanding.

Beyond the bipolar distinction between order and chaos formulated thus far, must come the recognition that neither concept can give independently an adequate conceptualization of either man or ultimate being. In Tillich's terms, we can never with justification isolate freedom from destiny.[12] Or, more ultimately, we can never speak of either process or chaos without at least implying some structure in which this is to be understood. Or, stated in Whitehead's terms, order and disorder (chaos) are essentially correlative terms, as are necessity and chance.[13] One without the contrast of the other would be meaningless. "An *absolutely* orderly world," states Hartshorne as well, "would deprive the concept of order of any significance."[14] This essential interplay of order and chaos, recognizing particularly the profound ontological function of chaos, is reviewed in contemporary philosophy of religion by Kuntz.[15]

The necessity of correlative contrast between order and chaos is meaningful not only as a logical polarity but also as an ontological, developmental reality. Reality as well as personality may be fruitfully understood as developmental in its movement through periods of stability, through the unsettling bursting of that stability due to the imbalance of

[12] Paul Tillich, *Systematic Theology*, 3 vols. (Chicago: University of Chicago Press, 1951–63), 1:182–86.

[13] Alfred North Whitehead, *Process and Reality* (Cambridge: At the University Press, 1929).

[14] Charles Hartshorne, "Man and Nature," in *Experience, Existence and the Good*, ed. I. C. Lieb (Carbondale, Ill.: Southern Illinois University Press, 1961), p. 98.

[15] Paul Kuntz, "Religion of Order or Religion of Chaos," *Religion in Life*, Summer, 1966.

disorganized expansion or contraction, and through the further formation of new and fuller organismic integration, which gives new stability. Order, the chaotic breaking of order, and resolution in further stages of order are constantly intermingled. The unbroken rigidity of the one would be as destructive as the unchanneled diffusion of the other. A dialectic of both must be maintained.

Order and Chaos in the Process of Psychotherapy and Salvation

To return to the psychological problems in which this discussion was initiated: there are important implications for the process of healing. The restrictive order characterizing psychopathology may be conceptualized in terms of the prototaxic communication of an individual,[16] and needs to be understood before it can be broken through in freeing the person. As language functions within the culture to enable persons to have some ordered view of reality which differentiates the significant from the insignificant, so the person who has experienced increasing personality dysfunction develops a language, which, if understood from the inside, may enable the therapist to differentiate what is significant from what is insignificant in the person's ordering of himself and reality. It becomes apparent that, if the psychotherapist is to understand accurately the nature of an individual's illness, he must enter as carefully and as empathetically as he can into this personally ordered world, seeing how distorted perceptions function within the client's psychic life. This is a process of phenomenological sensitivity or of existential encounter, which transcends subject-object dichotomies and allows participation in another's frame of reference.

Those therapeutic orientations which do not recognize the importance of understanding the private ordered world of the client, rely on an ordering system imposed from the outside. In these cases the therapist imposes an order which differentiates the significant from the insignificant in the illness on the basis of his therapeutic orientation, rather than from

[16] See Sullivan, *Interpersonal Theory of Psychiatry.*

the point of view of the person himself. It is obvious why such an externally imposed order, brought to the therapeutic situation by the therapist alone, creates "resistance" on the part of the client and may well set up conditions of parataxic distortion [17] in which the therapist talks right past the client, and the client, seeing the therapist as well as the rest of life only in terms of his own order, neglects or distorts what the therapist is saying, perhaps even including him in a delusional system. Therapists, we find, proceed more effectively by being sensitive to the individual's unique ordering of reality and its protective meaning.

In developing sensitivity to the client's internal ordering of life, it is frequently true that the client attempts to maintain as orderly a view of himself as he can, not letting himself or the therapist see those chaotic elements which lie submerged and out of awareness. For this reason the client frequently attempts to "look good" to the therapist. While admitting a few "presenting problems," which are relatively safe to look at, he omits a good many other things. It is tempting to discover quickly organizing principles which would help bring integration to the client. We know, however, that premature attempts at integration or interpretation and reorganization may tend to reinforce those mechanisms which have repressed the more seriously upsetting feelings in the first place. The therapist thus might miss those problems which lie more destructively at the heart of the disturbance. Furthermore, even after the root problems have come into view, therapeutic interventions which cut off the experience of sustained ambiguity connected with the problem may disrupt the therapeutic process by encouraging categorization or intellectualization on the part of clients, enabling them to talk about their difficulties, but not enabling them really to experience the ground of disturbed feelings which need eventually to be assimilated into a reconstructed order. What is frequently called for in the process of therapy, is an atmosphere of safety and freedom in which the client *can experience more fully the disordered chaos of his denied*

[17] *Ibid.*

experiences and feelings, and can become aware that these threatening experiences can be accepted and dealt with in their chaotic, frightening forms by both the therapist and himself in constructive ways. Indeed, it would appear that only from a creative resolution that emerges after experiencing the fullness and sustained ambiguity of these chaotic feelings can one truly come to reintegrate the most disordered material and move toward greater health in the sense of wholeness, self-awareness, self-affirmation, freedom, and stability. It is in this that the dialectic of chaos and order is existentially realized.

Similarly, in the process of salvation the same dynamic is evident. It appears essential that an individual open himself to the chaos of his own guilt, alienation, and meaninglessness before real healing, forgiveness, and redemption can occur. Repentance, in traditional terms, refers to one's brokenness and sorrow for sin. And one must experience the dark wilderness of this sorrow before new resolution may emerge. The temptation myth, common in nearly all religions and in most classical literature and drama, also exemplifies the crucial process of one's struggle with real chaos in the movement toward salvation and wholeness. But again, the process is not fulfilled if one merely remains lost or perhaps infatuated with the chaos of the wilderness. One must work through this, with gracious assistance, to eventually new integrative order.

Attention to the subtleties of the ordering process is also necessary within moment-to-moment therapeutic responses to a client and in the symbolic forms of preaching and teaching. Looking at contemporary literary criticism, it is noteworthy that *appropriate* order is increasingly considered necessary to a literary work, especially in providing images and forms which lend themselves adequately to the expression intended by the work. Images, symbols, and the general ordering structure must appropriately convey the meaning of the reality to which they point. It is similarly true in therapeutic and ministerial responsiveness that the images used to give order, both in particular responses and in the ongoing communication, must be appropriate to the meaning that is being uncovered and clarified. Although a therapist or minister is willing to live with the person through his experience of disordered events and feelings, he nevertheless at every moment is helping to formulate with more vividness, intensity, and focus, the genuine nature of those experiences. Some research has shown that fresh, colorful images used in therapeutic responses give greater adequacy to the expression of *feeling* than do expressions using therapeutic jargon or dull, hackneyed metaphors and phrases.[18] Through the freshness and accuracy of forms for ordering the experience, the helping person may provide a fuller language for the individual to use in a broadened awareness of himself and his relationships.

Finally, in the processes of psychotherapy and salvation, having broken through the conscious attempts at narrowly ordering life and having dealt with the chaotic undercurrents of real experience, one moves toward a gradual reintegration and reordering of life which includes the wider realities of one's total feelings and full participation in relation to persons and forces outside himself. In this process one develops a new and broadened frame of orientation. With a greater consciousness of those feelings and experiences which are an authentic part of himself, and with the possibility of perceiving more adequately what is going on around him, the individual is able to include in a larger gestalt both his self-concept and his concept of reality. The new frame of orientation should allow greater spontaneity and openness. It should enable one to have increasingly accurate perceptions of erupting chaotic feelings, without the insecurity that one will be overwhelmed by these, or the false expectation that one will inevitably be changed again by them. A healthy sense of order in personal life should give both the security that allows one to take a firm stand on who he is and what he is willing to fight for, and a sense of the irony of life which permits one to be humbly attentive to the continuing emergence of contradiction and new possibility which may de-

[18] Alice Wagstaff, "Successive Set Analysis of Verbal Styles in Psychotherapy" (Unpublished Ph.D. diss., University of Chicago, 1960).

mand further change on the basis of intelligent reflection and decision.

While contemporary psychotherapy has been one of the clearest voices speaking of the chaotic, irrational factors in life, it has even more clearly, both in its method and in its view of the end of psychotherapy, been a champion of the necessity of rationality and order in man's most comprehensive and fearless attempts to draw together all of the puzzling chaotic and potentially threatening elements that he finds in himself and his world. And if contemporary theology has also spoken clearly for process, openness, and freedom in our understanding of both man and God, it, too, has forcibly reminded us of the inevitability of structure, destiny, and responsibility. Chaos and order must progress in dynamic interaction both ontolgically and psychologically.

11

Religious Awareness and Small Groups:
Warmth versus Enlightenment

JOSEPH HAVENS

A Puzzle in Terminology

The word "religious" has lately taken on more fuzziness of
meaning than it had before. Because in this paper I apply it
to contexts and experiences usually thought of in "secular"
terms, and because "religious" awareness is the focus of the
argument, I begin with a definition.

I have heard college students argue that "religion" had
no place in their lives, but that "religious" questions were
extremely important to them. In his *Meaning and End of
Religion*,[1] Wilfred Cantwell Smith makes a persuasive case
against the use of the term "religion" in our contemporary
world, although he also feels that the adjective "religious"
has currency. (He argues that there are no longer entities
we might call "the religions of the world"; there are "traditions" and many forms of personal "faith"; but unities of tra-
dition-and-faith are rare and isolated.) In like manner I shall
confine my usage to the adjective, and by it designate experiences and encounters which William James subsumes under
"personal religion"[2] and Gordon A. Allport under "the religious sentiment." Allport, following E. Spranger, defines
the religious man as seeking unity: "He is mystical, and seeks
to comprehend the cosmos as a whole, to relate himself to
its embracing totality. Allport acknowledges that this search

[1] Macmillan Co., 1962.
[2] James, *The Varieties of Religious Experience* (London: Longmans,
Green & Co., 1902).

263

for ultimate meaning may be "decidedly immature." The religion may be "a self-centered construction in which a deity is adopted who favors the immediate interests of the individual, like a Santa Claus or an over-indulgent father." In such cases the religious sentiment serves mostly to enhance self-esteem, and may be merely utilitarian and incidental to one's life. But a more adequate personal religion "may be of such an order that it does provide an inclusive solution to life's puzzles in the light of an intelligible theory." The religious quest "is regarded as an end-in-itself, as the value underlying all things and desirable for its own sake."[3] As used in this paper, a religious awareness is one that serves to bind one experientially to the whole of things. The "whole" may be nature, human existence in all its vicissitudes, the human community, or the divine — or all of these together.

There is an interesting difference between the context of religious experience as defined by William James and the one assumed in this paper. James' now classical definition of religion reads: "the feelings, acts, and experiences of individual men *in their solitude*, as far as they apprehend themselves to stand in relation to whatever they may consider the divine"[4] (italics mine). Although the substance of the meaning of the "religious" is the same, my thesis assumes that important religious feelings and experiences can occur within and be engendered by *group* encounter. Such religious awarenesses concern the relation of a man to himself and to the human community, or to representative segments of it, as in the following account.

Not long ago I was sitting in an early session of a small discussion group of psychotherapists. My thoughts went something like this: "These people seem like giants. I feel very alone. I might just as well not exist. Why doesn't someone at least acknowledge my presence? They could at least speak to me, or sympathize with my feeling so uncomfortable, or ask me some questions. . . . It's stupid to feel left out.

[3] Allport, *Pattern and Growth in Personality* (New York: Holt, Rinehart and Winston, 1961), pp. 299–301.
[4] *Varieties of Religious Experience*, p. 32.

I'm as good as they are; in fact I could even put that last remark much better than he did. . . . But some of them talk
with such ease — as though they were perfectly at home
here! . . . Hell, I'll never get anywhere this way." Finally,
when I grew impatient talking only to myself, I plunged in
with a remark. Nobody paid the slightest attention. But fortunately I tried again. This time I was heard, responded to,
and drawn into the conversation. I learned I could be "in" if
I pushed in. This victory freed me from thinking so much
about me; I was able to listen to others. As I heard them and
watched their faces, it began to dawn: "Why, these people
are struggling with the same feelings I am! They're not as
comfortable with this group as I thought they were." Then
someone indicated that he had been comparing himself with
others just as I had! "And," I reflected, "some of them are
undoubtedly realizing, as I am, how irrelevant and stupid it
is to compete with each other." How alike we are when we
look beneath the surface! Then the discussion turned to our
fears of death, to the feelings of some that "time is running
out." And again I found myself sharing similar experiences. A
deep sense of closeness and brotherliness gripped me. How
absurd the competitive feelings seemed! We are *really* together and interconnected, despite our usual feelings of
separateness. Great wonder and joy!

This kind of religious awareness is not uncommon in small
groups which occur with sufficient time and intensity. Note
the strong emotional aspect (sharing, brotherliness, wonder,
and joy), but also a cognitive one (how alike we are;
absurdity of competitive feelings; interconnectedness of us
all). Although I would say that both aspects are "religious" in the broad sense, the word "awareness" is meant to
point to the latter — the new seeing or new knowing in this
experience. I shall return to this distinction later.

Religious awareness may be the beginning of a more inclusive sense of oneness with others, as in this instance. A thirty-
five year old management consultant exclaimed: "I saw this
old man today in our afternoon group. He is a, *a jerk*. He is a

fundamentalist, and he is *proud* of it. And I, I, (crying) *loved* him. I loved him. I love him."[5] Or religious awareness may border on the mystical, as in the following exclamation of a forty-six year old psychotherapist: "I can't look at you. It is like I am blinded by your face. You . . . It's like all the sorrow and all the beauty of the whole human race is in your face. *I'm* in your face! *I'm* the sun. I'm, I'm . . . I am beautiful. (cries)."[6]

One more comment about terms. The word "religious," partly because of its association in many minds with particular institutions or traditions, sets up boundaries in human *experience* where they do not belong. The word "transcendental," which will be used in this paper synonymously with religious, by its etymology poses the same problem. Other alternatives to these terms, "expanded awareness" and "widened consciousness," are advantageous in maintaining the continuity among levels of experience, and will be used in place of religious or trancendental awareness where this continuity is being stressed.

The Small Group Movement

The experiences described above occurred in what are imprecisely called "small groups." Face-to-face "basic encounter" groups have sprung up in a wide variety of forms and settings in the United States, particularly since World War II. Some of the better known are Alcoholics Anonymous, Synanon (the A.A. equivalent among drug addicts), group-dynamics groups, psychotherapeutic groups, "sensitivity-training" groups in industry, and cell or study groups in churches. ("Squares," that is, non-drug-addicts, have become so enthusiastic about what goes on in Synanon groups, that similar "games," as they are called, have been set up for them!) In some cases, already existing teams, for example, professional staffs in hospitals or mental health clinics, have

---

[5] Taken from James V. Clark, "Toward a Theory and Practice of Religious Experience," in *The Challenge of Humanistic Psychology*, ed. J. F. T. Bugental (New York: McGraw-Hill Book Co., 1964).
[6] *Ibid.*

become "small groups" in this special sense. Medical, nursing, and other students have in some schools been organized into such groups. The names sometimes given them are suggestive of their purpose: training groups, growth groups, search groups, listening groups, personal groups, fellowship groups.

The size of the groups vary from six to fifteen persons, and usually meet long enough for members to become deeply and personally acquainted (fifteen to twenty hours or more). The goals, though various, ordinarily include greater freedom of expression and openness to experience, greater sensitivity and closeness with others, and insight into oneself, the group process, and human behavior.

In his introductory essay to a recent volume on group psychotherapy, Gardner Murphy reflects that there is nothing new about small groups exerting "fundamental directive influences" on their members.

> In many periods like that of the "mystery religions" of the Greeks or the guilds of the Medieval Period, special interests and skills permitted a strongly inculcated sense of identification. The informal groups that gathered at a bridge on the River Cam in the thirteenth century developed a fellow feeling and gave strength and discipline to individual members.[7]

But two things are new: "the sense of *skill* or technique," and the "secular, rather than the religious, spirit in which individual aims are redirected." The former he sees as a part of the scientific and technological movement that began in the seventeenth and eighteenth centuries. By "secular" he refers to the clear focus on personal development or social scientific knowledge, without any reference to churchly or supernatural frames of reference. I am proposing that this broadly secular emphasis does not in any way preclude the possibility of religious or transcendental insights as we have defined them.

[7] Murphy, "Group Psychotherapy in Our Society," in *Group Psychotherapy and Group Function*, ed. Max Rosenbaum and Milton Berger (New York: Basic Books, 1963).

Religious Awareness in Small Groups

Some experimentation along this line has already been done. In 1962 in Los Angeles, J. F. T. Bugental and Robert Tannenbaum collaborated on a group-dynamics-oriented experiment, which moved beyond the usual group interaction toward such aims as "experiencing our relatedness to all men" and greater use of "feelings and moods, fantasy and speculation, tenderness and concern, sharing." Methods used or proposed included "sharing the creative products of our personal lives — paintings, writings, films, designs, pottery, theories, artistry, etc."; and "confronting existential moments — births, fear, stress, elation, death, helplessness, success, exhaustion, etc." All participants had previously taken part in more usual group-dynamics workshops, and had to some extent worked through emotional blockages and personal problems. They were characterized by the leaders as having "observing and curious egos manifesting desires for further self-exploration and greater self-actualization."

Bugental and Tannenbaum, and James V. Clark, quoted earlier, would all stress the continuity between personal growth that occurs in therapy and sensitivity-training groups *and* more transcendental insights. It is useful to see the transcendental openings as a further unfolding of more personal and psychological understandings.

I have tried in the following outline to scale the step-by-step *expanding awareness* that can occur in groups. The beginning is the state of almost total *unawareness* that characterizes some neurotics.

(1) 'Hysterical' blocking of awareness of most feelings and bodily sensations;

(2) Dawning consciousness of negative or erotic feelings, and/or repressed bodily sensations;

(3) Increased awareness of the impact of one's own behavior on others, and vice versa;

(4) Growing sensitivity to the whole group, particularly to the flow of feelings within it;

(5) Growing capacity to identify with others; momentary sense of oneness with others in the group;

(6) Uncompromising honesty regarding interpersonal "games," roles, and manipulations of others; confrontation with one's own contingency, limitedness and death;

(7) Experiential awareness that all men are "in the same boat"; a feeling of commonality; self-forgetful participation in the whole community and/or in nature;

(8) A sustained sense of oneness with history, nature, God, the cosmos; mystical union.

This sequence is variable. Several steps may be experienced concomitantly. Steps 2, 3, and 4 are usual in group therapy and group dynamics, and there is a considerable literature devoted to them.[8] The awareness of steps 5, 6, 7 and 8 we have tried to suggest earlier by examples. We turn now to a religious "opening," which will launch us into an exploration of the distinction between warmth-and-communication and enlightenment in group experience.

A Zen Experience

In an unpublished article "The Leicester Conference,"[9] Dr. Margaret Rioch of the Washington School of Psychiatry describes her experience of a two-week group relations conference in England. The leaders, associated with the Tavistock Institute of London, followed the Bion approach to group behavior.[10] We do not have space to comment fully on the theory and technique of leadership of the small groups in this conference. Bion hypothesized that in addition to working at its stated task, every group has hidden, unspoken agendas, which interfere with task accomplishment. On the basis of careful observation he conceptualized three different group emotional states or "basic assumption cultures" which, in addition to the work culture, characterize group members at a particular moment in time. The first of these is the De-

[8] See, for example, L. P. Bradford, J. R. Gibb, and K. D. Benne, eds., *T-Group Theory and Laboratory Method* (New York: John Wiley and Sons, 1964).

[9] Mimeographed paper in The Washington School of Psychiatry, Washington, D.C., 1965.

[10] See W. R. Bion, *Experience in Groups and Other Papers* (New York: Basic Books, 1961).

pendency assumption: the group exists in order to find support and direction from something or someone outside itself,
for example, the leader, external norms, its own past. The
second is the Fight-Flight assumption: the purpose of the
group is to avoid something by attacking or by fleeing.
The third basic assumption, Pairing, concerns the interaction
between two members of the group as the possible source
of exciting distraction or of some new "deliverance." The
Bion-type leader interprets directly and immediately to the
group where he feels the diversion to be. Frequently the interpretation implies criticism of the group in their relation to
him as leader or to their explicit task. For example, he may
charge the group with trying to make him into a Big Daddy
(Dependency), or with avoiding facing their task by playing
sexually titillating, intimate little games with each other
(Pairing), or with ganging together to attack him in back-
handed ways (Fight-Flight). Frequent interpretation of
these retreats from the task at hand reduces members to more
and more primitive forms of response. As their anxiety increases, they experience directly the fear of the "quicksands"
of opening themselves up to each other; they feel powerfully
their deep desire "to be the best one"; misperceptions of one
another and of the leader become painfully obvious. There
were periods, reports Dr. Rioch, of "almost psychotic drama."
A usually self-possessed and confident woman was found
standing alone with tears in her eyes, saying "she didn't know
anything about anything." "In a glance exchanged across the
table there was a Greek tragedy or a Shakespearian comedy
hidden, and at the same time displayed." And no relief for any
of this from the leader. But the chaos was endured, and deep
affection and a strong group feeling developed.

An important feature of the conference for Dr. Rioch was
the paradoxical demand placed upon members by the leaders, namely that they study group relations simultaneously
with their full participation in the group. Dr. Rioch compared
the total experience to Zen Buddhist enlightenment.

> The Zen student is placed squarely in front of a dilemma;
> he is given an impossible task. . . . The student tries

and tries and the more he tries the more he fails. . . .
When finally at long last, he really truly gives up the
struggle, the resolution of the conflict occurs. . . .
Something like this happened to some people in the Conference. It seemed that there simply was no right way
to do things, no right answer for which one could gain
approval. It seemed at the time that there was no way
to get an unequivocal reply from the staff which would
put a seal of approval on oneself. After much twisting
and turning to find answers, solutions, and good ways
of behaving, it became clearer and clearer that there was
no right turn, and that one did what one did; that however one tried to improve it or hide it, one was always
being oneself anyway. So why not be it whole-heartedly?
Again I do not mean to say that conflict ended once and
for all, but there was a glimpse, in fact there was a clear
look, into a state in which self-conscious, responsible
action became free and spontaneous.[11]

Dr. Rioch insists that there is a crucial connection between
the Bion kind of group and her Zen-like enlightenment. But
before we explore that, let us look at another approach to
groups.

Warmth and Communication versus Enlightenment: I

For many the term "group dynamics" has come to epitomize
the small group movement in this country. Since the forties,
the National Training Laboratories (official name of the best
known group dynamics organization) has pioneered the
study of human behavior in groups. Its stated aims were originally very similar to those of the Bion-style group relations
conferences ("increasing awareness and understanding of
intra- and inter-group processes"). But since its inception,
group dynamics has grown in many directions, and it is impossible to characterize it as neatly as the Bion approach. It is
probable, however, that the weight of the movement has
moved from research and scientific knowledge about group

[11] Rioch, "Leicester Conference."

processes to more practical emphases. In recent years, for instance, many group leaders stress "sensitivity training"; this phrase is applied to training groups of executives and supervisors in industry and government. The words highlight the emotional sensitivity and practical skill in human relations which are sought in the group experience. In contrast to the Bion method, leaders of T-groups (the small "training groups" of the N.T.L.) interpret what is going on within or between individuals as well as within the group as a whole. Sometimes one or another individual member is focused on by the group for "reaction" or "analysis." Many participants comment on the importance to them of learning to communicate deeply with others, to give and receive warmth and affection, and to become a part of a close-knit community. These personal, emotional needs have to some extent superseded the more theoretical questions of earlier years as the major goal of T-groups. As the 1965/66 brochure describes it: "NTL training methods . . . have demonstrated effectiveness as practical means for helping people apply theory (about personality, small groups, organizations, and about change processes) to problems of living and working together." One observer reported that he heard a number of participants at NTL workshops refer to them as "religious experience." The new affection and the free and open communication are a part of the unexpectedly religious character of the experience. This we shall refer to as the "warmth-communication pole" of group aims and group leadership.

In contrast to this, the Bion approach focuses more austerely on the task of comprehension of group processes:

> . . . human beings readily, all too readily, form groups . . . they form mobs which lynch, groups which glorify fanatical leaders, groups which easily slip into orgiastic experiences or into the warm glow of togetherness. On the other hand, the formation of a human group seriously and consistently dedicated to a serious task, without fanaticism or illusion, is an extremely difficult process and a relatively rare occurrence. . . . Whether or not members of such groups feel friendliness, warmth,

closeness, competitiveness, or hostility to each other is of secondary importance. It is assumed that these and other feelings will occur from time to time, but this is not the issue. The issue is the common goal to which each individual makes his own differentiated contribution.[12]

One can hardly probe human behavior in groups without gleaning some new understandings of human nature itself, or, more existentially, of "the human condition." In fact it may be just this combination of an immediate, experiential learning about human behavior in groups, with little explicit emphasis on individual dynamics and idiosyncracies, that provides an especially clear view of the human animal. In the same statement quoted above, the writers point out the conflict between "whole-hearted commitment" to a task or a group and "questioning" of the same. They conclude: "Recognition of the inevitability of such conflict brings with it appreciation of the tragic aspect of the human situation in which only courage can rescue us from the dangers of despair and superficiality." Dr. Rioch, in fact, suggests that a sense of the tragic may be a prerequisite for the fullest learning from the Bion-style group experience. I assume "tragic" to refer here to one's inner sense not only of the inevitable limitedness and contingency of life but also of the paradoxical enrichment and new insight which a confrontation with man's situation can bring. Participants in some groups may come to a new experiential knowing of their inner nature and their relation to the whole human community. This kind of new knowing I have called the "enlightenment pole" of group life.

Both poles are religious in some sense. But most contemporary institutions, including the churches, have focused on the improvement-of-human-relations aim of group life and have neglected, relatively, the enlightenment pole. An excursus exploring the current cultural situation will shed some light on this fact.

[12] From "Statement on Group Relations Conferences" (Mimeographed paper in The Washington School of Psychiatry, Fall, 1966).

The Changing Ethos: From Achievement to Affiliation

The bewildering changes of current history are most visibly seen in the mushrooming of cities, the Negro revolt, and the escalation of war. Less evident but no less important are the rapidly shifting inner attitudes of Americans. One of these is the gradual shift from a drive toward status and accomplishment ("achievement ethic") to a longing for communication and closeness ("affiliation needs").

In an important book, *The Achieving Society*,[13] David C. McClelland documents the decline of the achievement drive in twentieth century America. In a follow-up of that study, Stanley Rudin and others traced additional motivation changes in recent American history, using similar methods:

> Richard DeCharms and Gerald Moeller compiled the achievement scores and affiliation motivation scores for United States children for each twenty-year period from about 1800 to about 1950, by analyzing children's readers, such as the famous McGuffey's. They related these to a measure of economic productivity: the number of patents issued per capita. They found that the motive for achievement was low in 1800, began to rise about 1840, climbed steeply until a peak was reached in 1890, then went into a decline which was apparently still in progress in 1950. As with McClelland, the curve for actual achievement follows closely, about twenty-five years behind. What is even more interesting is that the curve for the power motive, which I derived, closely follows the curve for achievement, but peaks about twenty years later; and the affiliation motive peaks about twenty years after that.[14]

This study is only one thread in the fabric of evidence that, as the achievement drive in our culture has atrophied, affiliation needs have flowered.[15] For instance, a study by George

[13] Princeton, N.J.: Van Nostrand Co., 1961.
[14] Rudin, "The Personal Price of National Glory," *Transaction*, 2 (1965): 6.
[15] See also David Riesman, Reuel Denney, and Nathan Glazer, *The Lonely Crowd* (New Haven: Yale University Press, 1950); Kenneth

Spindler dealt with the changing values of college students. He hypothesized two value orientations closely related to "achievement" and "affiliation."[16] The second of these, called the "emergent" ethic as opposed to the "traditional" Puritan ethic, emphasizes sociability, self-expressive and aesthetic activity, "experiencing" for its own sake, orientation to the present, and a relativistic moral attitude. Recent research on Harvard students substantiates the existence of these as alternative value choices. Students pursuing this new ethic are more interested in literature, plastic arts, musical groups; they prefer humanities to sciences, define themselves by actions or qualities intrinsic to themselves as individuals, and value sensuous enjoyment, openness and receptiveness to others, and awareness of the world. My own observation of college students (and teen-agers generally) confirm Spindler's suggestion that this ethic truly is "emergent" among young people.

But it is not confined to them. I have been impressed with how hungry many people in middle age are for deeper "affiliation" with others. We sense a resurgent seeking for warmth, community, and a chance to share deeply with others. A mental health organization in San Diego televised a series of group therapy sessions, and then invited listeners to write in about setting up groups in their own localities without professonal leadership. Not only were eight or more of these groups formed, but it was found later that a number of groups had grown up spontaneously in bars, churches, etc.!

The dynamics of these value changes are obscure. Stanley Rudin speculates:

> What do people do when their world is a frightening jungle, but still one in which some inhibitions and repressions from earlier days still restrain them? Obviously, they will seek ways of lowering anxiety. . . . the most

Keniston, *The Uncommitted, Alienated Youth in American Society* (New York: Harcourt, Brace and World, 1965); and Jacob W. Getzels, "Changing Values Challenge the Schools," *School Review*, 65 (1957): 92–102.

[16] George Spindler, "Education in a Transforming American Culture," *Harvard Educational Review*, 25 (1955) no. 3, pp. 145–56.

basic way to achieve feelings of security and safety is through mutual support. By huddling together in groups offering mutual protection and emotional warmth, men can reduce anxiety and achieve refuge.[17]

(He then goes on to draw a parallel between our present age and the rise of Christianity in the last days of the Roman Empire: ". . . Christianity — which at the time stressed love, brotherhood, charity, and friendship for all men — corresponds to the period of heightened affiliation motivation.") Gardner Murphy, in the article cited above, makes the same point in a somewhat different way:

> It is fundamental to our modern way of living, let us say in the growth of America since the disappearance of the frontier, that we have preferred to solve our problems in a group rather than individually. This is the theme of David Riesman's impelling analyses of Western culture, and of American life in particular, in his volume on *The Lonely Crowd*; it is the theme of Holly Whyte's *The Organization Man* and of many studies of "suburbia," of families of young executives, and of the lost quality of those who must find solidarity in groups, however tenuous, because they are no one by themselves alone.[18]

The phenomenon is a complex one, with many determinants. Strong self-control has long been a part of the American ethos. It emerged in Puritanism and has served well the entrepreneurial demands of technological society and the responsibilities of world power. But a reaction has set in. (Rudin tabulates the cost of strong ego-controls and high achievement: ulcers, hypertension, alcoholism, etc.) The affluent society and freedom from material want have allowed Americans to attend to other long-repressed needs. In many quarters we hear a clamor for freer self-assertion and emotional expressiveness, less parental or authoritarian controls. But the inertia of society is massive; social inventions responsive to the new needs are slow to emerge. In spite of the new con-

[17] "The Personal Price of National Glory."
[18] "Group Therapy in Our Society."

cern with human relations in some quarters of the "public sphere" (business, government, education, the professions), competitiveness, bureaucratization, and the insistence on ego-controls still dominate. In some subcultures family life provides the alternative to the demanding roles and masks of public life; but in many other segments of the culture, families fail tragically to nurture emotional closeness or to give opportunity for sharing of personal feelings. Hence the rise of small, face-to-face groups in many settings as a direct expression of these sociocultural groundswells. They reflect, Gardner Murphy says, a "response to loneliness, helplessness in the face of the vastness of today." And they function as "de-repressors," that is, as culturally sanctioned vehicles for the expression of newly emergent feelings and needs.

Warmth and Communication versus Enlightenment: II

The foregoing picture may help us to understand why the warmth-communication aspect of small group life has had the widest appeal. The churches have tended to use groups for the same sensitivity-training purposes as other American institutions. The fresh affection and caring for one another which may arise in groups is highly consistent, of course, with the love ethic of the Old and New Testaments.

But there has always been a knowledge or enlightenment side to religion. We have referred to it above as the wider awarenesses that illuminate for a man his own nature and bind him to the human community, to the process of evolution, or to God. At its highest reaches it is called mystical knowing, and is found in Catholic (for example, St. Theresa, François deSales) and Protestant (for example, Jakob Böhme, the Quakers) circles in Christianity, in gnostic (Jñana) forms of Hinduism, and in Zen Buddhism. At less lofty heights it is the cognitive dimension of experienced faith. It is immediate and personal and not to be acquired second-hand. Epistemologically it has something in common with intuitive and aesthetic knowing. In contrast, the warmth-communication pole is partly represented by devotional forms of worship — much popular Catholic devotion, Bhakti Hinduism, "Pure Land" Buddhism, and so forth. (I am not suggesting that the warmth and communication of small groups is an equivalent of emotional or pietistic forms of worship. But they tap some of the same areas of experience; small group encounters are for some moderns a humanistic religious experience.)

It is likely that the religious "openings" we are discussing are restricted to fewer persons than religious feelings attached to secondhand ideas or beliefs; perhaps also in this anti-metaphysical age they are more suspect. But if, as I would assert, some knowledge about God and man based on one's own experiencing is an ingredient of a fully developed religious life (of any fully human life I would say), then we may conclude: groups which nurture these wider awarenesses can bring to fruition the unexplored spiritual potential of group experience.

Can Religious Awareness in Groups be Nurtured?

A good deal is known, as I have said, about the kind of leadership needed to move a group through tentativeness, intellectual sparring, and sharing of anxieties and hostilities, toward deeper understanding and affection. We also know more and more about how to run groups or conferences that can increase dramatically a participant's understanding of how groups operate. But it is problematic whether one can set up a group that can permit or nurture the transcendental understandings we have been discussing. Only a few general comments can be made at this time.

First, the setting. We cannot assume that an apparently religious setting, a church, for example, is necessarily related to transcendental experience in groups. On the positive side, some successful small groups have existed in church congregations and have met in churches or synagogues. Genuine personal concern for one another is frequently found among church members. Also in some churches one may find a longing for and thus an openness to personal or mystical encounters which transcend safe creeds and respectable levels of faith; the upheavals of contemporary theology tend to support such an openness. On the negative side, in many religious communities there is a deeply engrained pattern of what is and is not proper in personal encounter. In Quaker Meetings, for instance, where one might assume a greater openness and interest in religiously oriented groups, there are important inhibiting factors: particular attitudes toward war and civil rights are prescribed; marital difficulty is considered a weakness and is seldom discussed openly; four-letter words are taboo. In other groups a Christian faith may be assumed to exist in everyone, and a serious questioning of the "fundamentals" of that particular community cannot be openly voiced. Tradition may narrowly channel experience; ideology may inhibit free expression. Attitude studies indicate that in some communities church people are the most conservative, morally and politically; this outward conservatism is likely to be correlated with an inner reluctance to enter into emotionally open and risky interaction with others. These difficulties may be overcome by a group in time. But such considerations suggest that a nonchurch setting may be more freeing for some individuals.

It is possible to make only the broadest generalizations about the expectations and assumptions with which potential members enter small groups. I first believed that dissatisfaction with things as they are is the prime requisite — including dissatisfaction with one's religious orientation. I now believe that some sense of the possibility of wider awareness, of transcendental insights, is important. Further investigation is needed here. In any case, a commitment of time and willingness to venture oneself in the group enterprise, to brave the "quicksands" of becoming vulnerable, is necessary. Freedom from anxiety is not implied. But the capacity to endure anxiety in the interest of further growth is probably an essential.

We have already mentioned concern for the other as one of the possible positive attributes of church people in groups. The view that such a concern is essential would be disputed by some small group leaders. They would hold that caring about others will arise naturally in the course of the group life, whether or not it is felt at the outset. This seems to me too easy an answer. I suspect that a successful group depends heavily upon the concern for individuals which still permeates a good deal of American life. Such caring may be deeply buried under a self-seeking or destructive posture, but I believe that it could not be elicited by group experience unless it had been nurtured in early years by parental care. My guess is that a basic encounter group would have rough sailing in Dobu or Kwakiutl society. In one way or another the invention of small groups in contemporary life arose out of the conflict between a high valuing of the individual person and personal relationships, and the necessary impersonality and self-masking demanded in our competitive and bureaucratic social life. Without the first of these, most groups would fall apart or be destroyed.

The requirements of leadership can only be touched upon here. In most small groups, explicit leadership of some kind is necessary at the beginning, but may become less and less significant. (The San Diego groups, referred to above, were leaderless from the beginning; yet considerable therapeutic gain was reported in ten sessions.) A major function of the leader is consistently to stimulate and help to maintain honest, here-and-now interaction at the feeling level.

For groups fostering wider awarenesses, it is important that the leader himself have some experiential sense of them. He need not conceptualize or state this aim explicitly, however. If he does so, he may, for reasons given above, risk encouraging a kind of intellectualized religiosity on the part of some members. His legitimate function is to be aware of the transcendental possibilities, to trust the group's ability to move toward them, and, occasionally, to point out the wider referent or meaning of a particular group experience. Let me give an example.

During a long weekend retreat, a group of about fifteen college students discussed at length their problems with religious faith and other personal binds. One girl in an early session described her guilt over having just broken with a boy. Several group members tried in various ways to reassure her, but without avail. They were bothered by her discomfort, and were trying to reassure themselves also. Because most of the participants liked to think of themselves as loving persons and of the group as a loving community, they were uneasy. This feeling came out in the final session, and all were surprised when the original confessor stated that she felt *very much* supported and loved, even though her guilt had not at the time been assuaged. *Being with her* in her immediate distress, she said, was much more important than solving her problem for her. At this point, but not before, a religious interpretative statement — by the leader or by a perceptive group member — would have been in order. It might be: "I feel I know a little more what a Christian community is like, that is, one in which we can share the burdens of one another."

We have made certain suggestions about setting, assumptions of group members, and leadership as these relate to the emergence of religious awarenesses. We need much experience, experimentation, and observation before we can be more definitive.

The following, final section explores the problem of language in the religious interpretations of group events.

Symbols of the Ultimate: Traditional or New?

Within the Christian Church, small group experience has been used by some ministers almost systematically as a preliminary to a study of the Bible or of theology. In a recent, excellent article, Robert A. Edgar describes the "speaking the truth in love" and "bearing one another's burdens" which "comes about not only through human sharing, but through the presence of the Holy Spirit." He goes on:

> The group can be a laboratory for the dying to self. Members begin to live "in Christ" — they share in His resurrection, becoming the fellowship of the forgiven and the resurrected in the colony of the living. . . . Our work indicates that the experiences of listening and being listened to in the listening structured groups are essential psychological and spiritual preparation for understanding the Christian faith. In a very real sense,

one first discovers the meaning of Christ's love in these groups. Then one is introduced to the meaning of one's experience in Biblical and theological study groups. After one has had eighteen months to two years in a listening group, he may then be able and ready to participate in some group study in depth.[19]

This statement illustrates in an unusual way the point made above, namely that interpretation ("the meaning of one's experience in Biblical and theological study groups") should follow experience ("discovering the meaning of Christ's love"). This kind of theological interpretation makes much sense for those participants whose background and present commitment are solidly Christian — and for *some* who are not Christian. But Jewish and Christian symbols seem to have lost their power for many. With some individuals and groups, traditional formulations will seem inevitably hollow or contrived. In these cases participants — and sometimes a group as a whole — will want to find their own analogies, symbols, or metaphors.

James V. Clark, whose paper we have already quoted, states it in this way:

The symbols of religion are symbols for the unachievable infinite. . . . For so many, these symbols are no longer participated in vividly enough to arouse ultimate concern. For faith to be present — faith now being considered as the centering act of the personality and not as simple belief in something for which there is no scientific evidence — there must be, in Tillich's terms, an ultimate concern with an ultimate, a subject and an object. And for that to be felt the ultimate must be symbolized. Sensitivity training offers an environment in which an individual may produce symbols of a personal nature which open the gate for him to experience an ultimate outside of the self he has been experiencing. In the peak experiences quoted above, these were usually transformed

[19] Edgar, "The Listening Structured Group," *Pastoral Psychology*, June, 1964.

relationships with an other or with one's own core but they became symbols of something toward which the person moved after the experience was over.[20]

These symbols or images may be the "memory of an encounter, or his own sense of action which resulted in the encounter, of his own increasing sense of I-ness." Let me give an example. Shortly after I had pushed my way into the group (in my experience quoted earlier), I had the following fantasy: All of us were in a swirling, rapidly flowing river with many eddies and backwaters. I had been in a backwater; but when I plunged in with my remarks, I found I was able to move into the mainstream: I wasn't imprisoned as I had thought! Whether I stayed in the back eddy or flowed with the current was *my* choice! The almost physical feeling of pushing into the stream of action stays with me; it applies not only to groups but to the flow of life itself; it is one metaphor of my relation to the world.

The psychologist Henry Murray asserts that all our present "myths" and "mystiques" are obsolete. He charges the traditional religion with "senescence" and calls for new symbols and mythologies "to bring forth a new vision of a better world," and "to guide individual self-development and self-conduct in the light of an acceptable ideal." He believes that

. . . the creative imaginations which participate in the formation of a *vital* myth must be those of people — often alienated and withdrawn people — who have *experienced* in their "depths" and on their own pulses, one or more of the unsolved critical situations with which humanity at large or members of their own society are confronted.[21]

This statement I believe is relevant to many who are driven into basic encounter groups by their own inner needs, but who emerge with a deepened understanding not only of themselves but of human existence.

[20] Clark, "Toward a Theory and Practice of Religious Experience."
[21] "Possible Nature of a 'Mythology' to Come," in *Myths and Mythmaking*, ed. H. A. Murray (New York: George Braziller, 1960).

A similar sentiment about modern art and contemporary symbols of the ultimate is expressed from a very different quarter. The writer is Mircea Eliade, a historian of religion:

> . . . artists are no longer interested in traditional religious imagery and symbolism. . . . This is not to say that the "sacred" has completely disappeared in modern art. But it has become *unrecognizable*; it is camouflaged in forms, purposes and meanings which are apparently "profane." The sacred is not *obvious*, as it was for example in the art of the Middle Ages. One does not recognize it *immediately* and *easily*, because it is no longer expressed in a conventional religious language.[22]

It takes little translation to apply this description to small group encounters: spiritual experience is embedded in group forms, purposes, and meanings which are outwardly "profane." Because the language that some group members use about their experience is not conventionally religious, it is not recognized, sometimes even by members themselves, as referring to the "sacred." The premature use of a traditional formulation must not be allowed to obscure or preempt the fresh imagery and symbol that may emerge from group experience. Experiences in groups have their contribution to make to the new mythology that will emerge from the present crisis of faith.

I was drawn to small groups originally by my own need for deep communication and closeness with others. The "expanding awarenesses" I have described came unbidden; they now seem of paramount importance. It is not clear to me to what extent new and wider awarenesses can become an explicit aim of group interaction and leadership. But at the very least we can begin to envision small groups not only as a tool for learning interpersonal skills or as communities for the deepening of affection, but also as a context within which one can experience his true relation to himself and to the ultimate.

[22] "The Sacred and the Modern Artist," *Criterion*, University of Chicago Divinity School, 4 (1965), no. 2.

Biographical Notes

JERALD C. BRAUER was born in Wisconsin in 1921, graduated from Carthage College and Northwestern Lutheran Theological Seminary, and received his Ph.D. from the University of Chicago in 1948. He taught at Union Theological Seminary, 1948–50. He is professor of the history of Christianity and dean of the University of Chicago's Divinity School. His publications are in the area of English Puritanism, Reformation, and religion in America.

LeRoy ADEN is associate professor of practical theology at the Lutheran Theological Seminary in Philadelphia. He holds the B.D. degree from Wartburg Theological Seminary, and the M.A. (1959) and Ph.D. (1961) from the Divinity School of the University of Chicago. Before taking up his present position, he was instructor of pastoral theology at the Divinity School, University of Chicago, and director of the Pastoral Counseling Center, Pittsburgh. He has published articles in *Pastoral Psychology* and other journals.

FRED BERTHOLD, JR., is professor of religion and chairman of the Department of Religion at Dartmouth College. He received his B.S. from Dartmouth, his B.D. from Chicago Theological Seminary, and his Ph.D. from the Divinity School, University of Chicago. Before moving to Dartmouth, he was instructor in philosophy at Utica College of Syracuse University. He is the author of *The Fear of God*, and *Basic Sources of the Judeo-Christian Tradition*. He has published articles in the *Journal of Social Psychology* and the *Journal*

285

of Religion, and contributed chapters to *Contemporary Problems in Religion* and *The Constructive Aspects of Anxiety.*

FRANK M. BOCKUS received his B.A. from Southern Methodist University, his B.D. from Union Theological Seminary, New York, and his Ph.D. (1965) from the University of Chicago's Divinity School. He was associate professor of pastoral theology at the Institute of Religion, Texas Medical Center, before joining the General Board of Christian Social Concerns of the Methodist Church, Washington, D.C. He is the editor of *The Total Self and Total Care: Basic Considerations in Rehabilitation Medicine,* and has published articles in *Christian Advocate.*

DON BROWNING is assistant professor of Religion and Personality and, from 1966 to 1967, was acting director of the Doctor of Ministry program at the Divinity School, University of Chicago. He received his B.S. from Central Methodist College, and his B.D. (1959), his M.A. (1962), and his Ph.D. (1964) from the Divinity School, University of Chicago. From 1963 to 1965 he was assistant professor of theology and pastoral care at the Graduate Seminary of Phillips University. He is the author of *Atonement and Psychotherapy,* and has published articles in *Journal of Pastoral Care, Frontiers, Christian Century, Journal of Religion, Pageant Magazine,* and *Pastoral Psychology.*

LELAND ELHARD received his B.A. and his B.D. from Capital University, Columbus, Ohio, and his M.A. (1963) and Ph.D. (1965) from the University of Chicago's Divinity School. Before taking up his present position as instructor of systematic theology and pastoral theology at Evangelical Lutheran Theological Seminary, he served in the pastorate for five years. He has published articles in the *Lutheran Quarterly.*

JOSEPH HAVENS is clinical psychologist for the University Health Services, University of Massachusetts. He holds the B.S. degree from the Massachusetts Institute of Technology, the M.A. from the University of Southern California, and the Ph.D. (1958) from the Divinity School of the University of Chicago. He has been assistant professor of psychology at Wilmington College, Ohio, and college counselor and assistant professor of psychology at Carleton College. His articles have appeared in *Pastoral Psychology, Journal of Counseling Psychology, Journal of Social Psychology, Journal for the Scientific Study of Religion,* and *The Christian Scholar.*

PETER HOMANS is assistant professor of Religion and Personality at the Divinity School and currently on the staff of the Counseling and Psychotherapy Research Center, University of Chicago. His degrees include the B.A. from Princeton University, the B.D. from Virginia Theological Seminary, and the M.A. (1962) and Ph.D. (1964) from the University of Chicago's Divinity School. He served as psychologist at the William Healy School, Institute for Juvenile Research, Chicago (1961–62), before becoming lecturer at Trinity College, University of Toronto (1962–64), and then assistant professor of theology and psychology and director of Student Counseling at the Hartford Seminary Foundation (1964–65). He has published articles in the *Journal of Religion, Studies in Public Communication, Motive,* and *Look.*

PERRY LeFEVRE is academic dean and professor of constructive theology at the Chicago Theological Seminary. He received his B.S. from Harvard, his B.D. from the Chicago Theological Seminary, and his Ph.D. (1951) from the Divinity School of the University of Chicago. He has served as instructor at Franklin and Marshall College (1948–49), associate professor at Knox College (1949–53), and associate professor at the Federated Theological Faculty, University of Chicago (1953–61). He is the author of *The Prayers of Kierkegaard, The Christian Teacher, Understandings of Man,* and editor of *Philosophical Resources for Christian Thought* and the Chicago Theological Seminary *Register.* His many articles have been published in such journals as *Pastoral Psychology, Journal of Religion, Religious Educa-*

tion, Journal for the Scientific Study of Religion, and *Children's Religion.*

LEIGHTON McCUTCHEN is assistant professor of theology and psychology and counselor to students at the Hartford Seminary Foundation. He previously served pastorates in Alabama and Indiana. He holds a B.A. from Davidson College, a B.D. from Union Theological Seminary in Virginia, and a Ph.D. (1965) from the Divinity School, University of Chicago. He has published articles in *Crossroads.*

WILLIAM R. ROGERS is associate professor of Religion and Psychology and director of Student Counseling at Earlham College, Richmond, Indiana. Before this he was a teaching fellow and counselor to students at the Chicago Theological Seminary and a staff member of the Counseling and Psychotherapy Research Center, University of Chicago. He holds the B.A. degree from Kalamazoo College, the B.D. from the Chicago Theological Seminary, and the Ph.D. (1965) from the Divinity School of the University of Chicago. He has published articles in *Motive,* the *Journal of Religion,* and the *Journal for the Scientific Study of Religion,* and has contributed to *The Impact of the American College on Student Values.*

CHARLES R. STINNETTE, JR., as professor of pastoral theology and psychiatry and chairman of the field of Religion and Personality, holds a joint appointment in the Divinity School and the Department of Psychiatry at the University of Chicago. His degrees include the B.S. from North Carolina State College of Agriculture and Engineering, the B.D. from Union Theological Seminary in New York, the S.T.M. from the Hartford Seminary Foundation, and the Ph.D. (1950) from Columbia University. He has served as professor of religion and chaplain at the University of Rochester (1948–50); rector of the Episcopal Church of the Ascension, Rochester (1950–52); associate warden of the College of Preachers, Washington Cathedral, Washington, D.C., where he was installed as a canon (1952–56); and professor of pastoral theology at Union

Theological Seminary in New York (1956–59). He is the author of *Grace and the Searching of Our Heart*; *Faith, Freedom and Selfhood*; *Anxiety and Faith*; and *Learning in Theological Perspective*. His many articles have appeared in such journals as *Anglican Theological Review, Journal of Religion, Christian Scholar, Journal of Pastoral Care, Pastoral Psychology,* and the *Lutheran Quarterly.*

Acknowledgments

Many of the articles in this volume were first presented at the Alumni Conference of the Religion and Personality Field, January 27–29, 1966, celebrating the seventy-fifth anniversary of the University of Chicago and the hundredth anniversary of the Divinity School of the University of Chicago. The conference was greatly enriched by two public lectures by Rollo May and Seward Hiltner. Unfortunately it was not possible to include these lectures in the volume. Thanks are also due to those members of the conference who served as discussants on these papers. Limitations of space made it impossible for their comments to be included.

Special thanks are due to Mr. Leonard Scott, who, as editorial assistant, offered many helpful stylistic suggestions and carefully prepared the manuscript for publication.

Index

Acceptance, and judgment, 88, 89
Analogy of faith, applied to insight and revelation, 87, 90
Archetype: as primordial images, 226; of the God-man, 237, 240–41; in Christ and man, 240–41

Barth, Karl: his view of sin, 17–19; his understanding of the Gospel, 30–32; his understanding of religion, 70; compared to Schleiermacher, 130–34
Bultmann, Rudolf: on the object of theology, 12; on faith, 126; on demythologization, 186–87; mentioned, 71n, 104

Christic event, as the presence of Christ, 49
Creativity: in client-centered psychology, 73–74; as motivation, 114–15; ontological, 255; in therapy, 261

Dialogical studies: in the Divinity School, 1; the context of, 2–3; methodology in, 4–5; and Sigmund Freud, 8; psychology as the base for, 9–10
Dream: the telling of the, 183–85, 209–13, 216; and wishing, 186, 188–89, 190, 196–97, 206; and health, 208. See also Myth

Ego-identity, description of, 137–47
Erikson, Erik H.: on early infancy development, 24–25, 26; on

identity, 74, 121, 138–46; on hope, 197

Faith: as the object of theology, 84, 106, 107; the structure of, 125–30; and identity, 125–34, 147–61
Freud, Sigmund: importance of, 8; on the goal of therapy, 35; on two levels of psychic reality, 59; on the transference-god, 64–69, 80; on regression, 76; on religion, 83–84, 93, 255; on motivation, 112–13; on dreams, 190, 198, 201–5

Gospel, the heart of, 30–32

Identity: as the object of psychotherapy, 84, 106, 107; and Jesus Christ, 90, 91; and knowing, 120–25; and faith, 125–34, 147–61. See also Ego-identity
Images: the dynamic question of, 75–81; psychology of religious, 76–77; as fantasy, 76–77; and Rorschach psychology, 78; and the concept of God, 79; and the transformation of man, 90; and archetypes, 235. See also Symbol
Insight: in psychotherapy, 34, 38–39; kinds of, 35; as a way of life, 39; and revelation, 86–91, 97; defined, 87; phenomenology of, 91–96

Judgment, and acceptance, 88, 89

293